A fascinating blend of interviews and perspectives on where economics – and the economy – is heading. A must read for anyone who thinks economists are out of touch with today's reality or don't have competing compelling visions for the future.

SIMON JOHNSON
Ronald Kurtz Professor of Entrepreneurship
at MIT's Sloan School of Management,
former chief economist at the IMF

Arnold Kling and Nick Schulz show you how to think like a new economist, updating the conventional scarcity toolkit with their "one big story" on innovative entrepreneurship. This is the antidote to shallow, static pessimism about our economic future. Books about economics have proliferated in recent years, but *From Poverty to Prosperity* finally tells us about the important new ideas proliferating among economists. In this series of interviews with breakthrough thinkers inside the profession, Kling and Schulz offer the single best summation of new thinking on growth and development that I have seen, and their presentation is fantastic.

BOB LITAN, Ph.D.
Vice President, Research and Policy, The Kauffman Foundation, and
Senior Fellow, Economic Studies, The Brookings Institution

If more taxpayers read this book they'd be better prepared to vote for policies that keep America a place where workers become more, not less, productive, when they arrive here from their countries of origin.

IRA STOLL
editor of FutureOfCapitalism.com

The central thesis of this book is that mainstream economics, with its emphasis on labor and capital and its focus on the efficient allocation of an economy's output, is not so much wrong but utterly misleading in its understanding of modern economies, especially that of the United States.

RICHARD COOPER
ForeignAffairs.com

INVISIBLE WEALTH

The Hidden Story
of How Markets Work

Arnold Kling and Nick Schulz

ENCOUNTER BOOKS · *New York · London*

First American edition published in 2009 by Encounter Books,
an activity of Encounter for Culture and Education, Inc.,
a nonprofit, tax exempt corporation.

Encounter Books website address: www.encounterbooks.com

Manufactured in the United States and printed on
acid-free paper. The paper used in this publication meets
the minimum requirements of ANSI/NISO Z39.48-1992
(R 1997) (Permanence of Paper).

LIBRARY OF CONGRESS CATALOGING-IN-PUBLICATION DATA

Kling, Arnold S.
Invisible wealth : the hidden story of how markets work / by Arnold Kling and
Nick Schulz.
p.   cm.
Originally published in hardback in 2009 as: From poverty to prosperity :
intangible assets, hidden liabilities and the lasting triumph over scarcity.
Includes bibliographical references and index.
ISBN-13: 978-1-59403-527-2 (pbk. : alk. paper)
ISBN-10: 1-59403-527-X (pbk. : alk. paper)
1. Creative ability in business. 2. Technological innovations—Economic
aspects. 3. Success. 4. Economics. I. Schulz, Nick, 1972– II. Kling, Arnold S.
From poverty to prosperity. III. Title.
HD53.K583 2011
338—dc22
2011002275

10 9 8 7 6 5 4 3 2 1

Contents

For Lauren, Olivia, Gwendolyn, Ryan,
Jackie, Rachel, Joanna, and Naomi:
The Ultimate Sources of Prosperity

Acknowledgments

I have many influences, but two that I particularly treasure are those of my father, Merle Kling, and my undergraduate economics professor, Bernie Saffran. Both encouraged a spirit of open inquiry, and it saddens me that they are no longer with us to see this product.

ARNOLD KLING

Jim Glassman, Justin Peterson and Ryan Grillo understand the importance of growth to poverty alleviation and have worked hard across the globe to bring it about.

Christopher DeMuth has taught me that there is nothing more powerful than the production of new knowledge.

Arthur Brooks, Bob Litan and Carl Schramm have unlocked the secrets of entrepreneurship and its capacity for civic and economic renewal.

Kim Dennis and David Gerson have helped me see the myriad ways in which freedom is both a value in and of itself and a force for good worth protecting.

My friend Jonah Goldberg has convinced me that while there are no lasting victories in intellectual combat, one should always enjoy the fight (and the only scarcities that truly matter are those of grilled meats and a good Gibson).

Bill Bennett has been a mentor for over ten years now and

Acknowledgments

has offered generous friendship, wise counsel and shown me the spiritual abundance available everywhere, from the desert valley to the mountaintop.

My parents, Bill and Lynne, were the original sources of any hidden assets I might claim to have (any liabilities – intangible or otherwise – are solely my own). My wife Lauren and three kids have taught me that human love is capable of something miraculous — increasing returns to scale.

NICK SCHULZ

Preface to the Paperback Edition

THIS BOOK first appeared in the fall of 2009 as *From Poverty to Prosperity*. Because it was written before the recession started, it turned out to be one of the few books on the economy published at the time that did *not* portray the financial crisis and the recession as a vindication of everything that the authors had believed for years. We did not anticipate the financial crisis. In fact, an early draft of this book had a paragraph that reflected the conventional wisdom of the day: that the crisis would be confined to the underworld of subprime mortgage lending, without affecting any major regulated financial institutions. Eventually we deleted that paragraph, but in retrospect it might have been useful for historical purposes to have let the paragraph stand, as testimony to what most economists believed in 2007.

If as many commentators had been as certain about what was happening several years ago as they claim to be today, the crisis would never have occurred. For example, when the Glass-Steagall Act was repealed in 1999, this action was commonly viewed as a mere formality, ratifying changes that had already taken place, rather than creating a new playing field in finance.*

---

* Glass-Steagall was Depression-era legislation that separated commercial banking (taking deposits and making loans) from investment banking (raising capital for firms by marketing stocks and bonds). Financial institutions

We think this is still the appropriate analysis of that legislation.

Other commentators claimed that they had warned about the dangers of Fannie Mae and Freddie Mac. Their warnings, however, were focused on the interest rate risk embedded in the portfolios of those government-sponsored enterprises, which turned out not to be the problem. Instead, it was credit risk that ultimately doomed Fannie and Freddie.

A number of well-known doomsayers warned of dangerous financial imbalances. But their focus was on international capital flows, and they expected the key triggering event to be a flight from the dollar. This is not what happened.

In hindsight, it is easy to see the instances of regulatory failure.† In real time, however, regulations that later proved to be dysfunctional – such as the Basel rules for risk-based capital and requirements for market-value accounting – were regarded as sophisticated and conducive to safety.

In this book, we contrast three views of the relationship between markets and government:

> (1) "Markets work. Use markets."
> (2) "Markets fail. Use government."
> (3) "Markets fail. Use markets."

At first, the financial crisis was widely viewed as a refutation of (1) and a vindication of (2). This assessment has not held up well, however, as government policies have failed to prevent a deep recession. Indeed, it is possible that the government's

---

were forbidden from engaging in both activities at once. This boundary gradually eroded in the four decades preceding its formal repeal.

† See, for example, Arnold Kling, "Not What They Had in Mind: A History of Policies That Produced the Financial Crisis of 2008," September 15, 2009, http://papers.ssrn.com/sol3/papers.cfm?abstract_id=1474430.

reaction to the crisis has prolonged it – for example, by postponing a bottom in housing prices.

Defenders of the bailouts and fiscal stimulus (policies which we opposed) must make desperate use of counterfactual arguments, such as: "It would have been worse without government action," or "A bigger stimulus would have worked." We think it is more likely the case that the government's unwillingness to permit large firms to fail – and markets consequently to correct themselves – helps explain the scope and severity of the economic problems that emerged in 2007 and continue today.

Going forward, we believe it is far more likely that markets, not government, will lead the way to renewed economic growth. Moreover, we believe that the period of high unemployment, however long it may last, will not stop the march toward greater wealth and prosperity. We believe that the dislocations of the current recession will prove temporary. They will be alleviated not by government action, but instead by two of the factors that we emphasize in this book, namely entrepreneurship and innovation.

Chapter 1:

AN INTRODUCTION
TO ECONOMICS 2.0

ECONOMICS IS NOT what it used to be. Over the last few decades, economists have begun a significant reorientation in how they look at the world. This shift rests on a large and growing body of research that we will explore with you in this book. And it has significant implications for politics, policy, and how we view the world around us.

To understand this change in orientation, consider one of the most basic notions in first-year economics, an economy's so-called "factors of production." We used to teach that there are three factors of production: land, labor, and capital. We described an economy consisting of amber waves of grain, routine unskilled work, and belching, clanking machines inside of giant factories.

But most people today do not live in that economy. Instead, we work in quiet offices situated on land whose value has nothing to do with its agricultural fecundity, doing tasks that are highly specialized and differentiated.

For years, the story economists told to describe the world around us was incomplete. What we had left out of the story were the positive forces of creativity, innovation, and advancing technology that propel economies forward. We did not describe the dynamic process that leads to new pharmaceuticals, cell phones, Web-based information services, computerized logistical systems that fill stores with inexpensive merchandise, and financial innovations that give more people access to credit.

We also left out the negative forces that can hold economies back: bad governance, counterproductive social practices, and patterns of taking wealth instead of creating it. We took for granted secure property rights, honest public servants, and the willingness of individuals to experiment and adapt to novelty.

This book presents the main ideas of what we call Economics 2.0. Economists have developed these ideas in order to explain the enormous differences in quality of life over history and across countries.

Economics 2.0 says that these differences reflect intangible assets and invisible liabilities. The intangible assets are knowledge bases. This category includes formal scientific findings, such as the quantum mechanics and chemistry that help engineers design integrated circuits. It also includes less formal learning from experience, such as the know-how that enables general contractors to put up housing developments on schedule and within budget.

Invisible liabilities, on the other hand, are institutional and cultural impediments to innovation and productivity. These range from the structure and conduct of government to the attitudes and customs of ordinary citizens.

Economics 2.0 offers a completely fresh perspective on the role of markets in society, one that will become clear over the course of this book. Traditionally, the debate over markets has been between the "Chicago school" and the "Harvard–MIT school." The Chicago school says, "Markets usually work. That is why we need markets." The Harvard–MIT school says, "Markets often fail. That is why we need government."

Economics 2.0 says, "Markets often fail. That is why we need markets."

What do we mean by this? Economics 2.0 says that overcoming market failure requires innovation. Innovation is best delivered by markets. It is rarely delivered by government. Hence, the paradoxical conclusion is that markets are often the best solution to market failure.

Economics 1.0, whether at Chicago or Harvard, looks at the market as a mechanism for allocating a given amount of resources. Most importantly, the market is said to operate with a fixed, known set of production technologies. The debate between Chicago and Harvard centers on whether or not the government can out-guess the private sector in coming up with the best possible allocation.

In Economics 2.0, the market is a mechanism for stimulating and filtering innovation. Entrepreneurs are at the heart of the economy, pumping innovation through the system. Large bureaucracies, on the other hand, whether they belong to corporations or government, are more like cholesterol – inhibiting the circulation of new products and new methods.

If what you are looking to read is the next *Tipping Point* or *Freakonomics*, don't look here. Those books offer a smorgasbord of fascinating findings in economics and sociology. Each is a collection of interesting stories that are only loosely connected with one another.

Instead, this book tells one big story. It is a story that we have assembled out of a number of overlapping strands of research, undertaken by many economists who have received little or no attention in the media. A major goal in writing this book is to introduce these economists and their ideas to a broader audience.

A central figure in this story is Douglass North, who is practically unknown outside of the economics profession. Even among academic economists, North is little recognized, in spite of having been awarded a Nobel Prize. North's main area of research is economic history, a field that was overlooked by

Economics 1.0. Many other economists you will meet in this book focus on economic development, another field which, like economic history, has been neglected by mainstream economics. Conventional economists prefer the comfortable precision of mathematical abstraction to the messy complexity of the real world, with all of its uncertainties, unknowns, and ongoing evolution.

Antecedents of Economics 2.0 can be found in the work of a group of economists known as the Austrian school. Joseph Schumpeter emphasized the importance of entrepreneurs, innovation, and what he called "creative destruction." Friedrich Hayek emphasized the roles of cultural norms, institutions, and "spontaneous order." However, the focus of this book will be on the ideas of living economists, and we leave it to curious readers to explore the intellectual genealogy themselves.

ECONOMICS 1.0 VS. ECONOMICS 2.0

Economics 1.0 is about scarcity. To understand what we mean by that, consider that textbooks define economics as the study of the allocation of scarce resources among competing ends. So if a society wants to produce more guns, then it will have less labor, land, and equipment with which to produce butter. When first-year students are given a quiz on the opening textbook chapter that asks them to state the economic problem, their answer is supposed to revolve around scarcity, often phrased as "unlimited wants but limited resources."

Economics 2.0 is about abundance, which arises from technical progress. Maybe there is no free lunch, as the saying goes; but we do not have to work nearly as hard to put food on the table as we used to. Just two hundred years ago, over half of all Americans worked in agriculture. Today, the figure is less than two percent. Sixty years ago, a social studies teacher looking for a movie that would motivate students to sympathize with *struggling with deprivation*

the plight of the unfortunate in America might have chosen "The Grapes of Wrath." Today, it would be "Supersize Me." — *struggling with abundance*

Conventional economics is focused on how we can allocate resources efficiently. In this view, the story is that markets facilitate trade and thereby foster efficiency but do little else. With painstaking graphs and numerical examples, the professor shows that both sides of trade benefit from the exchange, whether trade takes place within a national border or across it. These calculations explain why it is better to outsource your ironing to a laundry than to do it yourself. Economics 1.0 explains that trade is based on comparative advantage.

Economics 2.0 says, yes, it is more efficient to send your shirts to a laundry than to iron them yourself. But have you heard of permanent press? Thanks to technical progress, many shirts today do not need to be ironed at all. Perhaps in another decade or two they will not need to be washed. Given the likely progress of nanotechnology, there is a good chance that shirts manufactured in 2020 will be "permanent clean." That's Economics 2.0.

THE SOFTWARE LAYER

Another way to think about Economics 2.0 is that it emphasizes the importance of the "software layer" of the economy. The economy can be understood as consisting of hardware and software, like a computer. Yet the software layer is glossed over in economics textbooks, which attempt to describe the production and allocation of goods and services in terms of the use of tangible inputs – things you can see and feel, like factory conveyor belts, machine tools, and individual workers.

But building a car takes more than just the machines and workers that you see sitting inside a factory. It also takes research, design, contracts, specifications, quality-control systems, and worker training – all of which are components of what we call the software layer. Moreover, when consumers come to a dealer to buy a car, both parties operate under a set of expectations and rules about negotiating, financing, and post-purchase obligations. These expectations and rules are also part of the software layer.

How important is the software layer? Over the past fifty years, many economists, including those you will meet in this book, have come to believe that the software layer explains most of the significant differences in economic performance over history and across countries.

To grasp the magnitude of these differences, consider for a moment what it would be like if you were forced to live like a typical American of one hundred years ago. Think of how many goods and services that you rely on today that could not have been found a century earlier. Call this the "Hundred-Year Gap." We can also go back in history and consider the Hundred-Year Gap between, say, A.D. 1000 and A.D. 1100. (That gap is much smaller than the most recent Hundred-Year Gap.)

Alternatively, imagine if you were forced to live like a typical citizen of an underdeveloped nation today. Call this the "Development Gap." For example, in Africa the average income is less than $2,000 a year per person, while in the United States it is more than $30,000. Even in rapidly growing countries, such as India, hundreds of millions of people lack many things Americans take for granted, such as reliable electricity and safe drinking water.

The Hundred-Year Gap and the Development Gap have never been as large as they are today. The Development Gap, in particular, is one of the most pressing economic issues of our time. Increasingly, we have come to recognize that much of what accounts for the Development Gap is to be found in the software layer.

The Hundred-Year Gap and the Development Gap reflect intangible assets and invisible liabilities. We may think of the intangible assets as recipes or algorithms. These recipes for satisfying human wants are far more sophisticated and efficient than the recipes that humans possessed one hundred years ago.

The invisible liabilities are social arrangements and political institutions. Societies are held back by government corruption, resistance to innovation, and the habit of rewarding those who expropriate wealth more highly than those who create it. Institutions are to the economy what an operating system is to a computer. A clumsy or buggy institutional environment will hinder economic performance.

The magnitudes of these intangible assets and invisible liabilities are staggering. A study published by the World Bank estimates that the average citizen in many advanced industrial countries has over $400,000 in *intangible* net worth. Meanwhile, the intangible net worth of people living in the poorest, most ill-governed nations of the world is actually negative. Their social and political institutions are like software that has so many bugs and viruses that you would be more productive without any computer at all.

There is another key difference between the hardware and software layers of the economy. The hardware layer obeys the laws of scarcity. The labor, machinery, and factory space in an automobile plant are scarce, in that they cannot at the same time be used to make frozen food or television sets. Moreover, when you double the amount of hardware used in production, you typically get less than double the level of output, which is the phenomenon known as diminishing returns.

If only hardware mattered, rich countries would face limits to growth and progress would decelerate. The standard of living would be improving fastest in the poorest countries, where small incremental gains in hardware would have the largest impact relative to a low base.

The software layer, by contrast, does not obey the laws of scarcity. As a result, we can (and do) observe growth accelerating in developed countries while some underdeveloped economies stagnate or even decline.

Only looking at the hardware layer, economists typically take progress for granted as something that just happens. Yet this raises the question of why the benefits of progress are so much greater in some countries than in others. Consider that we can profitably employ an immigrant in construction in the United States at a wage far higher than what that person could earn in his home country. Our building methods are not exactly nuclear secrets. Nor are the low-cost techniques of our retailers, our utilities, or our banks. How is it that so much of the world lags behind?

Economists used to try to explain underdevelopment in terms of hardware. Poor countries lacked the necessary tangible "stuff" needed to grow, such as steel mills and power plants. Today, we increasingly focus on the software layer, particularly government function and social norms. It turns out that where property rights are weak and government expropriation is unchecked, as in Zimbabwe or North Korea, prosperity is elusive. On the other hand, countries that are relatively poor in resources can nonetheless achieve a high level of affluence. The examples of Hong Kong, Singapore, and Israel demonstrate that with a constructive software layer, economic success does not require a natural resource base.

Rather than taking technological innovation as given, Economics 2.0 looks at the process by which innovation arises and spreads. Often, innovation is the result of the unplanned trial-and-error learning that takes place among new enterprises, rather than the organized research and development efforts of large organizations.

The hardware-driven story of textbook economics can be told without the entrepreneur. In contrast, entrepreneurs are the main characters in the story that we tell about the software layer. Entrepreneurs push innovation past the resistance of skeptics and entrenched interests.

We recognize that in order to function, modern markets need a robust operating system, consisting of rules, customs, norms, standards, and protocols. It is true that government provides part of this operating system in the form of laws and regulations, but the private sector also supplies much of the operating system that enables markets to function well.

In providing its segment of the economic operating system, government has the advantage of economies of scale: it can offer definitive, universal solutions. The provision of meat inspections and bank deposit insurance and regulation are examples of practices where the United States government has developed effective systems on which all of us rely.

However, the institutional software needs of markets are evolving. Improving an operating system requires innovation, and innovation is best delivered by trial-and-error experimentation and competition, which largely takes place in markets. Governments are not known for extensive trial-and-error experimentation (indeed, there are often good reasons for government not to engage in such experimentation). Hence, our paradoxical conclusion is that markets are often the solution to market failure.

Douglass North speaks of the *adaptive* efficiency of the economy. This is an important concept for understanding how Economics 2.0 differs from what came before it. The standard theory of public goods and private goods looks at how to allocate existing resources. Instead, we ask how well the software layer is suited to creating new wealth and raising the standard of living. Some economies are far better at generating wealth and rising living standards; these economies are said to have adaptive efficiency and not just allocative efficiency. They are more dynamic than their static counterparts.

North describes what he does as "the New Institutional Economics," emphasizing the role of institutions. Indeed, it is difficult to overstate how important institutions are to modern economies. But our scope is somewhat broader than institutional economics. We want to include the role of ideas and innovation in driving economic growth. We like to use Paul Romer's term "recipes" to point up the knowledge component of the economy.

Moreover, the term "institutions" as used by North differs somewhat from the term as it is employed in ordinary discourse. In standard usage, an institution is often a discrete social organization, such as a religious institution or an institution of higher learning. That is not really what North is referring to when he speaks of institutions.

A better term for North's concept might be "protocols." In ordinary speech, the term protocol is used to refer to unwritten customs for behavior among ambassadors ("diplomatic protocol"), written agreements ("the Geneva protocol"), formats for exchanging information between computers ("the Internet protocols"), and recommended procedures for medical treatment ("protocol for administering beta blockers"). All of these usages of the term "protocol" are relevant here.

We think that the term "operating system" provides a good metaphor for the sorts of institutions or protocols we have in mind. The concept of an operating system captures the fundamental importance of basic economic institutions. Just as your ability to use clever computer applications, such as email and spreadsheets, depends on having a working operating system, an economy's ability to use the latest innovations depends on having well-established property rights and the rule of law.

In short, we will describe the software layer as consisting of recipes and an operating system. We use "recipes" to refer to innovation, ideas, know-how, science, and technology. We use "the operating system" to refer to customs, rules, norms, laws, regulations, and methods of intermediation.

One important form of intermediation is financial intermediation. A recent tradition in economics treats financial intermediaries as "transparent," with investors always able to see through the intermediary to the underlying risks of the projects being undertaken. Instead, we take the opposite view. We think that the role of financial intermediaries in the economy necessarily involves disguising risk. We believe that this explains why financial markets are fragile, and that this in turn can help explain economic booms and slumps.

The Plan of the Book

The plan for the rest of the book is as follows. Chapter 2, "Economics 2.0 in Practice," explores the nature and significance of the software layer, using examples and data. We go on an imaginary tour of a food court at a shopping mall, pointing out some of the many recipes and protocols that are necessary for its operation. We proceed to look at the measurements of the software layer in national economies. We present the evidence for the significance of the software layer as if in a courtroom trial. Also included in this chapter are interviews with two Nobel laureates. Economic historian Robert Fogel provides evidence of the enormous progress that humans have made over the last few centuries. Robert Solow, who first identified the large intangible component of wealth, discusses the origins and implications of his research.

Chapter 3, "From the Meadow to the Food Court," looks at how the economy has evolved from one of scarcity to one of abundance. The meadow, in which people are imagined like a grazing herd, is a metaphor for Malthusian subsistence. The food court, in which a plethora of recipes allows for easy substitution among ingredients, is a metaphor for the abundance generated by knowledge, the intangible asset. This chapter explains the role that science, technology, and innovation play in raising our standard of living. It emphasizes the experimental nature of economic progress, with ideas being adopted and discarded on a trial-and-error basis.

Chapter 3 includes interviews with Paul Romer and Joel Mokyr, two enthusiastic and articulate exponents of the role of knowledge and discovery in creating prosperity. Mokyr points out that knowledge often is developed without anyone anticipating how that knowledge will be used. This means that economic development inevitably has an unplanned aspect. Romer points out that although the supply of physical matter on earth is finite, the number of ways to re-arrange matter is infinite. This implies that our intuition, which expects prosperity to run into physical limits, is wrong. Instead, over time, economic constraints tend to recede in the wake of new discoveries.

Chapter 4, "Bugs in the Software Layer," looks at explanations for poor economic performance in underdeveloped countries. In these countries, output falls far short of the potential represented by their traditional factors of production – land, labor, and capital. We will examine how dysfunctional operating systems drive people away from productive activity and toward the informal or underground economy.

Chapter 4 includes interviews with William Easterly and Nobel laureate Douglass North. Easterly argues that local people working close to a problem have the incentive and the knowledge to solve it, while conventional government-administered foreign aid must go through a process that inevitably breeds corruption. North relates how studying the history of shipping led him to realize that curbing piracy was very important to development. This then led him to appreciate the significance of the broader issue of economic "piracy," including crime and government expropriation.

Chapter 5, "The Heart that Pumps Innovation: The Role of the Entrepreneur" stresses the significance of entrepreneurs. The most important role of entrepreneurs is to overcome resistance to change. Resistance comes from bureaucracies, where new ideas get shot down by those who are threatened or simply confused by innovative thinking. This chapter includes an interview with Amar Bhide, who emphasizes how entrepreneurs gravitate toward situations that are dynamic and ambiguous, such as the commercialization of the Internet.

Chapter 6, "Financial Intermediation," looks at the role of financial institutions in reducing the cost of taking risks. Financial intermediation is a critical component of the software layer. However, the very nature of financial intermediation is characteristically fragile, because investors cannot "see through" the intermediary to fully understand the underlying risks. The economy can benefit from government regulation that balances the need for innovation with the need for stability and reliability in the financial sector.

Chapter 7, "Adaptive Efficiency and the Role of Government," describes the market as a process for sifting through new ideas. We show how the structure of jobs changes radically over time, as some occupations experience rapid growth while others undergo rapid decline. Government, as an institution, tends to resist this kind of change. Whenever the press notices that interest groups are lobbying the government for protective regulation, people see this political favoritism as something that can and should be stopped. Economists, on the other hand, see lobbying as inevitable; we call it "rent-seeking." Because incumbents are typically better than entrepreneurs at "rent-seeking," this behavior is an important impediment to progress. Restraining government from siding too strongly with incumbents and against innovation is a constant challenge.

In the United States, two industries that are most in need of adaptive efficiency are education and health care. Both industries are complex and challenging, with many possible avenues for improvement. In these important sectors, we surely could benefit from the development and diffusion of innovation. Education and health care would be invigorated by reducing the role of government.

This chapter includes an interview with William Lewis, whose focus on particular industries, notably retailing and construction, enabled him to identify striking differences across countries in their ability to adopt new, efficient techniques.

Chapter 8, "Challenges for the Future," identifies some important issues pertaining to the software layer that need further study. For underdeveloped countries, a key challenge is how to reconcile the need for order with the fact that economic progress requires rapid learning and change, which necessarily undermines old and established ways of conducting business and other transactions. For the advanced countries, challenges include adapting to the increasing share of income devoted to health care as well as to the rise of the "information" component, relative to the physical component, of economic output. This chapter includes an interview with William Baumol, who observes that there are some situations in which the best outcome is likely to come from openness and collaboration among firms, and other situations which are likely better served by secrecy and competition.

About the Hardware/Software Metaphor

How is the economy like a computer?

Both the economy and computers have enabled us to enjoy more goods and services with less effort, although not without occasional frustrations.

Both have shown exponential improvement. You would not want to trade a computer made in the last three years for one made twenty years ago. Nor would you want to trade the economy of today for the economy of one hundred years ago.

(At times, economists have treated the market as a mechanism for processing information. However, this is not an idea that is pursued or assumed in this book.)

We should stress one important difference between a computer and the economy. A computer is the product of conscious design, but the economy is not. An economy emerges from the decentralized actions of individuals and small businesses as well as the organized planning of large corporations and government. In Friedrich Hayek's term, the economy is a spontaneous order.

How are the traditional factors of production – labor, land, and natural resources – like hardware?

Both are visible and quantifiable. One can count the number of hours worked, the number of acres of land, and the supply of fresh water or diamonds or oil in the ground. Similarly, one can quantify the speed and storage capacity of the hardware components of a computer.

Both are what economists call rivalrous. If I use land for an office building, then you cannot use it for a farm. If I use a cash register for a clothing store, then you cannot use it for a bookstore. If I am using a computer's hardware component, such as the keyboard, then you cannot use that same component.

Increasing output with traditional factors of production means "doing more with more." That is, you add more labor, more capital, more land, or more computers. "Doing more with more" is subject to the law of diminishing returns: you cannot keep doubling the strawberry harvest by doubling the number of strawberry pickers. Similarly, increasing computer operations with hardware means adding memory circuits or storage capacity.

How are recipes (ideas, innovations, and so forth) like software?

Both are invisible and difficult to quantify. Counting the number of patents issued in a year or the number of lines of code in software is feasible, but it's not especially informative.

Both are nonrivalrous. If one person uses a spreadsheet, that does not stop someone else from using a spreadsheet. If one firm uses an efficient inventory-control system, that does not stop another firm from using the same approach. Indeed, according to researchers such as William Lewis, better inventory control across many players in the retail sector helps explain the productivity gains America has enjoyed in recent decades, something that has contributed considerably to economic growth.

Increasing output with better recipes means "doing more with less." A better recipe allows a firm to increase the value and reduce the cost of its product or service. "Doing more with less" explains how, in spite of the law of diminishing returns, economic growth continues to accelerate. A better software program makes more efficient use of the computer's resources and of the time and effort of the people who interact with the program.

Both recipes and software are costly to produce, but nearly costless to reproduce. Undertaking research and clinical trials to develop a valuable medical treatment takes a lot of resources. Actually manufacturing the drug or administering a new protocol costs relatively little. Similarly, developing a new software solution or application can take many person-years of effort. However, the costs of distribution and training new users can be low.

Both software development and recipe creation can benefit from broadly applicable innovative ideas. For example, until the 1980s, every computer application used its own program to manage data. This tied up programmers who were, in effect, "reinventing the wheel." Eventually generic database programs came into use. This freed computer programmers to write more specific applications, yielding widespread improvement in efficiency. In economic history, the electric motor, the internal combustion engine, the personal computer, and the Internet are all "general-purpose technologies." They were applied in many fields, resulting in a broad increase in productivity.

How are laws, regulations, written agreements, and unwritten rules like an operating system?

Both are invisible and difficult to evaluate objectively. Researchers have attempted to construct indices that measure corruption or the difficulty of obtaining a business license. But such measures are tenuous and incomplete.

Both are nonrivalrous. When one citizen benefits from a society's respect for private property, a good work ethic, and honest government, there is nothing that prevents these protocols from benefiting another citizen.

Both can be difficult to repair when not working properly. Software "bugs" are notoriously difficult to locate and to fix. Similarly, it is difficult to "debug" the poorly performing economies of the underdeveloped world. Until relatively recently, most development experts were not even looking for bugs in the software layer. Instead, they were focused on hardware – particularly capital.

Both are hard to convert from one entity to another. When two companies, such as banks, merge into one organization, they eventually need to consolidate their software systems into a single operation. Typically, this turns out to be very costly. It would be particularly difficult if one company used Microsoft's operating system and another company used Apple or Linux.

One might naively suppose that after a merger, all an executive has to do is select one company's system (the winner) and convert the other firm's software (the loser) to that system. In practice, however, such conversions are not so easy. Software that has been in use for a long time tends to be filled with patches and idiosyncratic features that reflect the evolution of business practices beyond what was anticipated at the time the system was first designed. There will be data structures and sections of code that might have seemed appropriate when first implemented but which no longer make any sense. When undertaking a conversion, you will find that some of the loser's peculiar features are so deeply embedded that they have to be carried over to the new system. Conversely, some of the features of the winner's system may prove to be quite awkward when applied to the loser's business.

By the same token, regulatory policies that may be effective in one cultural setting may be counterproductive elsewhere. An operating system that works on one computer will also work on a similar machine. Countries do not have that same degree of similarity.

Even if an underdeveloped country wants to adopt the operating system of a successful country, it is not clear how this can be done. Perhaps the U.S. model of bank regulation is a good one to follow. But are our agricultural subsidies worthy of emulation? Our housing market subsidies? Our telecommunications regulations? Our approach to health care regulations and insurance?

The merger between East and West Germany illustrates the difficulty of changing operating systems. East German wages were converted to West German marks at a one-to-one ratio, which meant that East German wages were far too high relative to productivity. When this wage structure was reinforced by the institution of strong unionism, the result was massive disorder and unemployment in the East.

One way in which the hardware–software metaphor is *not* helpful is in describing the role of education. From the hardware–software perspective, the cumulative knowledge available at any given time – what you can find in libraries or on the Internet – is software. Yet the skills and knowledge of a particular *individual* might be classified as hardware. It is true that skills and knowledge are invisible and difficult to quantify. But a brain surgeon's experience can only benefit one patient at a time, so the brain surgeon's know-how – what economists call "human capital" – is rivalrous. Also, increasing output by increasing know-how means "doing more with more." People need more formal schooling or more on-the-job training to increase their human capital. In economic terms, acquiring human capital incurs an opportunity cost – you have to give up time and resources in order to increase your skills.

Metaphorically, it would seem that individual know-how is software. After all, it is not physical. The World Bank includes it in its measure of intangible capital, which we will refer to in the next chapter. In economic terms, however, the process of acquiring skills is more like obtaining hardware. Therefore, for individual education and skill acquisition, the metaphor of human capital may be more apt than the metaphor of software.

Why this book, and why now? For many years, economists did not do an adequate job explaining how the world worked. This was not their fault; often they were working with the best tools at their disposal. Even today, our understanding of how modern economies work – and how and why some economies don't work – is not total or complete.

But we believe that in beginning to see the world through the lens of Economics 2.0, you will come away with a more thorough and penetrating understanding of the world around you. We believe that it may influence how you think about business and technology as well as your approach to politics and policy. But mostly we think you'll enjoy what is, in our view, a remarkable journey of intellectual discovery. Let's get started.

19

Chapter 2:
ECONOMICS 2.0 IN PRACTICE

LET'S BEGIN WITH an imaginary tour of a food court at a shopping mall. During this hypothetical field observation, we will look for both the hardware and software layers embedded in the workings of the food court.

The hardware layer consists of the tangible factors of production at work. These are land, labor, and capital. Some of the food stalls occupy more valuable positions than others, which illustrates that land varies in value. The workers who staff the cash registers and cook the food are the labor. Ovens, refrigerators, soda-dispensing machines, tables, chairs, and other equipment constitute the capital in the food court.

Next, we think about all of the intangible factors that make the food court possible. These are the recipes and protocols that make up the software layer. We use the term "recipes" as a metaphor for all of the knowledge that is embedded in the food court. To be sure, there are literal recipes for cooking the dishes on the menus in the food stalls. But there are many more metaphorical recipes at work here.

The workers follow routine procedures – for example, the sales clerk will always ask the customer what he or she would like to drink. Such procedures also are recipes of a sort. How equipment is installed, operated, maintained, and replaced makes up another set of recipes.

How does the owner of a food stall make sure that the right amount of food supplies are ordered – not so little that they run short but not so much that they have to throw away a lot of spoiled food? There have to be recipes for predicting demand and managing inventory.

The developer of the shopping mall used a recipe for selecting the site and designing the food court. The lawyers who wrote the contracts between the developer and the stall owners used a recipe for composing such agreements.

The contracts, in turn, are part of the protocols of the shopping mall. Protocols are the written and unwritten rules that govern the food court. These rules apply to customers, workers, and owners.

For example, although the food stalls are separate, they share some equipment in common: chairs and tables, trays, and trash containers. The responsibility for cleaning the common dining area is not borne by individual stall workers. Instead, it is shared between customers (who throw away trash and put trays on a central shelf) and generic food court workers (who clean floors and tables and redistribute trays to food stalls).

How are these common resources provided? We assume that there is a central management company that supplies the shared equipment and cleaning crew, paid for by monthly fees from the stall owners. This arrangement is an example of what we mean by a protocol.

We notice that each stall has an identical soda-dispensing machine, with the same brands on offer. We surmise that the stalls have a collective contract with a supplier, in which the supplier gets exclusive rights to serve the food court in exchange for sharing revenue with the owners of the food court stalls. This contract is another example of a protocol.

If a hamburger stall decides to expand its menu to include

pizza, does the owner need to get the approval of the owner of the pizza stall? What mechanisms are there for preventing or resolving disputes between stall owners? Written documents probably answer some of these questions. Other issues may be resolved informally.

Some items, such as straws, napkins, and small packages of condiments, are placed out in the open to be taken by customers as needed. Customers generally take only small quantities of these items, and typically only from a stall where they have made a purchase. This reflects unwritten protocols that customers have learned to observe.

Unlike other paper products, drink cups are held by cashiers and not left in the open for customers to take. Perhaps owners measure cup usage and compare it with soda purchases as a way of keeping tabs on their employees.

The workers appear to follow a number of rules concerning sanitation. Those who handle food use plastic gloves. There are signs in the bathrooms saying that employees must wash their hands before returning to work.

Some of the cleanliness regulations come from the government. Stall owners must exert effort to comply with government regulations. In return for that, they enjoy the confidence of consumers that stalls must maintain certain standards in order to retain their licenses. Other government regulations include rules for tax payments and labor practices.

Some stalls are franchises of large, national chains. We presume that capital costs and profits are contractually shared between the local operator of the franchise and the national firm. These agreements serve to allocate the risks and rewards of each franchise.

Does the stall owner borrow from the national franchise in order to finance equipment and inventory? Or does the owner rely on a bank for a loan or a line of credit?

A few stalls do not appear to belong to national franchises.

Instead, they have names that are unfamiliar. Sometimes, such stalls offer free samples of their food. We presume that, in the absence of a well-known brand, many consumers would be reluctant to try an unfamiliar stall without first sampling the food.

We wonder about the management arrangements in the food court. How do the owners of the stalls ensure that their workers do not skim money for themselves or give away food to their friends?

We notice that there is an automated teller machine (ATM) near the entrance of the food court. The same ATM accepts cards from many different banks. Obviously, the banks have agreed on a shared set of protocols.

We also notice that most of the stalls will accept credit cards. They use machines to verify the credit card purchases. Back in the 1980s, fast-food outlets only took cash.

Overall, the software of the food court fills three types of needs: interoperability, property rights, and trust.

Interoperability means that machinery from different companies works well together. For example, someone with a deposit at bank XYZ can obtain money from the ATM operated by bank ABC. In manufacturing industries, interoperability creates efficiency in many ways at all stages of production. Interoperability is what allows companies to standardize procedures and reduce the time it takes to perform operations. Where interoperability is absent, as when doctors find that different health insurance companies require different forms to be filled out, productivity suffers.

Property rights serve to establish who owns what. For the napkins, straws, and small packages of condiments left in the open, the property rights are enforced by informal norms. For the relationship between the stall owners, the shopping mall developer, soda suppliers, and the national fast-food franchises, property rights are allocated contractually.

Trust is at issue in the consumption of restaurant food, the performance of workers when owners are not present, and in various methods of payment. National fast-food chains have reputations that consumers trust when choosing food. We speculated that cups are carefully dispensed because otherwise stall owners might be unable to trust their workers to charge properly for drinks. The credit card verification machines are used to improve trust in that form of payment.

Government plays an important role in promoting trust in the payment system. The ATM is accessed by customers of banks. Their bank deposits are insured by a federal agency, which in turn monitors and regulates banks in order to minimize the risk of having to bail out an insolvent bank.

Government also is responsible for making sure that cash can be used safely in transactions. It establishes money as legal tender, meaning that merchants are required to accept it. But if the government were wanton in its printing of money, inflation could be high and unpredictable, making the process of setting prices and paying in cash much more difficult to trust.

Consumer trust in food also is bolstered by government institutions. Food production and distribution are regulated and inspected at various stages by federal and local agencies. Restaurants are inspected and regulated by local officials.

In addition, government is involved in ensuring that property rights are trusted. Although private parties typically negotiate contracts without government involvement, they know in the back of their minds that any disputes between the parties will be adjudicated peacefully and impartially by government courts.

The impartiality of government is something that we take for granted in the United States. In other countries, government officials may take bribes. Worse, they may decide matters on the basis of clan loyalty or the interests of a narrow ruling clique, leaving the majority of citizens without institutional protection of their property rights or their interests as consumers.

The recipes and protocols that make up the software layer

of the food court are clearly important, even though they are not visible. Next, we will look at evidence that the software layer has contributed greatly to the improvement in our well-being.

Fifty years ago, when economists searched for explanations for differences in output per worker over time or across countries, the focus was on hardware, primarily the stock of capital. What they have found over the last half-century, however, is that variations in the stock of capital account for less than a fourth of differences in worker productivity. Instead, over time, the most important factor is the development of new recipes. Across countries, the usage of recipes varies. To a large extent, the failure to use the best recipes reflects dysfunctional protocols – in particular the absence of trust and property rights.

The software layer is a major factor in the economic well-being that we enjoy. It is difficult to overstate how much living standards have improved in how brief a span of time. If anything, as you'll see below, we underestimate how much conditions have improved.

This chapter lays out evidence in order to tell the following story:

1. The Industrial Revolution was a very big deal. Sometime around 1800, human living standards began to improve in a sustained, rapid way never before observed.

2. Economic development tends to be either imperceptibly slow or extremely rapid. As a result, the gap between underdeveloped and developed countries in terms of living standards is very high.

3. Differences in the average standard of living across countries have widened, as growth has continued in rich countries while the poorest economies have stagnated and in some cases declined.

4. Most of the differences in the standard of living across countries cannot be traced to tangible factors such as resources or

capital stocks. Intangible factors, what we call protocols, appear to have greater explanatory power.

5. One of the intangible factors is the environment for entrepreneurs. The harder it is to start a legitimate business, the lower a country's standard of living.

6. Economic growth is accompanied by dramatic changes in occupations. The nature of work changes rapidly.

1. The Industrial Revolution was a very big deal. Sometime around 1800, human living standards began to improve in a sustained, rapid way never before observed.

EXHIBIT A. Historical Levels of GDP per Capita[1]

YEAR	GDP PER CAPITA, WORLD AVERAGE
5000 B.C.	$130
1000 B.C.	$160
A.D. 1	$135
1000	$165
1500	$175
1800	$250
1900	$850
1950	$2,030
1975	$4,640
2000	$8,175

Our first exhibit shows the historical improvement in living standards as measured by the standard economic performance gauge, Gross Domestic Product (GDP) per capita. Think of it as the value of all of the goods and services produced worldwide in a given year, divided by world population as of that year. Because of new inventions and other factors, the comparison of

GDP over long historical time periods is an art, not a science.

Note that the average standard of living in 1500 was only about 35 percent higher than in 5000 B.C. But over the fifty-year period at the end of the twentieth century, average living standards increased to almost 400 percent of their 1950 level.

GDP numbers can seem abstract, and issues of comparability across time can lead to doubts. The next exhibit looks at goods that were available over a period of one hundred years. It estimates how long it would have taken to earn enough to buy each good at the average American wage.

Brad DeLong, who compiled this data, calls the ratio of the number in the first column to the number in the second column the "productivity multiple." For example, for the Horatio

---

*EXHIBIT B. Changes in the Cost of Goods
Over the Past 100 Years*[2]

COMMODITY	TIME TO EARN (HOURS) 1895	TIME TO EARN (HOURS) 1997
Horatio Alger books (six volumes)	21.0	0.6
One-speed bicycle	260.0	7.2
Cushioned office chair	24.0	2.0
100-piece dinner set	44.0	3.6
Hairbrush	16.0	2.0
Cane rocking chair	8.0	1.6
Solid gold locket	28.0	6.0
Encyclopædia Britannica	140.0	4.0
Steinway piano	2,400.0	1,107.6
Sterling silver teaspoon	26.0	34.0
Oranges (dozen)	2.0	0.1
Ground beef (one pound)	0.8	0.2
Milk (one gallon)	2.0	0.25

Alger books, the productivity multiple is 35. In other words, if that commodity were used to measure the standard of living, a worker in 1997 was 35 times as well off as a worker in 1895. Overall, DeLong estimates that the productivity multiple for the last one hundred years in the U.S. is between 14 and 25 – that we are between 14 and 25 times better off than we were just a century ago.

EXHIBIT C. Life Expectancy[3]

COUNTRY	1750	1900	1950	1990
England or UK	37	48	69	76
France	26	46	67	77
U.S.	51	48	68	76
India		27	39	59

In addition to becoming significantly wealthier, we are living much longer. The increase in longevity corroborates the increase in world average G D P per capita as an indicator of the improvement in living standards over time.

The prevalence of serious health problems has rapidly diminished in recent generations. So as we get wealthier and live longer, we are living healthier as we age as well. We're aging better than we used to.

In the table below, the difference between the first and the second column reflects how the state of health changed between cohorts of military veterans over this seventy-five-year period. The difference between the second and third column shows the contribution of health care in alleviating disorders among the more recent cohort. The combination of better overall health and better care has greatly reduced the prevalence rate of chronic disorders, as can be seen in the difference between the first and the third column.

EXHIBIT D. Health Status[4]
Prevalence Rates of Disorders
Among Veterans Age 65 or Older

TYPE	PREVALENCE RATE		
	1910	MID-1980S PRIOR TO ALLEVIATING INTERVENTIONS	MID-1980S AFTER ALLEVIATING INTERVENTIONS
Musculoskeletal	67.7	47.9	42.5
Digestive	84.0	49.0	18.0
Genitourinary	27.3	36.3	8.9
Central nervous system, endocrine, metabolic, or blood	24.2	29.9	12.6
Circulatory	90.1	42.9	40.0
Respiratory	42.2	29.8	26.5

In the early twentieth century, for example, large majorities of those age 65 or older would experience digestive disorders. As the twentieth century came to a close, fewer than one in five elderly people had such disorders.

Overall, around 1900, the average U.S. male between the ages of 65 and 69 had 6.2 chronic conditions. By the mid-1990s, this had fallen to 1.9 chronic conditions. Economic growth has produced improvements in health status as well as longevity.

Some improvements in living standards are not captured in statistics such as GDP, so GDP numbers understate how much things have improved. The table below quantifies the value of the improvements in health status that we discussed in exhibits C and D. These improvements in health are not counted in measured GDP.

EXHIBIT E. *The Value of Improvements in Health and Life Expectancy*[5]

YEARS	AVERAGE ANNUAL PERCENTAGE INCREASE	
	CONSUMPTION	VALUE OF HEALTH STATUS
1900–1925	2.0	2.3
1925–1950	1.8	3.3
1950–1975	2.4	1.9
1975–1995	2.0	1.7

How important are these improvements? Including these values would roughly double our estimate of the improvement in living standards over the past century. So if Brad DeLong is correct that the productivity multiple has gone up by a factor of 20, then including health and longevity improvements, we are about forty times better off than people living one hundred years ago.

EXHIBIT F. *Improvement in Nutrition*[6]

YEAR	DAILY AVERAGE CALORIES CONSUMED PER CAPITA IN GREAT BRITAIN
1700	2,095
1800	2,237
1850	2,362
1909–1913	2,857
1954–1955	3,231
1965	3,304
1989	3,149

Calorie consumption is another indicator of economic growth. How much better are our diets after a few centuries of economic growth? Fogel points out that people today could not survive on the diets of three hundred years ago. At our size,

2,000 calories would barely maintain our bodies, leaving no energy left for work.

EXHIBIT G. Improvement in IQ – the Flynn Effect[7]

COUNTRY	TIME PERIOD	INCREASE IN AVERAGE IQ (15 points = one standard deviation)
Belgium	1958–1967	7 points
Netherlands	1952–1982	21 points
Israel	1970–1985	9 points
Norway	1954–1980	12.5 points
Britain	1942–1992	27 points
New Zealand	1936–1968	7.7 points

The rise in average IQ is known as the Flynn effect. It provides strong evidence that environment can influence IQ. Not only are we much healthier and living far longer than our ancestors, but we're smarter than they were, too. The rise in IQ over time is a plausible consequence of economic growth in general and better nutrition in particular. That is, the rise in average IQ likely represents another benefit of economic growth.

As if it weren't enough that we are richer, healthier, and living longer than ever before, we also have significantly more leisure time. We'll reserve judgment about how well or wisely people spend this additional leisure time, but there's no denying that as the table below shows, in addition to more GDP per capita, we have over three times more leisure.

It is important to recognize how much less effort it takes to acquire the necessities of life now, relative to a century ago. Fogel notes that one hundred years ago it took 1,700 hours of work to purchase the annual food supply for a family. That's over ten months working a standard work week. Today, it requires just 260 hours – less than a month and a half.

Exhibit H. More Leisure Time[8]
Activities on Which a Typical Male Head of Household
Spends Time During an Average Day

	HOURS SPENT PER DAY	
ACTIVITY	IN 1880	IN 1995
Work	8.5	4.7
Illness	0.7	0.5
Sleep, meals, chores, and travel to and from work	13.0	13.0
Leisure	1.8	5.8

Exhibit I. The Shift Toward Leisure[9]

	PERCENTAGE OF CONSUMPTION	
CATEGORY	IN 1875	IN 1995
Food	49	5
Clothing	12	2
Housing and durable goods	13	6
Health care	1	9
Education	1	5
Other	6	7
Leisure	18	68

Less dramatic increases in productivity have occurred in clothing and in durable goods. But the overall result is that we have much more time for leisure, and we can afford to spend more on health care and education.

This increase in leisure, like the increases in longevity and health status, goes uncounted in GDP. Thus we have even more evidence of dramatic improvement in our standard of living over the past 125 years.

EXHIBIT J. *Improvements From Innovation*[10]

YEAR	TECHNOLOGY	LIGHTING EFFICIENCY (lumen-hours per BTU)
1750 B.C.	Oil lamp	17.5
A.D. 1800	Tallow candle	22.2
1815	Whale-oil lamp	39.4
1875	Kerosene lamp	46.6
1883	Electric light, carbon filament	762.0
1920	Electric light, tungsten filament	3,463.7
1992	Compact fluorescent bulb	20,111.1

More people today can consume more goods and services for less effort than one hundred years ago. But the change is so great that we actually consume in different ways.

William Nordhaus writes, "almost three-quarters of today's consumption is radically different from its counterpart in the nineteenth century." This makes measurement of the value of innovation particularly important.

Nordhaus believes that consumer price indexes are strongly biased over long periods to overestimate inflation and underestimate real growth. He calculates alternative estimates based on different estimates of this bias. "In terms of living standards, the conventional growth in real wages has been by a factor of 13 over the 1800–1992 period. For the low-bias case, real wages have grown by a factor of 40, while in the high-bias case real wages have grown by a factor of 190." In other words, using DeLong's estimate of GDP per capita of $250 in 1800, real GDP per capita today would be about two hundred times that, or $50,000 (compared with DeLong's estimate of $8,175 for 2000).

Overall, it seems fair to say that our economic lives have changed dramatically in the past one hundred years. By comparison, all of the economic progress from the dawn of civilization through the eighteenth century seems tiny. The rapidly accelerating rate of economic advance that began around 1800 is a significant historical event.

2. *Economic development tends to be either imperceptibly slow or extremely rapid. As a result, the gap between underdeveloped and developed countries in terms of living standards is very high.*

EXHIBIT K. Productivity Growth in Nail Production[11]

PERIOD	PRODUCTIVITY INDEX	PERCENTAGE INCREASE
1200–1249	100	–
1400–1449	147	47
1600–1649	351	139
1800–1849	1132	223

Human beings can become more productive over time at widely varying rates. These rates of increase are important. They help determine how much and how quickly living standards will improve.

To get a sense of increases in productivity over time, Clark estimated output per worker in nail production in England. The productivity index for the half-century of 1400–1449 was 47 percent higher than its value two hundred years earlier. The increase over the next two hundred years was 139 percent. Over the two hundred years ending in the first half of the nineteenth century, productivity accelerated even more quickly, for a cumulative gain of 223 percent for those two centuries.

It is this speed-up in productivity that is characteristic of rapid economic development.

For individual countries, getting rich used to be a lot harder than it is today. Parente and Prescott point out that the process of development has sped up over the years.

EXHIBIT L. Industrialization Rates in Various Countries[12]

COUNTRY	YEAR INCOME REACHED $2,000	NUMBER OF YEARS TO REACH $4,000
New Zealand	1821	65
Australia	1831	42
United Kingdom	1835	54
Netherlands	1855	64
Belgium	1856	55
United States	1856	44
Syria	1961	12
Jordan	1964	15
Taiwan	1965	10
Turkey	1965	23
South Korea	1969	8
Thailand	1977	13

Shown above are the first and most recent countries to achieve $2,000 in average income and to subsequently rise to $4,000 in average income. Note how much more rapidly the doubling occurred in the more recent arrivals.

The table below shows that economic growth has been quite rapid in much of the world, even though poverty is still widespread. The growth in China and India has been particularly impressive, as those nations achieved in the past fifty years what it took the OECD countries hundreds of years to accomplish. On the other hand Latin American economic growth in the past fifty years has been disappointingly slow.

The second table in exhibit L says, for example, that the OECD countries in 1727 were at the level of GDP of African countries in 1950. It took the OECD countries the next 133

EXHIBIT M. Speed of Growth in Various Countries[13]

COUNTRY OR AREA	GDP PER CAPITA 1950	GDP PER CAPITA 2001
Average of 18 OECD countries	$5,150	$20,110
Africa	949	1,796
Middle East	1,533	18,289
India	619	1,957
China	438	3,583
Japan	1,920	20,683
Latin America	3,673	6,947

COUNTRY OR AREA	YEAR OECD COUNTRIES REACHED 1950 GDP LEVEL	YEAR OECD COUNTRIES REACHED 2001 GDP LEVEL	YEARS OF OECD GROWTH 1950–2001
Average of 18 OECD countries	1950	2001	51
Africa	1727	1860	133
Middle East	1858	1950	92
India	<1500	1847	>350
China	<1500	1917	>400
Japan	1920	2001	81
Latin America	1919	1957	38

years to achieve the same amount of growth that the African countries achieved from 1950 to 2001. China and India started out in 1950 from an even lower base than Africa, and they grew even faster from 1950 to 2001. What exhibits K and L tend to show is that economic development, once it gets going, takes place relatively rapidly. The pattern seems to be for countries to remain trapped for long periods with a low standard of living, but when growth is sustained it tends to accelerate.

3. *Differences in the average standard of living across countries have widened, as growth has continued in rich countries but the poorest countries have stagnated.*

Exhibit N. Rich Countries and Poor Countries[14]

Once countries get on a stable growth path, they get much richer compared with poor countries that haven't. As Lant Pritchett points out:

Measured in purchasing-power-parity terms ... the ratio of the per capita income of the richest country (the United States) to the average per capita income of the poorest countries grew from around 9 ($2,181 compared with $250) in 1870 to over 50 ($16,779 compared with $325) in 1960.

Between 1960 and 1990, income grew, on average, 2.6 percent per year in the Organization for Economic Cooperation and Development (OECD) countries, and 1.8 percent in other countries. Among the poor countries, 43 percent have grown more slowly than the slowest-growing OECD country, and 70 percent have grown at a slower rate than the median for OECD countries.

Exhibit O. Rich and Poor Countries[15]

According to David Henderson and Charley Cooper, "900 million people live in 28 high-income countries, with an average income per person of $9,361 per year or greater. But 3.5 billion of the world's 6.1 billion people live in countries with incomes of less than $760 a year per person. Of these, 1.2 billion people live in countries with average incomes of less than $1 a day. The official poverty line in the United States is more than twenty times higher than that."

4. *Most of the differences in the standard of living across countries cannot be traced to tangible factors such as resources or capital stocks. Intangible factors, what we call protocols, appear to have greater explanatory power.*

EXHIBIT P. *Intangible Wealth around the world*[16]

INCOME GROUP	WEALTH PER CAPITA	NATURAL RESOURCES SHARE	PRODUCED CAPITAL SHARE	INTANGIBLE CAPITAL SHARE
Low-income Countries	$7,532	26%	16%	59%
Middle-income Countries	$27,616	13%	19%	68%
High-income Countries	$439,063	2%	17%	80%
Switzerland	$648,241	1%	15%	84%
Denmark	$575,138	2%	14%	84%
Sweden	$513,424	2%	11%	87%
United States	$512,612	3%	16%	82%
Germany	$496,447	1%	14%	85%
Niger	$3,695	53%	8%	39%
Congo	$3,516	265%	180%	-346%
Burundi	$2,859	42%	7%	50%
Nigeria	$2,748	147%	24%	-71%
Ethiopia	$1,965	41%	9%	50%

When many people think of wealth, they think of things they can touch and feel, such as homes or rental properties. Or they think of securities, such as stocks and bonds, that represent shares in companies with impressive offices and factories. This is tangible wealth. But wealth comes in other forms. Sometimes wealth is intangible. Indeed, the most important forms of wealth are intangible.

As an individual, your wealth could include several sources: the land that you own (natural capital); financial assets that entitle you to the returns from investments in business plant and equipment (produced capital); and intangible capital, which includes the value of your skills and education as a worker as well as the quality of the economic institutions in the country where you happen to live. Note that the average level of wealth per person in high-income countries (about 25 countries in the Organization for Economic Co-operation and Development) is more than 15 times that of the wealthier non-OECD countries and more than fifty times that of the poorest non-OECD countries. Note also the very high share of intangible capital in total wealth.

Intangible wealth is measured as a "residual." This means it represents the difference between the value of national output and the value that would be produced by unskilled labor, given the nation's endowment of natural resources and produced capital.

The hundreds of thousands of dollars in intangible wealth per person in Europe or the United States reflects "human capital," including education and know-how. It is the value of the recipes that we have accumulated to facilitate production and exchange.

But look at the chart again. Some of the countries have negative intangible wealth. How is this possible? The negative value of intangible wealth per person in countries like the Congo or Nigeria reflects dysfunctional government and social conditions. These conditions are so bad that their adverse effect on the average worker's output more than offsets the positive boost to output that workers would otherwise enjoy from natural resources and produced capital. Again, think of a computer that is so hampered by bugs and viruses that it actually makes anyone who tries to use it less productive. That is how damaging the software layer in these countries has become.

In addition to those listed in the table above, countries with extremely low shares of intangible capital include Russia (16%), Venezuela (10%), Syria (-15%), and Algeria (-18%).

The method used by the World Bank authors to calculate wealth is focused on what they term "sustainable consumption," which includes national saving. Because the rate of national saving is higher in many countries than in the United States, the United States falls below three Scandinavian countries in national wealth. This approach might be disputed on the grounds that the United States generally makes more efficient use of its saving because of its vigorous competition and free-flowing capital markets.

How important is the quality of economic and social institutions as a source of wealth? DeLong's idea is to compare the standard of living produced by different economic systems. The "matched pairs" represent an attempt to control for other factors. If the only remaining difference between each country on the left and the matching country on the right is in the form of economic organization, then this table provides powerful evidence of the adverse effect of communism on average living standards.

Note, however, that by 1997 many of the countries in the left-hand column were no longer communist. Note also that some of the "matches" that DeLong makes are between countries with very different resource bases and ethnic compositions. On the other hand, had he undertaken such an analysis prior to the fall of the Berlin Wall, the contrast between East

EXHIBIT Q. The Effects of Communism[17]

COMMUNIST COUNTRY	GDP PER CAPITA	MATCHED NON-COMMUNIST COUNTRY	GDP PER CAPITA
North Korea	$700	South Korea	$13,590
China	$3,130	Taiwan	$14,170
Vietnam	$1,630	Philippines	$3,520
Cambodia	$1,290	Thailand	$6,690
FSR Georgia	$1,960	Turkey	$6,350
Russia	$4,370	Finland	$20,150
Bulgaria	$4,010	Greece	$12,769
Slovenia	$11,800	Italy	$20,290
Hungary	$7,200	Austria	$22,070
Czech Republic	$10,510	Germany	$21,260
Poland	$6,520	Sweden	$19,790
Cuba	$3,100	Mexico	$8,370

and West Germany would have provided a strong example in support of the point that communism as a system of government has adverse effects on the standard of living.

EXHIBIT R. Trust and Living Standards[18]

The level of trust in a society is affected by many different factors, including culture, history, norms, and legal institutions. But whatever affects the level of social trust, there is strong evidence that a higher level of trust yields enormous economic benefits. William Easterly writes:

Suppose that we measure the level of trust by the percentage of people responding "yes" to a survey question asking whether, generally speaking, most people can be trusted. Countries with very high trust have about five times the level of per capita income as countries with very low trust. In rich Denmark, where trust is so high that mothers leave babies unattended on the street while they shop, 58 percent say they can trust people. In the poor Philippines, only 5 percent are trusting.[19]

EXHIBIT S. Effect of Financial Institutions on Living Standards[20]

INSTITUTIONAL CHARACTERISTIC	ADVANTAGE OF COMMON-LAW TRADITION VS. NON-CASE-LAW TRADITION
Transparency of corporate accounting	30%
Enforcement of contracts	20%
Enforcement of property rights	50%
Rule of law	50%

Another intangible source of wealth comes in the form of financial and legal institutions that are conducive to productive economic activity.[21]

EXHIBIT T. Democracy and Living Standards[22]

QUARTILE RANKING IN DEMOCRACY	AVERAGE INCOME PER CAPITA, 2002
Bottom 25 percent	$1,000
Second quartile	$1,600
Third quartile	$3,700
Top quartile	$12,000

This table shows that more democratic countries tend to be more prosperous than less democratic countries.

EXHIBIT U. Productivity Differences Across Countries[23]

COUNTRY	LABOR PRODUCTIVITY OF RETAIL SECTOR AS A PERCENTAGE OF U.S.	LABOR PRODUCTIVITY OF HOUSING CONSTRUCTION AS A PERCENTAGE OF U.S.
United States	100	100
Japan	50	45
Korea	32	70
Poland	24	25
Russia	24	8
Brazil	14	35
India	6	8

Regulations and rules can have a strong impact on productivity. This table shows that relative to the United States, other countries make much more intensive use of labor in the retail and construction industries. This suggests that there are barriers to the adoption of best practices. Lewis' book enumerates numerous regulatory barriers.

5. *One of the intangible factors is the environment for entrepreneurs. The harder it is to start a legitimate business, the lower a country's standard of living.*

EXHIBIT V. Cost of Obtaining a Business License[24]

This study, summarized in the following table, looks at the time and cost of obtaining legal status to operate a firm in different countries. Time is measured in days, and cost is measured as a share of per-capita GDP in that country.

COUNTRY	GDP PER CAPITA, 1999	TIME (days)	COST (share of per-capita GDP)
U.S.	$30,600	4	0.0049
Canada	19,320	2	0.0145
United Kingdom	22,640	4	0.0143
Germany	25,350	42	0.1569
France	23,480	53	0.1430
Russian Federation	2,270	57	0.1979
Japan	32,230	26	0.1161
India	450	77	0.5776
Kenya	360	54	0.5070
Egypt	1,400	51	0.9659
Top quartile of GDP per capita	24,372	24.5	0.10
Second quartile of GDP per capita	5,847	49.3	0.33
Third quartile of GDP per capita	1,568	53.1	0.41
Bottom quartile of GDP per capita	349	63.8	1.08

The study's authors find that:

> heavier regulation of entry is generally associated with greater corruption and a larger unofficial economy, but not with better quality of private or public goods. We also find that the countries with less limited, less democratic, and more interventionist governments regulate entry more heavily, even controlling for the level of economic development.[25]

The size of the informal sector, as measured by its estimated percent of GNP, is an indicator of institutional weakness. The

EXHIBIT W. The Underground Economy[26]

REGION/COUNTRY (regional lowest and highest countries shown)	INFORMAL SECTOR AS A PERCENTAGE OF GNP, 2000
Africa, average	42%
South Africa	28.4
Zimbabwe	59.4
Asia	26
Japan	11.3
Thailand	52.6
Latin America	41
Chile	19.8
Bolivia	67.1
Eastern Europe	38
Slovak Republic	18.9
Georgia	67.3
Western Europe	18
Switzerland	8.8
Greece	28.6
U.S.	8.8

larger this underground economy, the more likely it is that property rights are not secure. The absence of secure property rights makes black market activity more attractive.

The estimates in the table indicate that insecure property rights and underdevelopment tend to go together. Countries and regions with a high percentage of their GDP in the underground economy tend to be poorer than comparable countries or regions where it is easier to operate a legitimate business.

6. Economic growth is accompanied by dramatic changes in occupations. The nature of work changes rapidly.

Exhibit X. Change in Women's Work[27]

As of 1900, the method of doing laundry in 98 percent of households took 4 hours of labor for a 38-pound load, with another 4.5 hours for ironing. With electric appliances, this time fell to 41 minutes for washing and drying and 1.75 hours for ironing.

In 1900, the average household spent 58 hours a week on meal preparation, laundry, and cleaning. In 1975, this figure was 18 hours.

Exhibit Y. Jobs Destroyed, Jobs Created[28]

New techniques and technologies improve productivity and fundamentally alter how, where, and how much people work. According to the report cited above, "[p]roductivity has also allowed Americans to reduce the average workweek from 76 hours in 1830 to 60 in 1890, 39 in 1950 and just 34 today."

These productivity gains can destroy jobs, but they also create new jobs and entirely new industries:

> From 1979 to 2003, Americans filed more than 114 million initial claims for unemployment benefits, a figure that captures just a fraction of the number of job losses. Yet during this same period, America created enough work for a growing labor force, with total employment rising from 91 million to 130 million.
>
> Over the past decade, an era of rapid technological change and globalization, big employment gains came in occupations that rely on people skills and emotional intelligence. We added 512,000 registered nurses and 248,000 people in financial-services sales. Others in growing occupations include lawyers, educational and vocational counselors, and recreation workers.
>
> The past decade also saw gains in jobs that involve

imagination and creativity – designers, architects, pho-
tographers, actors and directors. The hairstylists and
cosmetologists category rose by 146,000 jobs. Many
occupations that use analytic reasoning have continued
to grow, too, but computer operators and others are
beginning to see their numbers fall.

The occupations in eclipse are generally those that
involve muscle power, manual dexterity and formulaic
intelligence. The number of secretaries and typists, for
example, has fallen by 1.3 million since 1992, as more
computers, printers, voice mail and other office machines
have entered the workplace. The ranks of sewing machine
operators have declined by 347,000, those of farmers by
182,000.

JOB CATEGORY	GROWTH IN THOUSANDS OF EMPLOYEES, 1992–2002	PERCENT GROWTH, 1992–2002
People Skills/Emotional Intelligence		
Registered nurses	512	28
Financial-services sales	248	78
Lawyers	182	24
Educational and vocational counselors	48	21
Recreation workers	35	37
Imagination/creativity		
Designers	230	43
Hairstylists and cosmetologists	146	19
Architects	60	44
Actors and directors	59	61
Photographers	49	38

JOB CATEGORY	GROWTH IN THOUSANDS OF EMPLOYEES, 1992–2002	PERCENT GROWTH 1992–2002
Analytic Reasoning		
Legal assistants	159	66
Electronic engineers	147	28
Medical scientists	22	33
Metallurgical engineers	-2	-8
Computer operators	-367	-55
Formulaic Intelligence		
Cost and rate clerks	-16	-24
Health records technicians	-36	-63
Telephone operators	-98	-45
Bookkeepers	-247	-13
Secretaries and typists	-1,305	-30
Manual Dexterity		
Tool and die makers	-30	-23
Lathe operators	-30	-49
Typesetters	-34	-62
Butchers	-67	-23
Sewing machine operators	-347	-50
Muscle Power		
Garbage collectors	-2	-4
Stevedores	-3	-17
Fishing workers	-14	-27
Timber workers	-25	-32
Farm workers	-182	-20

EXHIBIT Z. Another Look at the Evolution of Work[29]

CATEGORY	PERCENTAGE OF U.S. EMPLOYMENT, 1910	PERCENTAGE OF U.S. EMPLOYMENT, 2000
Professional, technical	4%	23%
Service workers	3	13
Clerical	5	17
Managers, officials, proprietors	6	14
Sales workers	4	6
Craftsmen, foremen	11	10
Operatives	15	10
Laborers	10	3
Private household workers	5	1
Farmers	15	1
Farm laborers	17	1

The table above shows the dramatic reallocation of labor that took place between 1910 and 2000.

EXHIBIT AA. Market Work, Housework, and Leisure[30]

YEAR	MARKET WORK	NON-MARKET WORK	TOTAL
1965	34.24	23.52	57.76
1975	32.13	20.30	52.43
1985	32.13	20.64	52.77
1993	34.02	17.94	51.96
2003	33.01	18.00	51.01
Difference, 2003–1965	-1.23	-5.52	-6.75

The table above shows the average weekly hours spent in market work and non-market work (household chores) for U.S. adults from 1963 through 2003. The decline in necessary housework is an important benefit of economic growth.

EXHIBIT AB. Non-market Work, United States Versus Germany[31]

COUNTRY/ GENDER	MARKET WORK	NON-MARKET WORK	LEISURE
U.S. males	39.1	14.1	114.4
German males	35.2	17.9	113.7
U.S. females	25.4	26.8	115.4
German females	17.7	36.1	113.3

The German data are from West Germany in 1991–92; the American data are from a survey in 1994. Both sets of data are for an average workweek. The data show that although Germans work less in the market, their overall leisure time is constrained by non-market work.

Interview with
ROBERT FOGEL

ROBERT FOGEL is the Charles R. Walgreen Distinguished Service Professor of American Institutions at the University of Chicago Booth School of Business. Fogel also heads the Center for Population Economics at Chicago Booth. He was awarded, with Douglass North, the Nobel Prize in economics in 1993 for their pioneering work using statistical analysis to study economic history. Fogel first attracted attention in the early 1960s with his statistical analysis of the impact of railroads on nineteenth-century American economic development. In the 1980s, he began to focus on what he called "the problem of creating and studying large life-cycle and intergenerational data sets." His research has led to numerous publications on the topic of economics and aging. He is the author of The Escape From Hunger and Premature Death, 1700–2100, *a remarkable story of human, scientific, and technological change.*

ARNOLD KLING & NICK SCHULZ: The title of your book is somewhat dry, but it's about an important development in human history. It tells an extraordinary story. Can you tell us how you got interested in looking into this subject and what, broadly speaking, you discovered?

ROBERT FOGEL: Well, a group of other people in demography economics and the biomedical sciences and I began collaborating back in the mid-1970s to first measure the decline in mortality in the United States. Prior to that work there was very little that was known about what happened to mortality before the middle-to-late nineteenth century in the U.S. And so we found sources of data that permitted us to recreate time series on that, and we discovered that the pattern of increase in life expectancy was puzzling. And in the effort to explain these puzzles we produced many new lines of research, some of which are summarized in the book *The Escape From Hunger.*

AK & NS: And what exactly was puzzling about this pattern of increase?

RF: Well, life expectancy appears to have increased pretty steadily from the early eighteenth century until maybe around 1820. And then it started cycling. We had actual decreases in life expectancy before we returned back to a path of increase in life expectancy, beginning in the late nineteenth century, and from then on it was a pretty steady pattern of increase. In both good times and bad times, we have a substantial increase in life expectancy.

For example, during the Great Depression of the 1930s, which in some ways was not new but in some ways was surprising – you would think that in such hard times with such a large percentage of the people unemployed, many for a long time, it would've had a negative health effect. But, whatever negative effect there might have been was swamped by more positive factors that led to an increase of more than six years in life expectancy, in a decade.

AK & NS: You mentioned that, after years of increase starting in the early eighteenth century there was a decline. What prompted the decline, if anything? Were you able to tease out the answer?

RF: It was a combination of things. One was large-scale immigration. Many of the immigrants brought with them diseases. The most spectacular case was the cholera epidemic of 1849–1852, which became endemic to about 1857.

Two boats from Germany – one landed in New York and when people got off of that boat, cholera broke out in New York City, and the other went down to New Orleans, and people boarded the riverboats going upstream, and every place that the boat docked to leave people off, cholera broke out, all the way up to St. Louis. And then, up the Ohio River to Pittsburgh. So, you had a pretty graphic example about how sick immigrants could introduce serious diseases.

The other, quantitatively more important [factor], was the rise of urbanization. If you look in third-world countries today, cities are healthier than the countryside. But, in the nineteenth century it was the opposite – there was a mortality gap, with the cities having higher morbidity and mortality rates than the countryside down to World War II. It's only in the 1940s and 1950s that the cities become healthier than the countryside, which is still the case.

AK & NS: And yet people still came to cities, despite the fact that living conditions were so bad and that it could be hazardous to your health?

RF: Right. Well, in the United States, most of the people who came to the big cities were foreign migrants. In Europe, they were the poorest of the countryside being pushed out of the countryside and into the cities. The city of London had a mortality rate that was higher than the fertility rate, and the city population only grew because of net in migration during the nineteenth century.

AK & NS: The first chapter of the book is called, "The Persistence of Misery in Europe and America Before 1900." What was so miserable about life before the twentieth century?

RF: Well, first of all, it was short. The life expectancy, if I can go back to 1700, was only about 35 years at birth. In 1900, two hundred years later, it had increased by about twelve years – it was in the neighborhood of 47 in Western European countries. And today it's 77 or 78, so in a century we added thirty years to life expectancy, maybe a little bit more.

AK & NS: That's obviously unprecedented for life expectancy to increase by such a large amount in one century. What were the primary drivers of that?

RF: Public health reform, cleaning up of the water supply, cleaning up of the milk supply. But if you said what was the single most important factor, it's technological change.

Let me give you one small example. We complain a lot about air pollution today, but there were two hundred thousand horses in New York City at the beginning of the twentieth century, defecating everywhere. And when you walked around in New York City, you were breathing pulverized horse manure – a much worse pollutant than the exhaust of automobiles. Indeed, in the United States, the automobile was considered the solution to the horse problem because pulverized horse manure carried a lot of deadly pathogens.

So technological change made it possible to greatly increase the food supply and permit levels of nutrition that were not previously attainable. Secondly, it made it possible to have a safe water supply. We needed a more modern technology to be able to carry away waste water and provide safe water, both through filtering and chlorination. Still another area was the development of vaccines, which made it possible to inoculate the very young against diseases. And with better nutrition, you greatly improve the physiology of human beings.

AK & NS: That leads to our next question, which is, what was the significance of malnourishment on work, productivity, and economic growth in human history? You found some interesting things when you looked into this question of nutrition and malnourishment.

RF: Right. With the kind of agricultural technology that exists in Malthus's era, we could only feed 80 percent of the population with enough energy that they could work. The level of nutrients available for work was about a third of what it is now, so even people who worked were much less productive.

AK & NS: They would literally not have enough calories to work?

RF: The poorest 20 percent of the population was slowly starving to death. They were beggars that littered the streets. They had enough energy for maybe an hour of strolling and then sitting down and begging. But not enough energy to work.

AK & NS: And this is in Europe and the United States?

RF: Yes, Western Europe down to around the middle of the nineteenth century. And in the United States in the bigger cities. The countryside was pretty well-fed from the beginning. But when we began to develop the big cities, we had a problem of urban poverty that was not solved until well into the twentieth century.

AK & NS: So a lot of these technological factors came together at the same time. Now, we know this is a highly debated question in the academy, but why were the conditions such that these things came together in Europe and the United States when they did, at this time in history?

RF: Well it's based on a long history of improving knowledge. The accumulation of knowledge is the basis for modern technology. Later on it becomes not just empirical knowledge, but also science which gives us theories about what to do. And these theories become increasingly effective guides to technological advance.

But technological advance is the basis for all economic growth, including the derived growth that I referred to, as you will have technologies that improve productivity in agriculture. It's possible to improve human physiology so there is an interaction, a synergy.

AK & NS: Right, and you coin a term in this book called "techno-physio evolution."

RF: Right.

AK & NS: Explain what that is and explain why it's important.

RF: Well, it's the interaction between improvements in technology and improvements in human physiology. The average stature of adult males in Western Europe increased by close to a foot between 1864 and the present.

AK & NS: That's an enormous percentage of body height.

RF: Yeah, that's a very big increase. The current giants are the Dutch. Dutch males, on average, are over six feet tall. They used to be only about 5 foot 4 inches in the mid-nineteenth century, so they've come quite a ways.

And with that is an improvement in the strength of electrical signals across membranes – our lungs are stronger, our hearts are stronger, the central nervous system is more effective. All these things were permitted by changes in technology, which improved nutrition.

Now, improved nutrition is not only an improvement in the diet, but in the proportion of the diet that's metabolized. If you have a lot of diarrhea, your food won't be metabolized. If a pregnant woman has diarrhea, the fetus will be severely underfed and will probably produce a child that will be not only at high risk to die in infancy but at high risk to have severe chronic diseases at a relatively early age. So the chronic diseases of people who reached age 65 in 1900 came ten to twelve years earlier than they do today.

AK & NS: The same diseases?

RF: Yes, talking about things like arthritis, coronary heart disease, respiratory diseases. Not only do they now come ten to twelve years later, but the proportion that gets them is smaller. So a larger proportion of people live until death, or nearly death, in good health – whereas in 1900, about 80 percent of the population of males age 65 and older were severely impaired by chronic diseases.

AK & NS: On this nutrition question, today we hear a lot of concerns about over-nutrition or obesity, especially in the developed world of the U.S. and Europe, but you point out that even in the developed world today, there are still some problems with under-nutrition. Is that right?

RF: Right. It's a much more limited problem than in third-world countries. But we still have enough inequality in this country that there are malnourished children, undernourished children.

AK & NS: On the subject of techno-physio evolution, you say in the book that "this evolution is likely to accelerate in this century." Why is that?

RF: Well, first of all, our technology is accelerating.

AK & NS: How do you measure that? How do you know that it's accelerating?

RF: Well in the book I give a diagram and show it visually. I have on the Y axis the size of the population, and on the other axis time. And I show the curve of population – from about 1700 on, that curve becomes almost vertical on the scale that's shown in the book. And then along that scale, I put in scientific innovations.

One of the points I make is that it took four thousand years to go from the invention of the plow to figuring out how to hitch a plow up to a horse. And it took 65 years to go from the first flight in a heavier-than-air machine to landing a man on the moon. Not only did that happen in such a short period of time, but over a billion people all over the world watched it happen. So we had a communications revolution in a very short period of time. I could work out a precise metric, but it wouldn't mean much. It wouldn't give you more information than that diagram does.

AK & NS: Sure, or than those anecdotes themselves do.

RF: Right.

AK & NS: In the book you see a growing demand for leisure and retirement, and education and health care. Now, in current debates, especially in Washington, that sounds like more Social Security, more education spending, and more Medicare. Can we avoid heading towards more government involvement in things? How do you see that?

RF: Heading towards it. You've got to distinguish between the rhetoric and the facts.

We currently have passed legislation that delays the onset of full Social Security [benefits] to age 68, and there is a good deal of talk that we're going to push it to 70 – a good deal of talk in Congress. At the same time, people are retiring earlier. The average age of retirement is now around 62, which is pretty high compared with Western Europe. It's 59 in France. So, it's very likely that by the time my son retires, there'll be ten years of no government support for retirement which he'll have to finance himself. That's more than 50 percent privatizing the retirement system.

We're probably going to shift gradually, despite the opposition to it, to private accounts, which exist in some countries, which require everyone who enters the labor force to put aside 30 percent of their income into a fund to cover retirement, health care, and education. In some countries, they permit you to borrow against that fund to buy houses. It's approaching what American academics have. You cannot teach in American universities without having TIAA-CREF. In American universities, you're required to put aside between 12.5 and 17 percent (it varies from university to university) into this fund so that when you retire you don't end up with a tin cup sitting on the administration building saying, "I was a good teacher once, please help me." That's a forced retirement system. It has the advantage over Social Security that the government can't take it away.

Secondly, 24 hours a day I can call up and find out what am I worth today. It's my money, and I can leave it as a legacy to my children or grandchildren. Not only that, everyone who did as I did, when CREF became available, and took three-quarters in equities and one-quarter in bonds, is a multi-millionaire today.

AK & NS: So all of those teachers are multi-millionaires?

RF: Well, if they're still alive. Not all of them are still alive. But the rate of return has been over 10 percent per annum, for decades. Figure it out. You're doubling the value every seven years. So it's been a very successful investment.

AK & NS: And you see that as a potential model for Social Security or public pension programs?

RF: Right. Now, there is an argument which says it's not as secure as the guaranteed government program. Well, ultimately, what the government can pay depends on how the economy performs. If we continue to grow as we have, in the neighborhood of 2 percent per annum per capita over the past fifty years, we won't have any difficulty paying for it either, as a governmental program or in private accounts. If the economy goes into long-term stagnation, then the government is not going to be able to sustain it because the tax base for it won't be there. So you need to have a successful and rapidly growing economy in order for standards of living for the elderly to improve.

I think the odds that we will are very high. I think we're already actually underestimating. I mean, when I gave you the figure of 2 percent per annum, that figure does not take into account improvements in the quality of health care or in the quality of education, or in the quality of many manufactured goods. So, if you take these quality improvements into account as I've tried to do roughly in one paper, the real rate of growth is 3.1 percent, not 2 percent.

AK & NS: You talk a lot about technology and biotechnology in your book. There's concern about some humans over-enhancing themselves, and we see this in the debates over the steroid controversy in baseball or Leon Kass's worries about medical innovation. Do economists have anything to contribute to these ethical debates?

RF: There are a lot of different ethical issues. The debate over whether we should do stem cell research from fetal material is only one of them. It's going to happen; whether we do it or not, it's going to happen. The Chinese are doing it. Other countries are pursuing it, so these scientific lines of research are going to take place.

The U.S. has the most heavily endowed scientific research program in the biomedical areas, and we are subsidizing the whole world. And we'll continue to do so for the foreseeable future. I'm not too worried about scientific progress; we're at the leading edge of most frontiers. It would be incredible if we were at the leading edge of every frontier. No country has ever been.

AK & NS: As you've looked at some of the history of it, these concerns about technological advance – have you seen any precedent for it, or are we in terra incognita here?

RF: No, there is always concern over scientific experimentation and adverse – either unethical or undesirable – consequences. It's part of the fear of the unknown.

Look, one thousand years ago, nothing happened. Each generation experienced life more or less as the previous ones had, with maybe some random factor thrown in for weather and pestilence. But, it's only in the past three hundred years that science has become so powerful that it could influence the course of events. And it has, and I expect it to do it at an accelerating rate. We have a powerful scientific establishment, and we're making new discoveries daily, even short of genetic engineering.

By the way, genetic engineering is hundreds of years old. It's just that our new techniques speed up the process of mutation. We've been tinkering with cross breeding plants and animals for a long time. But even if you take the existing best technology – not what's going to come out of what's generally referred to as genetic engineering, but just the diffusion of best practice – that can produce a rate of growth of 2 or 3 percent in productivity.

China is a good example of what can happen. The Chinese population just about doubled since 1961, and the per capita food consumption of this doubled population is up 80 percent. So China has a much bigger population and a much better standard of food intake and life expectancy. In half a century, life expectancy increased from about 45 years to 72. It took the Western world 150 years to make that leap.

AK & NS: Let's shift to declining populations. How important is the population decline that is happening in Western Europe?

RF: It's terribly important to Western Europe. Italy – I mean, Italy, the home of the Vatican – has a total fertility rate of

1.4. To maintain the population, you have to have a total fertility rate of 2.1, so Italy is facing a rapid decline. The Italian government is doing everything it can to promote a higher fertility rate. Otherwise, in one hundred years, Italy will have a third of its current population – assuming no migration into or out of the country, just from natural progression.

Among the rich countries, we're the only country that's not shrinking inherently. By the way, the age structure enters into it. Even if you have a total fertility rate that says you should shrink, if you have a lot of women in their child-bearing years, the shrinkage won't happen until the age structure changes, which may take a third to half of a century.

But Asia is still growing, and Africa, despite its age, is growing very rapidly because of a very high fertility rate. And Africa will be a much more – in terms of the percentage of the world population, it'll be more than double what it is in half a century, whereas Western Europe, if current trends continue, will shrink. And Asia – Southeast Asia and South Asia – will increase.

So, not only will per capita income be rising in countries like China and India, but because of the population increase, they'll be the dominant economies of the world.

It's already reflected in the extent of Western capital that's rushing into these countries. General Motors' main expansion plans are in Southeast Asia and Latin America, not in the United States, the same thing as Ford, Volkswagen. All the big auto companies are reading the tea leaves in the same way.

AK & NS: Are there broader implications of these population changes for Europe and the U.S.?

RF: The U.S. is going to be the technological leader, probably through the end of the twenty-first century. Maybe China

63

will catch up in some directions and maybe we will cede to them in some directions like stem cell research, but we still have a huge advantage in terms of investment and in terms of human resources in these areas. The country remains devoted to a policy of heavy investment in science, especially in the biomedical sciences and in science in general.

AK & NS: So you're still optimistic about the United States with respect to technology and the future?

RF: I picked the right century to be born in, and my grandchildren have also picked the right century. Not only the twentieth but the twenty-first will be American centuries in terms of the scientific heights that we scale and in terms of the success of our economies.

But watch out for China. If its current growth rate continues and if we take Western European and U.S. growth rates and assume they will continue, China will be bigger than the United States and Western Europe put together by about 2030 or 2040. That means the market will be bigger. It doesn't mean per capita income will be higher.

AK & NS: When would China achieve parity in per capita income with either the U.S. or Western Europe?

RF: You know, I haven't calculated that and so I don't have an answer to it. But if you take what I think is the true growth rate of the U.S, rather than the one that we publish in the National Income and Product Accounts, I don't think it'll happen this century.

AK & NS: We have one last question for you. It's kind of an unconventional question, but it's one that we like to ask folks we interview, and you can take a second to answer it. Who are your heroes?

RF: You know, my reaction is that scientists don't really have heroes because all scientific knowledge is incremental. You're aware of how dependent each individual is on all of the other people.

We tend to heroize the person who gets there first, but usually there are a dozen people who were so close that you can feel their breath on the back of their neck, so that if one guy stumbled, it wouldn't be that that scientific stream wouldn't materialize. It would be that some other scientific group or individual is the one whose name is attached to it.

I really think science is a collective enterprise. What you can do depends not only on what happened before you but on what everybody else around you is doing. You're talking to each other and hoping you'll be a little luckier, or a little cleverer, to the extent that we're in competition with each other.

Interview with
ROBERT SOLOW

ROBERT SOLOW began his teaching career in 1949 at the Massachusetts Institute of Technology, where he became a full professor in 1958. He is now professor emeritus at MIT. He served on the Council of Economic Advisers in 1961–62 and was a consultant to that body from 1962 to 1968. In a paper published in 1957, "Technical Change and the Aggregate Production Function," Solow observed that much economic growth cannot be accounted for by increases in capital and labor. He attributed this unaccounted-for portion – now called the "Solow residual" – to technological innovation. Solow was awarded the Nobel Prize in economics in 1987 for his work on economic growth theory.

ARNOLD KLING & NICK SCHULZ: In some ways, the new case for markets can be traced to your 1957 paper.

First, we have seen an evolution in thinking about economic development as an institutional process rather than as a process of capital formation. As recently as December 2005, the World Bank published a study that argued that over 80 percent of the wealth of rich countries is "intangible." The study cited education and the rule of law as factors that might account for the "residual" as they estimated it.

Second, the focus on technical change and economic growth has promoted interest in the process of innovation. Some economists see entry and exit as important elements in the diffusion of innovation and growth in productivity. This leads them to be skeptical of government policies that protect incumbent firms.

In what ways has the focus on intangible factors in economic development helped to increase understanding of the development process?

ROBERT SOLOW: When I first began to think about these questions long ago, the standard view was that developing economies suffered primarily from doing too little saving and investment. "Investment" meant conventional plant and equipment. The standard remedy was to supplement meager domestic saving by foreign aid to finance investment. We now know that there are flaws in this simple story. Without appropriate institutional infrastructure, without the right local incentives, without complementary human capital, aid and investment will be wasted, and little or no sustained growth will take place. In short, poor countries are not only poor in capital, they are poor in the factors that make for "total factor productivity."

AK & NS: What is still poorly understood about economic development?

RS: My answer almost follows from the preceding one. We need to understand more about the factors that make for high and rising total factor productivity. It is not enough to speak generally in clichés like rule of law, property rights, incentives. Some versions of law, property rights and incentives lead directly to skimming, Swiss bank accounts and conspicuous consumption. I have no doubt that developing countries need all three, but I doubt that the same version of all three will do for each country. You could say that we understand the institutional economics of economic development pretty poorly. The West had the luxury of evolving concepts of rule-of-law, property rights, and useful incentives over centuries, with plenty of backward steps and no assurance that we have got them right even now. Poor countries can't wait, but neither can they simply copy our solutions.

AK & NS: What do you think of attempts to correlate economic development to things like indices of economic freedom, measures of how long it takes to incorporate a business, measures of corruption, or other indicators of institutional support for private enterprise?

RS: I suppose in principle there is no harm in doing those correlations. The possible harm comes from forgetting the distinction between correlation and causation. Causation almost certainly goes both ways between successful economic growth and sound institutions. Moreover, to go back to earlier remarks, a phrase like "institutional support for private enterprise" does not define anything unique. That cat can be skinned in several ways, and those ways can lead to different results in terms of both prosperity and equity. Those correlations are not my favorite instrument of research.

AK & NS: When economists focus on property rights and other libertarian sources of development, what might they be overlooking?

RS: Above all, they are overlooking the distributional impact of alternative solutions to the problem of effective property rights and other "libertarian" devices, and they are forgetting that those distributional effects can dominate the kind of development that ensues. To take the recent example, we may have turned Russia into one version of a growing "capitalist" society, but not into a place you would want your grandmother to live. We could have tried for a better version of a growing market economy.

AK & NS: Have you paid attention to the disagreement between Jeff Sachs and William Easterly on development policy? What comments would you have?

RS: Not in detail, though I have read many of Jeff Sachs's writings and Bill Easterly's book. I do think that Sachs is too given to massive top-down solutions (though he could with some justice deny this), and I liked Easterly's more piecemeal, skeptical approach. Maybe there is a possible synthesis: more resources and more local variation.

AK & NS: What do you think of the view that vigorous competition is necessary for the adoption of productivity-enhancing innovation?

RS: I agree with it strongly. That is one of the main conclusions of the McKinsey Global Institute, in which I was an active participant.

AK & NS: Apart from vigorous competition, what other factors are important in promoting such innovation?

RS: My belief is that innovation does not flourish in a macro-economically weak economy. A slack economy is more likely to foster protectionism, monopoly, defensive strategies. A weak labor market has the same effect of fostering restrictive workplace policies, both from private and public sources. So I am a strong believer in full employment and full utilization of capacity. That doesn't happen automatically. How to get these without inflation (which is bad for innovation) is not obvious, but letting the economy drag along is no solution.

AK & NS: What adverse consequences of innovation should be mitigated by government policy?

RS: The usual ones: consolidation of monopoly power, possible environmental degradation, excessive inequality, the purchase of government by the successful, to name a few. More broadly, equity is a social concern, not always looked after in an individualistic society. Innovation may be neutral or perhaps favorable in this respect, but there is no automatic guarantee that it will not be unfavorable.

AK & NS: What would you say to someone who says that the key to prosperity is the adoption of innovation, the key to that is competition, and the best thing that government can do to promote competition is to leave the private sector alone?

RS: It is far from obvious to me that the way to foster competition is to leave the private sector alone. The private sector does not much like competition; it has its own ways of creating monopoly power, restricting access to wealth (and therefore to political rights), and preserving vested interests. It is no easy matter for a society to get the benefits of competition without the disadvantages of oligarchy, and there is no reason to believe that *laissez-faire* will do the trick.

Chapter 3:

FROM THE MEADOW
TO THE FOOD COURT

TRADITIONALLY, ECONOMISTS HAVE focused on the problem of scarcity. Humans have unlimited wants but limited resources, so that every time we choose something, we have to decide what to give up in order to obtain it.

But we now live in an age of abundance. The rate at which we have increased our longevity, health, and comfort is remarkable. Moreover, we can expect future progress to be at least as rapid as what we have recently experienced. These improvements come from ideas and inventions, which emerge in the software layer of the economy.

One may think of an economy without a software layer as a meadow, in which the limited supply of grass constrains the well-being of the herd of grazing animals. In contrast, we describe the software-based economy as a food court, in which a variety of recipes and substitution possibilities give rise to abundance.

THE MALTHUSIAN MEADOW

Prior to around 1750, average life spans were short and food was scarce. Many children died in infancy. Others perished of childhood diseases. Most people barely consumed enough calories to enable them to work during the day. The focus of most people and most economic activity was on trying to produce food. The uncertainty of life meant that parents had to have many children in order to have a high likelihood that some heirs would survive.

In this Malthusian economy, human ecology resembled that of a herd of animals grazing in a meadow. In a meadow ecology, the animals' standard of living depends on the amount of grass per animal. If there are many animals in the herd, then each animal will have relatively little grass to eat. If there are relatively few animals in a herd, they will have more grass to eat.

If the animals tend to have more offspring and live longer when there is abundant grass, then the meadow will tend toward a Malthusian equilibrium. This means that the population will expand to the point where each animal is grazing at a subsistence level. When there are too many animals, grazing is below the subsistence level, and animals will die off. When there are few animals, food is abundant, and the population expands.

Economic historian Gregory Clark has pointed out that the Malthusian environment has some perverse characteristics. War, plague, and natural disasters thin the herd. These catastrophes thus make life better for the survivors; the standard of living is higher in a herd that has been thinned by disaster than in a normal herd. Of course, this higher standard of living only lasts until population growth restores the herd to the point where each animal can eat just enough to subsist.

In the view of Clark and a number of other economic historians, humanity was stuck in a Malthusian equilibrium until the Industrial Revolution. Although human ingenuity steadily increased the yield per acre of food crops, increased population dissipated these gains. As the meadow yielded more grass, the herd expanded. For the average person, food consumption remained close to subsistence levels until nearly 1800.

Recall the Hundred-Year Gap, which is the difference between the average standard of living at one point in history and the average one hundred years earlier. In the view of Clark and other economists who have undertaken similar calculations, the Hundred-Year Gap was small as late as 1700. The quality of life for the average person living in 1700 had little or no advantage over that of someone living centuries earlier. Food was no more plentiful. Shelter from heat and cold was hardly better. Sanitation in the big cities of the seventeenth century could scarcely have been worse. Travel over land was primitive, slow, and uncomfortable.

Increasing production in the meadow economy requires more physical effort. It means doing more with more. The meadow economy is ruled by the law of diminishing returns. The supply of land is fixed. We cannot keep doubling the food supply by doubling the amount of labor applied to a fixed amount of land.

The Food Court

Today, we live in a food court economy rather than in a meadow economy. In a food court economy, better ideas are a substitute for more physical effort. This means doing more with less. The law of diminishing returns does not place an upper limit on growth. A food court economy is characterized by many substitution possibilities and by increasing returns to knowledge.

Unlike the meadow, where there is only grass to eat, a food court offers many choices of meals. There are a large number of ingredients and many ways to combine ingredients into meals. As a result, when one ingredient is in short supply, there are many avenues of substitution. If one type of cheese is unavailable, the pizza maker can use a different type of cheese.

Alternatively, consumers could eat less pizza and more chicken. Abundant opportunities for substitution help to defeat the law of diminishing returns.

In fact, a food court economy shows symptoms of increasing returns. For example, a more cost-effective way to process credit card transactions will make every food stall more efficient. A new recipe in itself creates new opportunities without taking away any other opportunities. Indeed, a recipe can increase the value of other recipes.

The transition from the meadow economy to the food court economy took place relatively recently, in what is called the Industrial Revolution. Economists have long debated the causes of this transformation. For over a century, most explanations were focused on the hardware layer. Economists emphasized steam engines, railroads, steel mills, electric motors, power plants, automobile factories, and other tangible forms of capital.

However, tangible capital obeys the laws of diminishing returns. The mere accumulation of capital, without innovation, can produce only limited economic growth. Ultimately, capital does not allow people to escape the scarcity of the meadow. To explain the Industrial Revolution, we need a factor that can generate abundance.

Scientific understanding and applied know-how, which we refer to as recipes, do not suffer from the laws of scarcity. Recipes can be used repeatedly without being used up. If one food stall develops a recipe for a new food item, that item can be incorporated into the menus of similar food stalls in any food court. Better training procedures, inventory control methods, and other operational recipes can likewise be adopted in any food stall without making such recipes less available elsewhere. Moreover, food stalls can tinker with and improve the operational recipes that they adapt from other places.

While scarce resources are used to undertake pure research or trial-and-error experiments, once ideas are developed, they may be freely incorporated into new products and new research. As the knowledge base gets larger, the process of adding new knowledge gets faster. Thus, the food court economy does not suffer from the limits to growth that constrain the hardware layer. The software layer creates the possibility that growth will accelerate. As more and more of the value in goods and services comes from ideas, our standard of living will tend to increase at a faster pace.

Ray Kurzweil, an entrepreneur and scientific writer, points out that the fraction of product value accounted for by materials is shrinking and that the fraction accounted for by knowledge is approaching 100 percent. He has written:

> It is estimated that raw materials comprise less than two percent of the value of [computer] chips . . . and less than five percent of the value of computers. As our computers become more powerful, the percentage of their value accounted for by raw materials continues to diminish, approaching zero. . . . [M]ore than half of musical instrument industry revenues are now from electronic products. If we look at the typical electronic musical instrument (a digital home keyboard, for example), it is basically a computer with at least 90 percent of its value based on its knowledge content. By the end of this decade, more than 90 percent of all musical instrument industry revenues are expected to be based on this type of technology.
>
> George Gilder (author of *Wealth and Poverty* and *Microcosm*) estimates that the cost of raw materials for automobiles is now down to 40 percent of total costs. Again, this figure will continue to decline with the increasing use of computers and electronics.[32]

Rodney Brooks, a robotics researcher, has an arresting way of describing where we may be headed in our use of knowledge to defeat material scarcity. He has suggested that later in this century we will have such exquisite ability to manipulate genes that "instead of growing a tree, cutting it down and building a table ... you just grow a table, digitally instruct the organism how to grow."[33]

And former Federal Reserve Board Chairman Alan Greenspan has pointed out that the opportunities for international trade have increased along with the knowledge content of products:

> As microprocessors became an increasing part of our national product the relative physical dimensions of our value added fell dramatically. The physical weight of our gross domestic product is evidently only modestly higher today than it was fifty or one hundred years ago.
>
> By far the largest contributor to growth of our price adjusted GDP, or value added, has been ideas – insights that leveraged physical reality. The consequent downsizing of output, of course, meant that products were easier, and hence less costly, to move, and most especially across national borders.[34]

The metaphor of recipes is useful for explaining the remarkable rise in the standard of living over the past two hundred years for people in the developed countries of the world. Recipes are re-usable. Recipes are cumulative. Recipes allow us to do more with less.

However, the importance of recipes only serves to deepen the mystery of the Development Gap. If we did not achieve high living standards by "doing more with more" (that is, primarily by accumulating capital), then how can we explain the backwardness of the less developed nations? That is the topic of the next chapter.

Interview with
PAUL ROMER

PAUL ROMER is a senior fellow at the Stanford Center for International Development (SCID) and the Stanford Institute for Economic Policy Research (SIEPR). His contributions to the field of economics include being the primary developer of new growth theory, which deemphasizes the traditional idea of the scarcity of objects and directs attention to the power of new ideas. In addition to pursuing a career in teaching and research, Romer founded Aplia, Inc., which is now part of Cengage Learning. Aplia, which develops and applies technologies to improve student learning, grew out of Romer's conviction that information technology can be used to raise productivity in education. This idea could have important implications for how societies keep up with the growing demand for highly educated workers – a demand that is driven by the use of new technology in all other sectors of the economy.

ARNOLD KLING & NICK SCHULZ: How much better off are we today than we were, say, two hundred years ago or one hundred years ago? What accounts for the changes and improvements?

PAUL ROMER: One very good indicator of changes in standards of living over time is to ask how much of any particular physical commodity or valuable commodity people can get from an hour's worth of labor. Fortunately, William Nordhaus has done this calculation extending far back, really as far back as we can go in human history, focusing on the particular commodity of light: How much light can somebody get from an hour's worth of work? Or more specifically, if somebody works for an hour to get the energy to produce light, how much light will that person be able to produce with that amount of energy?

AK & NS: And "light" means the light [needed] to illuminate a room?

PR: Yes. Just measured in the physical units that a scientist would use: lumens of light. And in the last hundred years, we've had striking improvement in the quantity of light that the average person can get from doing an hour's worth of labor. We saw big improvements during the nineteenth century, but dramatically more during the twentieth century, and looking back you see this process not just of more and more light being available per hour of work but an increasing rate of growth in the amount of light available per hour of work.

AK & NS: The velocity is changing, too.

PR: Yes. The puzzle is deeper than why do things keep getting better; it's why are things getting better faster and faster with each passing century? That's the fundamental issue to be resolved.

AK & NS: Why are things getting better at a faster rate?

PR: What's nice about that particular example – and by the way, he documents it all the way back to the Neolithic revolution, so that you can really trace all of human history, and you can see how remarkable the last couple of hundred years have been in terms of changes and standards of living. When you look in this particular domain and ask what was going on – how people were producing light two hundred or three hundred years ago – [you find that] they were using candles made from animal fat; then eventually they started using gas, like open gas flames; then gas burnt inside of a mantle, a little cloth bag; and you can see that with each new technology, each discovery, people found better ways to get light, and it was all about not doing more and more of the same old thing. We didn't get that much more light by producing hundreds of thousands of candles per person, but by switching from candles to gas; when we had gas, we learned that we could burn it just as an open flame, but if you burned it inside of a mantle, you could actually get much more light per unit of gas or per unit of energy.

Continuing on through the centuries, you see kerosene, eventually the electric incandescent light bulb, and then the fluorescent light bulb. At the time Nordhaus finished his paper, the compact fluorescent light bulb was the most efficient device we had for converting energy into light. And somebody reading his paper might well have said, "Well, surely we've reached the limit of how much more efficient we can get at producing light," but since he wrote that paper, there's a whole new generation of devices based on LEDs that produce light with even greater efficiency than the compact fluorescent light bulb does.

So what's behind the simple answer is that it's technological change, discovery, finding new ways to use the materials that are available here on earth that drives this process of giving more and more of the things we want – things like illumination, which lets us do things at night that we couldn't do before.

AK & NS: What is "new growth theory," and what insight does it give us about this process of technological change?

PR: New growth theory describes a body of work that started essentially in the mid-1980s, when a group of economists, including me, tried to understand that process of technological change and to use the standard tools of economics, incentives and institutions to understand what would speed up or slow down the rate of technological change. And we started out – I started out specifically with this question: what would make that rate of technological change increase over time? Before, there had been a tendency to treat technological change as this force that came into the economic system from outside, and we had no basis for answering any question about what influenced its rate – [it was] what they called "exogenous technological change." It just came in from the outside. People acted as if economic analysis couldn't help us understand why the rate of technological change might be speeding up, whereas I looked at this and said, this may be the most important question in human history: why have we had technological change and why has it been speeding up over time? So new growth theory was an attempt to use the tools of analysis to answer questions like, why is growth and technology speeding up over time?

I think the explanations that we've come to after poking around at that question for twenty or more years now are these. First, it may be inherent in the process of discovery that the more we learn the faster we can learn. It's a notion that was captured by Newton when he said that he could see farther because he stood on the shoulders of giants. That was the first model that I tried to articulate for the speeding-up phenomenon, that the more we learn, the more we *can* learn. That makes sense in the realm of discovery, even though it's a story that wouldn't make sense if you were talking about discovering oil. For the discovery of ideas it makes sense, but for the discovery of oil it wouldn't, because in a physical exploration process there's only a finite amount of oil to begin with and you tend to find the largest deposits early on and then work to the smaller ones later on, so you'd expect a slowing-down.

One of the first questions we had to address in thinking about this was, what are ideas? How do they differ from the physical objects like oil? And one clear sense in which they differ is that the set of possible ideas, the set of things there are out there to discover, is just so incomprehensibly large that we've only begun to explore the tiniest subset of possible ideas or discoveries.

AK & NS: How do we know that?

PR: Well, there's some simple calculations you can do if you ask, what are all possible ideas? Just ask yourself, how many mixtures could you make out of the periodic table? Just take a hundred elements out of the periodic table and then ask, how many different things could we mix up from that? So you might take some copper, you might take some oxygen, you take carbon, shake it up, mix it together, bake it, see what you get out of that. If you just try to do the calculation of how many mixtures you can make that way, there are more mixtures like that than there have been seconds since the Big Bang created the universe. Even if every human now alive had been trying a new mixture every second ever since the universe was created, we would still have only tried a tiny fraction of those possible mixtures. So if you think of ideas as recipes or instructions for taking the physical objects we've got and rearranging them, doing something like making a mixture, you can see that we've only explored a tiny fraction of what's possible.

We discovered that you could make bronze from tin and copper; that was one extremely valuable mixture that we discovered early on. The whole Bronze Age resulted from that discovery. Fifteen or twenty years ago, somebody discovered that if you took copper, barium, oxygen, and yttrium and baked them into ceramic, you could create a superconductor that was superconducting at temperatures that were far higher than anybody had ever thought possible until then. So we still are discovering things at a very fundamental level, like mixing copper and tin to make bronze.

In this case, it was to make these high-temperature superconductors. But that only begins to suggest the scope for discovery, because most interesting artifacts in our lives are not just random mixtures but things that are connected according to a particular kind of order or with a particular type of structure.

One example I use is this: I'll claim that there's a recipe out there that you could use to just assemble carbon, oxygen, and hydrogen atoms, and that if you just use the right recipe to put them together, it will make a factory that will be smaller than a car, that will be mobile, that will seek out some renewable input, that will convert [the input] into some chemical that humans want, that will be self-healing whenever it gets injured, that will maintain sterile conditions, and that will even make a replica of itself when one generation breaks down. So the question is, could you really put something together out of carbon and hydrogen and oxygen and atoms that would be that sophisticated?

If you describe that just in the abstract, many people will think it's not possible. But then you point out to them that it already exists in the form of a dairy cow. And then get people to think well, what is the recipe or the set of instructions for a dairy cow? Well, it's really just a DNA sequence that has a list of instructions for how to assemble raw materials together, and then you start to ask yourself, well, how many possible DNA sequences are there? Like other mixtures, most of them won't work, they'll be non-functional, but if you consider the universe of those – it's what physicists would call a hyper-astronomic number. There are more possible DNA sequences than there are elementary particles in the universe. You could never create them all because there aren't enough particles in the universe to make them, but if you imagine a set that large and think that, well, one element out of that set is something as astonishing as a cow, and another element is a bat that navigates by echolocation, and another element is a human – humans, who talk to each other and make music like Mozart did and so on – the conclusion you come to is that the set of all possible ordered structures we can make out of just the raw material here on earth is incredibly large.

Most of those ordered structures would be as useless as dirt. They would have no order, no structure, no value to us; but a small number, a small fraction of them, can be extraordinarily valuable to us, like LEDs or dairy cows or the like.

So it's that kind of analysis, thinking of ideas as recipes – really, instructions for combining together small numbers of physical objects – that persuades, I think, anybody who works through the logic that the number of things we could have even tried up to this point in time is so small compared with the number of things that are possible, that we're just extremely early in this discovery process. For as far as you want to project into the future of humans, we won't run out of new things to discover. And as I conjectured in the beginning, it may even be that the more we learn about this process – the science of DNA, the science of materials, our understanding of quantum mechanics – the more we learn about this stuff, the better we get at finding new, ever more valuable mixtures.

AK & NS: [Once you started] thinking about technical change and growth in terms of recipes, there was a conceptual change in economics with regard to what were traditionally thought of as the factors of production. Is that right?

PR: Yes. There was the question of how you link the fairly abstract kind of discussion I was just having with more standard traditional models of growth. We augmented the traditional factors of production that we list – land, labor, physical capital – with this kind of stand-in concept we call technology, and we explicitly distinguished that last input as technology. It has these characteristics that are different from the other inputs, which are fundamentally like physical objects, and the theory that we developed talks about the interaction between the accumulation of more knowledge, like more of these recipes, and these other more traditional inputs.

One thing I wanted to try and make clear is that part of this transformation was [moving] away from thinking of production as – we talk about an economy producing things, but in some sense we don't really *make* anything. Think of it just the way a physicist would; we don't produce anything, we just rearrange it. The way we create value is by rearranging the physical mass that's available here on earth, and the value-creation process amounts to using recipes for rearranging things, instructions for rearranging things, to put them in more valuable configurations than older ones, and that helps people understand why running out of stuff is not the problem.

The issue is that we've got the same amount of stuff, and it's just a matter of rearranging it in ways that we find more productive.

AK & NS: Julian Simon had his idea of the ultimate resource, which – to tie into the point you just made – was that human ingenuity is the ultimate resource. Human ingenuity has the capacity to rearrange what we already have in an almost infinite number of ways, so we won't run out of actual resources because we can keep moving things around and manipulating things. Is that right?

PR: Yes. Simon had a kind of intuition for this; he looked at the history and said, "look, you're concerned about running out of stuff" – going back to Malthus, it is always being suggested that things should be getting worse. Yet here things have been getting better and better at faster and faster rates, so it's human ingenuity which somehow is making the difference here.

He had that intuition right. But I think he didn't dig hard enough into the question of what it is about the physical world that makes it possible for human ingenuity to make a difference. You could imagine living in a physical world which was so barren, so sterile, that no matter how smart we [might be], there would be nothing we could do. There just wouldn't be many interesting recipes or rearrangements you could make without enough ingredients. Or maybe you couldn't mix them together in any interesting way. So what was lacking in Simon's story, I think, was a vision of what it was about the physical world that created this potential that human ingenuity could then take advantage of. And it also didn't lead to this sharp distinction between physical objects, of which there are scarce, finite quantities, and the set of possible rearrangements of those physical objects, which are virtually unlimited, virtually infinite.

There is this concept, coming out of mathematics, of combinatorial explosions. It says that if you take a small number of objects and ask how many ways there are to order them or combine them, the number of combinations grows extremely rapidly with the number of elements. Sometimes people speak of exponential growth as a growth process that takes off very rapidly. These combinatorics – how many combinations you can make out of a given number of objects – grow much more rapidly with the number of objects. It's combinatorial explosion combined with a rich number of raw materials here in the universe that gives us this enormous sandbox to play in. So human ingenuity has some useful productive challenges that it can try and solve.

When we formulated these models and were trying to boil down that complex argument into factors of production, there's some math we used to try to describe what we call the production function, how these things are linked to each other. What the mathematics pointed to were the fundamental senses in which ideas or recipes differ from physical objects. I described one of those senses, that there's unlimited scope for discovering new recipes – that's one sense in which [ideas] are different from the scarce, limited quantities of physical objects. There is another sense which turns out to be even more important, which is that a physical object can only be used by one person at a time. You've got a piece of lumber. I can use it to build my house or you can use it for yours, but we can't do both. But if I discover the Pythagorean theorem and use that as a carpenter to make right angles, as soon as I discover that, I can describe it to anybody, and everybody can make right angles at the same time with this one discovery.

That attribute of ideas is what we call non-rivalry – that you and I are not rivals for the use of the Pythagorean theorem. We can use it at the same time. It was the mathematics which sharpened our focus on that distinction between rival physical objects and non-rival ideas. And the mathematics also [drew our attention to] a very powerful theorem that traces back to Adam Smith, which says that in a well-defined sense, the best institutions you can craft for creating value out of scarce physical objects are ones which involve property rights and trade in markets. It's a really sharp and remarkable result about the power of markets and property rights as mechanisms for creating value out of scarce physical objects.

What was interesting and surprising about our analysis of non-rival goods is that this theorem just doesn't go through. It turns out that property rights in competitive markets in the traditional sense are not the ideal institutions for creating value if you simultaneously want to discover lots of new recipes and combine those recipes with these scarce physical objects.

AK & NS: Can you illustrate how that's so?

PR: Yes. You can look back at human history and ask, "So why have things been getting so much better over time?" A very important part of [that progress] was the discovery and implementation of the notion of a competitive market. Private property rights and market exchange are extremely powerful insights, and within the domain where they apply, they really are the best possible institutions. So part of it is the story of modern market capitalism, which is the discovery of markets and property rights, one set of institutions which grew up over time. But there was also a parallel set of institutions that I would call the institutions of modern science, and those developed along very different lines. There's no notion of property rights [in science]. For example, the modern university and research system was designed not to create property rights but to lead to the rapid dispersal of new information; academics were rewarded based on the priority with which they disclosed information, so that the first person to disclose gets all of the professional credit for discovering something new.

That's an institutional arrangement which is designed precisely not to keep things secret, but to lead to the broadest possible dissemination of any given new insight or idea. The power of that is, when that one person discovers the Pythagorean theorem, after she discloses it to everybody, she can keep working on it, using it to make right triangles or maybe to discover new mathematical insights, but at the same time everybody else can also be using it to make right triangles or discover new insights in mathematics. So it's better to have these new discoveries shared and used by as many people as possible all at the same time.

So there's one set of institutions, markets, and property rights which work very well for dealing with physical objects, but there are other institutions, the institutions of science, which work well for the wide dissemination and use of key insights and ideas.

[Let's return to] the question at the very beginning: why did growth speed up over time? As I said, my first story was that, well, it's just inherent in the discovery process that the more you discover the faster you can learn things. The second-round answer, which I think actually captures more of the truth, is that it may get easier to discover as you learn more things or it may not, but what we've done is created better *institutions* over time, so that we now exploit the opportunities for discovery much more effectively than we used to. This story says that, fundamentally, human institutions have gotten better, and because we have better institutions, we all use our energy more productively and better things come out of it.

AK & NS: Let's get into this a little bit. So what are these institutions? And just as importantly, both for the context of this conversation and for going forward generally, was it just the happenstance of history that these institutions emerged as they did and when they did – just dumb luck? Or did they arise in tandem with some identifiable things, so that we can generate these institutions where they are lacking and, possibly, expand them to areas where they don't currently exist?

PR: Let me take the last question. I would distinguish questions about development from questions about growth. Development is the set of questions around why some people, some nations have very low standards of living compared with others, and I think a very large part of the answer is that they don't have in place the kinds of institutions which we know work well – institutions where, again, the market economy with property rights, market exchange, will dominate a very large fraction of what goes on every day, or will dominate the attention and activities of most people in an economy. But there are also these other institutions, these institutions of science, which feed and support the market economy and which operate on different lines.

What's wrong in many parts of the world is they don't have these institutions, and of the two [kinds], it's much more the market institutions which are fundamentally lacking, because if you think about it, a poor country in sub-Saharan Africa could get enormous benefits from just making use of what's already known in the rest of the world without necessarily contributing to that body of knowledge itself. If they could just put in place institutions that let them essentially freeload, take advantage of what's already known, they could do much better.

AK & NS: In the book *Barriers to Riches* by Edward Prescott and Steven Parente, it is argued that if undeveloped or underdeveloped parts of the world could just harness the existing stock of knowledge, they wouldn't have to actually generate any new knowledge at all – they could attain the living standards that are enjoyed in Western Europe and the United States and Japan.

PR: Yes. And again, let's go back to the fundamental reason for that. It's the non-rivalry of knowledge. They can use all the same procedures, processes, formulas that we use without taking away anything from us and still get the benefits of them. The institutions that interfere with their use of these ideas – or the things that are missing – are the institutions of the market. So for the purposes of thinking about development, it's probably not a bad shortcut to say that the only institutions that matter are the institutions of the market. Get property rights, the basic institutions of security, personal security, a legal system that support property rights – get those in place and things will be fine.

In that sense, the simple message of Adam Smith's invisible-hand analysis is a pretty good starting point for doing a better job with development. But when you think about policy for the nations on the leading edge – or when you think about the historical question of how we did better and better over time – I think you really have to have a richer perspective, where you take into account both the institutions of the market and the institutions of science, which work together but which are to a certain extent in conflict with each other. And I think one of the most interesting and exciting questions right now from a policy perspective is, where do you draw the line? Where do you use the institutions of the market as opposed to the institutions of science, and how do you form an effective interchange between domains where [different sets of institutions] reign?

One place where you see these questions bubbling up would be open-source software, which is an attempt to produce software under the institutions of science rather than the institutions of the market. There are debates about patenting. To what extent do we want to have patent rights on new ideas or gene sequences? How strong do we want to make patent or copyright protection of various forms of intellectual property? There are interesting and subtle questions in this area, which is at the interface of science and the market. You might want some forms of property rights like patents or copyrights, but you might want to make sure that they're not too strong, too comprehensive, too limiting. Lots of interesting institutional decisions will be made in the coming decades about how precisely to structure things in this middle ground.

AK & NS: And is your best sense at this point that the [best] approach is almost entirely ad hoc, or are there principles that we can appeal to, to adjudicate where to draw the line?

PR: I think there are some principles that we can use here, but to be honest, I think they're not well understood. It's the job of people like me who started out in new growth theory to try to articulate those principles.

If you go back many years, many decades, the main mission in economics was to get across the idea of the invisible hand – that you don't need the government to regulate, you don't need the government to prescribe or to be a provider in the economy; just create property rights and stay out of the way.

That was an extremely important message to get across, and one that I still have to proselytize about and persuade policymakers and people of; but now what we're getting to is this new challenge, which is to try to explain this important exception to that general message – that there really is a role for action through government, essentially collective action that actually makes the economy better off.

[Here's] the vision you could paint for this: for many ideas, most ideas, what we [should] create are weak property rights, incomplete property rights rather than ironclad property rights. Take land – it would be just crazy to say that somebody's title to a piece of land expires after seventeen years. It would cause chaos, and you'd have the waste of the underlying land once nobody could have title to it. So it's kind of obvious that [this approach] doesn't make sense for physical objects. But limits on the length and breadth of patents and opportunities for people to borrow from each other's ideas – those kinds of weak property rights are probably a reasonable compromise in an economy, because they let private-sector incentives lead to the development of new ideas but prevent anybody from creating the kind of a monopoly that would impede the re-use of an idea into the infinite future.

If the great, great, great grandchildren of Pythagoras still had property rights in the Pythagorean theorem and everybody who did anything involving right angles had to go pay a royalty payment to his heirs, it would slow down the process of discovery in a way that wouldn't be beneficial. The modern science-based economy is driven by having relatively weak property rights for ideas, but still some property rights for ideas, and by the recognition that most of the discovery is actually not going to take place inside the university, not inside of the institutions of science – it's going to be market-based, and we still want to give relatively weak property rights for those ideas so that we can create new entrants, new competition, a Schumpeterian kind of turnover.

So that's the first part. Once you say that, you have to recognize that you won't get enough idea production in that kind of world. You've weakened the property rights of anybody who comes up with a new idea, so they'll only capture a small fraction of the benefits that they create when they come up with something new. Then you might say, "Well, gee, collectively we'd all be better off if we could encourage that process of idea creation." The mechanism that has worked well for that historically, I think, is for the government to subsidize the training of people who are educated in fields like science and engineering, [for the government] to say, "You know, we don't know exactly what these people will go out and do, but we'll create this university system, we'll subsidize it, we'll train a bunch of these people, and then they'll go out and they'll discover new things because these trained people are the key input in the discovery process. If we got more of these people out there, they'll discover more things and that will lead to good outcomes." On the private-sector return side, you're depressing innovative activity by having weak property rights. But on the input supply side of this discovery process, you've got the public sector feeding the supply of people. Again, the reason we have to do this is that having weak property rights slows down the discovery of new ideas – because everybody says, "Well, if I get something new, I don't get as big a return on it" – but that also [means] that that entire pool of existing ideas is available for you to make use of if you want to go out and find a new thing. So the rough institutional structure, I think, that emerges from theory and into history is one of property rights on ideas and private-sector discovery, but limited property rights on ideas, and subsidies of innovation through the training of people.

AK & NS: And is it your sense right now that anyone, say any one nation, does an adequate job of subsidizing? Could the United States do more or could Europe be doing more or less? And how do we know what the right amount is?

PR: One thing that I think is a danger right now is that there has been a very strong tendency towards strengthening intellectual property rights in the United States over, I'd say, the last twenty or thirty years. The proximate cause was the creation of a special appeals court for hearing all patent cases. The ultimate cause of this, I think, was the proselytizing by economists that property rights are good – just let the legal system create property rights and let things run on their own from there. So we've been on a trajectory where we've been strengthening patent rights considerably, and people are now starting to see that this could actually be counterproductive.

We're just starting to rethink how best to calibrate this notion of weak property rights, and you can see that there are special-interest forces [involved]: anybody with an existing property right always wants it to be stronger and longer-lasting. No pharmaceutical company with a patent on a given drug wants anybody else to discover something that's better, or to use what they've learned to discover something that's better. So I think one broad question for policy is, are we erring on the side of trying to lock [things] up, giving proprietary control over too much of the knowledge?

On the other side, we're going through this shift in the economy where the fraction of human effort that goes into actually physically rearranging things – bending metal, doing manufacturing, and so on – is going down over time and the fraction that's going into discovering the right formula or recipe is going up over time. And that's a really good thing, because all of the value really comes from finding the new recipes. If you picture the innovative activity of one hundred years ago and you think of it as U.S. Steel, most of the workers there were involved in literally bending or melting metal – doing the physical rearrangement – and a relatively small number of people were coming up with, say, better ways to extract iron from ore. If you shift ahead to the beginning of the twenty-first century and you think of a company like Genentech, very few of the workers actually physically stamp out the pills or make the injectable fluids. Almost everybody who works at a company like that is engaged in trying to figure out the right recipe for making some compound that will do something really beneficial for humans.

So we're going through this transformation where a larger and larger fraction of the labor force is engaged in problem-solving, sifting through possible ideas, and a relatively small fraction of people actually stamps out the pills or bends the metal. We have been training more and more people in the United States in higher education and producing more people with science and engineering degrees. [But] I don't think we've been doing it at a rate that has kept up with the opportunities that are available to us, and so you see the United States sucking in really talented people from all across the world, because domestically we're unable to take advantage of all the opportunities for discovery that are out there. I don't think the United States is keeping up in training the numbers of scientists and engineers that would be most beneficial for us from the point of view of society as a whole.

AK & NS: It's very difficult to get people to think of technology in a broad sense. Today, for example, I think your man in the street would say that technology is computers and bits and bytes, and it might be iPods and things like that. But there's a much, much broader way of thinking about technology, and I think it's important to think more broadly [in this way]. Could you talk about this broader way of thinking about technology, what it means and what its implications might be?

PR: You can think of technology as any set of instructions or procedures that people follow to try to create value, and those procedures could be as elaborate as how to mix together a superconductor or how to make an LED, but they can also be as simple as how to efficiently deliver hot, good-tasting coffee to people.

I've used this analogy: One piece of technology was somebody figuring out how to design the coffee cup so that different-size coffee cups could all use the same-size lid. It's kind of obvious once you think about it, but it was a piece of technology, it was a recipe, it was a formula, a procedure that somebody thought of – and once they thought of it, they slightly increased the productivity of the people working in the coffee shop. You have a smaller inventory of lids and spend less time going out and making sure that all three types of lids are out there and available, and in a competitive market, what that ultimately means is more competition between different coffee shops and coffee provided to people at slightly lower prices, because the workers there are slightly more productive. So we should think of technology as being everything from the very high-tech examples of superconductors and transistors and pharmaceuticals to the [simple] procedures that people follow when they're making coffee in a coffee shop.

When you look at [technology] in that broad sense, it becomes clear that the vast majority of that kind of discovery has to come from the private sector. This part of the traditional message carries over, that you have to allow some kind of property rights, or at least allow people to have some proprietary control. A lot of it is just trade secrets over ideas, or just [letting some time pass before] talking. You have to rely on private profit motives to lead to all of these kinds of discoveries.

You'd never want to let university professors or scientists be in charge of coming up with efficient ways to serve up coffee, but at the same time, you want things to be fluid enough; if Dunkin' Donuts had had an [indefinite] patent on serving coffee to people from a store, you could have never had an entry from Starbucks, which created a whole new kind of product and a whole new kind of experience for people. You have to find this vague balance, with incentives for the private sector to innovate but room for new innovators to come along and contest with the incumbent.

AK & NS: Do you think it's true to say that the easiest discoveries of new knowledge are behind us now – that we've tackled the low-hanging fruit? And if that is true, does it mean that growth will slow?

PR: This gets back to the two explanations I described at the beginning about why growth was speeding up. One [explanation] was that it's just getting easier and easier. I think there is something about this process of discovery which says that the more you know, the easier it is to discover new things. I still think there may be some truth in that. It may be true that you can keep the rate of discovery constant over time by virtue of this momentum within the discovery process itself. There are some interesting people who would argue the other side – but even if I'm wrong about that, and with the same amount of, say, resources going into discovery, the rate of discovery actually falls over time, what's offsetting that right now is that we're applying more and more resources to the discovery process. As long as we keep freeing up labor from bending metal and stamping out pills and put more and more [of it] into discovery, we can keep pushing up that rate of growth, by directing more and more resources in that direction.

I think that either through internal momentum or by adding more and more resources to the discovery process, we'll be able to sustain this accelerating rate of growth into the coming century.

AK & NS: And where might computers and the Internet fit into this? Do they make it categorically easier to develop and spread knowledge? And if so, do these inventions and platforms mean that growth will accelerate?

PR: That's an example of the first process, the internal dynamic – because we've learned how to use digital electronics, we can create devices now that make the process of discovery much faster than it used to be. A lot of discovery is still based on what the pharmaceutical companies would call mass screening – you just try a whole lot of different compounds until you find something interesting. They've now got this area of combinatorial chemistry, where they can create lots of different compounds to chemical reactions and then [use] screening systems to screen large numbers of those compounds. These new digital technologies will let us consider many more compounds per minute or per researcher than in the past. That's an example of how improvements in technology to date are making us even better at coming up with new technologies in the future. So I would treat the

Internet and digital electronics as a part of that general process of discovery, communication, getting better as technology evolves.

The one other thing that's happening is that we're getting more and more people worldwide engaged in the discovery process. The fraction of humans that really are engaged in discovery is still relatively small. If you think into the far future, and you think of educating the whole world population to the level of, say, the United States and then scaling up the total number of people engaged in the discovery process so that the fraction worldwide looks like the fraction here in the United States now; or to go one step further, if you project that fraction growing in the United States and then extend that all over the world, [it's clear that] we'll be able to have many more people engaged in this kind of discovery process. As long as people are coordinating their efforts, the more people you have out there discovering the better off we're all going to be, because if one person discovers it, we basically all get to use it in the end. If one person discovers a pharmaceutical that prevents Alzheimer's disease, then bang, we're all going to benefit from it, and the more people who are out there looking, the more likely it is that we'll soon come up with it.

The thing that you have to do, though, when you get that many people all trying to discover at the same time, is to coordinate their activities, at least loosely. You want people to be aware of what others are doing so that you don't end up with a whole lot of replication of effort. Part of what communications technologies are doing is coordinating these discovery efforts worldwide: as soon as somebody discovers something, it gets broadcast very quickly to others throughout the world, and people can change the directions they explore based on what they know others are doing.

So digital devices, digital screening, digital analytical

techniques, and computing techniques are inherently speeding up the productivity of researchers, while communications technologies are helping them coordinate their efforts and build on each other's efforts.

AK & NS: You have started your own firm. You're an entrepreneur.

PR: Yes.

AK & NS: Has that experience as an entrepreneur in any way changed or refined your outlook as an economist?

PR: Yes, it has, in lots of subtle ways. Creating the right incentives for people is a very subtle process. In one sense, my experience has reinforced what I knew from economics, which was that incentives really matter. People respond to incentives, and if you can harness those incentives you can get very good outcomes for everybody. That reinforces the basic invisible-hand market message. Markets work by aligning incentives in such a way that everybody benefits. The qualification that I've learned from being in business, I guess, is that setting up the detailed structures that create the right incentives for people is much more subtle and complicated than the usual economic analysis suggests.

For example, a firm as a whole faces a profit incentive. You know, we sell or we don't sell, we make a profit or we don't. But within the organization, there are all these small incentives you have to create to get people to work together, and you know, most workers aren't paid on a piece-rate basis, they don't share a piece of the profits. In Silicon Valley you can use things like options to get all your workers to have a little piece of the profit incentives; but it's still a very subtle process to set up all the internal incentives and get everybody working in the right direction.

In our particular industry, where we're trying to get professors to use technology to teach better, you can see the problems of misalignment of incentives on the other side. You see professors who – basically, nobody will ever know if they [can] do a better job teaching, and so they have no incentive to try to do a better job teaching. All they want to do is to minimize the total input of time into their activities. If the students could really understand how much they're learning and if they could prove to outsiders how much they learned and that it was important, the teachers who really did a better job of teaching would get rewarded more and you could solve these incentive problems. But modern higher education is filled with the misalignment of incentives, so professors don't always do the thing which is best for their students and students don't always get the quality of education that they might get if those incentives were better aligned.

AK & NS: Are there changes you would recommend for the system of higher education in the United States? Maybe it even applies to our institutions of science. Are there changes that you would advocate, concrete steps of any kind?

PR: Yes. I think there's a very general lesson about non-market organizations. When you can create a market, this may be less important – but even in a very market-oriented economy like the United States, a lot of interactions are actually non-market interactions; within the firm we don't have an internal market, and within the university we don't have markets, and so forth. Inevitably, there are still large domains of activity that are non-market activities. In those settings, the more you can measure and the more information you can make visible and observable, the better you'll be able to align incentives. You know, roughly speaking, you can't reward somebody for doing the right thing if you don't measure whether or not they do it.

Better measurement is fundamental to creating incentives that will lead to outcomes that are good in a broad sense. As I was saying a minute ago, you might have a professor who could do a much better job as a teacher than somebody else, or [better] than if she didn't put in any effort, but if nobody measures how well she does, then there's no way for her to get rewarded for that performance, and then there's no way for students to select that professor based on her being somebody who will teach them more. And the students might be able to show that they went to a good school, but they will have no way to prove to their employer, "We actually learned a lot more economics than somebody else in my school." If they can't show and she can't measure how much they learned, then the students really don't have any incentive to go out to get the job, or at least don't have any way to prove to employers that they learned more or have the incentive to learn more [in order to] get a better job or higher pay. So in these large non-market domains, better measurement and more information can be extremely beneficial.

Even in the market domains – in many cases private-sector agents have incentives to provide information, but not always. One interesting example of a beneficial government action was when the FAA started forcing the airlines to report on-time performance for their flights. This led to really big changes in how the airlines did their scheduling, and on-time performance went up dramatically, and all the FAA had done was mandate the disclosure of the on-time arrival rate for all these different routes that the airlines fly. So even in the market setting, sometimes there can be some benefit from collective decision-making, from a government that says, "We need to measure things and we need to make sure that the information is disclosed."

I think I have a deeper appreciation of the importance of that, having now been an entrepreneur and having struggled with both universities, as customers, and organizations, as the vehicles I use to try to develop new things.

AK & NS: What's been the biggest challenge in getting professors to adopt Aplia?

PR: It's fundamentally this problem, that most of them don't have any incentive to do a better job as teachers. A lot of them do it anyway because they just like being better teachers. They have a personal sense of integrity that makes them want to do it, but there's very little in the way of institutional rewards for doing a better job as a teacher, so . . .

AK & NS: If anything, is there the opposite?

PR: Well, yes; there's even a sort of stigma attached to being a better teacher. I think this gets back to some more pervasive questions. Go back to my original claim that [we should] have government subsidies for education. I do believe that, but then once we do that, we have to think hard about the question, what are the incentives in the institutions that actually deliver on those subsidies?

And so we have, for example, a public education system that, I think, suffers from an extreme version of this lack of measurement of what's really happening in the public education system. Many economists who've looked at publicly provided education have said, "Well, the problem here is that this is like a monopoly. There's no choice." Choice and entry by competitive providers is clearly one thing that makes markets work well, so they're onto something when they say that competition entry would be a good thing in education; but I think they actually miss the other piece of this, which is that without the measurement of what's happening, it's hard to have effective competition . . .

AK & NS: . . . and that there's no exit.

PR: Yes. If you can't tell who's doing a bad job, you don't have this exit process that will drive the less effective providers out of the business.

So I think choice and competition are good, but I think that we probably underestimate the importance of measurement in this educational activity, because it isn't easy to tell the difference between educational institutions that are really doing a great job and ones that are just plain fraudulent.

AK & NS: Are there one or two key things that our political class, broadly speaking, doesn't sufficiently appreciate or understand about economic growth?

PR: Well, one thing that's important to persuade everyone of is that everyone wants growth but nobody wants change, and you've got to have both or you've got to have neither – it's what I was talking about before, that it's all about rearrangement and finding better ways to rearrange things. The only way you can create new value with new rearrangements is essentially by doing things differently; and any time you do things differently, there will be change, so people have to buy into the idea that change accompanies growth. It's not going to be just more of the same for everyone. Everyone wants it to be like bread dough – so everybody's piece of everything gets a little bit bigger but nothing else changes – and it just can't be like that.

A slightly stronger version of that is to recognize that when you have change, there will inevitably be winners and losers. You have to have some tolerance for the idea that if there's something which is, on average, going to make the next generation much better off than this generation, we have to collectively commit to go for that even if some people who have extremely good positions right now are going to end up having less good positions down the road. Some [people] are going to move down and others will move up, and we can't let a small group of losers – either absolute losers or relative losers – stop the process of growth that will benefit most people going forward.

We have to agree that, one, there will be change, and two, there are some winners and losers and there are no guarantees: everybody who is engaged in economic activity takes a certain amount of risk. There are always winners and losers when there are risks. We all commit to that, and on average we're all going to be better off, but we don't let the losers have veto power over progress. This is clearly a very acute question right now in Europe, where the existing elite, the existing well-off, do have a very strong position of veto power, a choke-hold on change and innovation. I think people need to understand this commitment to change and to winners and losers.

I think that, by the way, you can simultaneously say we'll take risks, we'll have change, we'll have some winners and losers, and we will also make efforts as a society to keep extremes of income and inequality from opening up. Historically, commitments to collective financing for education have been very important in creating a growth process in which everybody could share in the benefits. And if we hadn't had any public provision or any public financing of education, things in the United States would look much more unequal now than they did before. We can say that collectively there are some measures we'll undertake, like continuing to help subsidize education for everybody, even people who come from disadvantaged or modest backgrounds. We can still make those commitments but not go so far as to say we're going to give every interest group, every union, every entrenched business, every incumbent veto power over any kind of change.

AK & NS: Are there any threats to progress and technical change on the horizon that you think are particularly worrisome? Or do you think that the benefits that come with growth are so great that we have reached a point where we'll be able to overcome any obstacles that in previous periods of history may have stopped or even reversed it?

PR: I have one small concern. In general, I'm very optimistic; despite political opposition and resistance to change and special interest groups, we've still had this process of accelerating growth over time. One factor that does worry me a little is the demographic changes that we're going through. Young people, I think, tend to be more innovative, more willing to take risks, more willing to do things differently, and they may be very important, disproportionately important in this innovation and growth process.

A smaller fraction of our population will be young in the future just because of slower population growth and longer life spans. That shift in the proportions is not necessarily bad. It could become bad if control structures were shifted towards the more entrenched, the older. Where might that show up? If you look at universities right now, for example, the average age of a principal investigator on an NIH grant has been moving up over time; instead of young scientists getting grant funding to go off and do whatever they want in their twenties, they're working in a lab where somebody in his forties or fifties is the principal investigator in charge of the grant. They're working as apprentices, almost, under the senior person. If we're not careful, we could let our institutions, things like tenure and hierarchical structures and peer review, slowly morph over time so that the old guys control more and more of what's going on and the young people have a harder and harder time doing something really different, and that would be a bad thing for these processes of growth and change. I'd like to see us keep thinking about how we could tweak our institutions to give power and control and opportunity to young people.

I must say that even though I'm worried about it in the long run, I think the United States right now is really remarkable – not just in how effective it is in creating good market structures, market institutions, compared with other countries, but also in how good it is at giving resources to young people when they come up with something that's a really powerful idea. One of our great strengths is that we really do create the space and the running room for young innovators when they come up with something new. I think the long-term outlook for the United States is good, but you want to keep aware of what the dangers could be.

This is, by the way, one of the subtle dimensions along which we differ from the rest of the world. It isn't just that Europe is more corporatist and more union-oriented and more collectivist and special interest-driven, but there's also just a lot more deference to age and respect for wisdom and received wisdom.

AK & NS: That's true in places like Japan as well.

PR: Yes. And it will be very interesting to see how this plays out in China, because China has the potential to be highly educated, highly innovative. They clearly are moving very rapidly towards markets, but they do have some of these same traditions of deference towards elders. It's the kind of culture that can tolerate rap music and extreme sports that can also create space for guys like Page and Brin and Google. That's one of our hidden strengths.

Interview with

JOEL MOKYR

JOEL MOKYR *is the Robert H. Strotz Professor of Arts and Sciences at Northwestern University. He holds a joint appointment in economics as well as a Sackler Professorial Fellowship at the Eitan Berglas School of Economics at the University of Tel Aviv. He is particularly interested in the economic history of technology and population, but he considers himself a general-purpose economic historian. A former editor of the Journal of Economic History, he served as the editor in chief of the* Oxford Encyclopedia of Economic History (*five volumes, 2004*) *and continues to be editor in chief of a book series published by Princeton University Press, The Princeton University Press Economic History of the Western World. He has served as chair of the economics department at Northwestern and president of the Economic History Association, and he is a member of the American Academy of Arts and Sciences. Among his publications are* The Lever of Riches (*1990*), *The* British Industrial Revolution (*1993; revised edition, 1998*), *and* The Gifts of Athena (*2002*). *He is currently working on two books:* The Enlightened Economy: an Economic History of Britain, 1700–1850 *and* Neither Fluke nor Destiny: Evolutionary Models in Economic History.

ARNOLD KLING & NICK SCHULZ: Describe the importance of what you call in your book, *The Gifts of Athena*, "useful knowledge." What's the importance of that to economic growth, and how is this knowledge generated?

JOEL MOKYR: I started to ask myself: if somebody put a gun to my head and said, "define technology," what would I say? And the only answer I could come up with that really satisfied me was that it's something in our own heads. It isn't really the artifact – that is to say, the machinery, the tools, the equipment, the lab; nor is it the books, nor is it anything else of that nature. It's really what's happening in people's heads.

Now, that doesn't mean that this knowledge can immediately turn itself into action without all kinds of intermediate steps. But it's the knowledge that really counts, and so what I wanted to do was to think about the fundamental unit by which you would define it, that entity which we call knowledge, without getting too much into the epistemological issue of what it is that we do when we think we know something. I gladly leave that to cognitive psychology.

I got this actually from a famous cognitive psychologist named Michael Polyani. He's the great mind behind this, though he didn't really care much about economic history, as far as I could tell. What Polanyi basically says is that there are two kinds of knowledge, and I used these in my book as "propositional" knowledge and "prescriptive" knowledge.

What I mean by prescriptive knowledge is really what technology's all about; you should think about it as a kind of recipe. But let's say essentially what a technique is: it's a set of instructions. It's how you produce. And that's a very broad [thing] to define. It isn't just how to bake a cake or how to drive from Cincinnati to Louisville. It's how to build a nuclear reactor and how to fix it when it's broken. Everything to do with production as we know it is going to be defined as a recipe.

You can think of a recipe – if you want to be geeky, think back to the time when we still wrote our own computer programs. It's a "do loop" – "do this, do that, do that" – and if you run it correctly, out comes something which we call production. Of course, these "do loops" may be nested, and they may have all kinds of internal subprograms and on and on and on, and they can be fiendishly complex. But basically, that is what a technique is.

That's one set of useful knowledge. The other part of useful knowledge is the base of it: How do you know that? How do you get to this technique? When the first person writes this down, what does he or she have to know? If you want to give somebody instructions about how to drive from Cincinnati to Louisville, there's some background knowledge [involved]. You know the layout of the land, you know where the highways are, and then you give these instructions. But there is some background knowledge that in itself is not a recipe, but is underlying. And that's what I call the epistemic base of techniques. It is what we know about natural phenomena and regularities that allows us to exploit nature for our own purposes and produce these techniques. Some of these are exceedingly simple and some of them are fiendishly complicated.

AK & NS: In your book, you describe it as the equipment we use in our game against nature.

JM: Yes, that's exactly right. My point was that those two entities are separate. Jointly they comprise what I call useful knowledge. If you wanted to partition [useful knowledge] into these two subsets, to use the language of formal economics, there is a prescriptive subset, which is essentially these recipes, and there is a propositional subset, which is all the knowledge we have about natural phenomena and regularities that we can bring to bear in order to write down these recipes.

Now, some of this knowledge can be exceedingly simple – like the knowledge that the sun rises in the east and sets in the west, or the knowledge that the winds blow in a particular direction over the Atlantic in the spring and a different direction in the fall, which you can utilize to sail across the Atlantic – and some of it has to do with deeply complicated stuff like quantum mechanics. But they all in some sense have a common denominator, which is that we know something about natural phenomena and regularities. Of course, science as we know it today is a subset of that knowledge, but nobody would argue that the knowledge that it's warm in Chicago in the summer and cold in the winter is science; it's common knowledge. It's much bigger than science.

But that is what I mean by useful knowledge. On the one hand, propositional knowledge provides the basis for prescriptive knowledge. But the degree to which the epistemic base has to be wide or narrow depends a great deal on the particular technique in question. And this is why history is so interesting; sometimes we invented something without having a clue as to why it worked. We just hit upon it by accident, by serendipity, by trial and error, or maybe by completely fallacious reasoning. The point is that inventions are made when there is a minimum epistemic base – which can be zero, but sometimes it's not. You cannot build a nuclear reactor by accident. You've got to know something about nuclear science. But you can invent aspirin quite serendipitously, without having the faintest clue about how it works.

Then you see something interesting happen: once a technique is invented, even on a very narrow epistemic base, if the institutions are right and if society is ready for it, there's a feedback going back from the technique into the knowledge, and people start wondering how and why it works. And this happens over and over again. In my book I give a few examples – about aviation, about steam engines, about aspirin – but one can multiply these examples *ad nauseam*. We invent something, and sometimes we know a little bit about how it works, sometimes we know nothing, sometimes we know quite a bit, but in all cases, as we use it more, the epistemic base gets wider. We get a better and better idea as to what exactly it is that makes this thing tick, and as we understand it better – and this is the key, where it links into the economy – it gets easier to improve it. It gets easier to apply it to other things. It gets easier to adapt it to changing circumstances.

There are lots of techniques in human history which we got to work but, because we didn't understand *why* they worked, that was it – they stopped. They didn't keep improving. But over the last two hundred years, the world is different: now we feel challenged that if something works and we're not sure why, we want to know why, and we'll carry out research to know why. Sometimes we're better at it and sometimes we are worse at it. We're always trying to figure it out.

I don't think anybody really has a good idea of how acupuncture works, for instance. Maybe you do. I don't. But we know – at least it is argued – that acupuncture works very well for some people and that there's still a lot to learn about the human body, and eventually – it might take another generation or so, but eventually – people are going to figure it out. We know that certain kinds of drugs work on the brain. We don't know exactly why, but we're trying to find out. When we find out, we will be able to make them better – and that, in my view, is how economic growth works.

One example that's in my book, and that I really like, concerns the use of engines. When the first engines were built – this probably dates back to 1712 and the first working Newcomen engine, although there were some models built earlier – what Newcomen basically did, as we see it today, is to find a way of converting thermal energy into kinetic energy. Now, that's a concept he did not have, right? That's the concept of thermodynamics, which was discovered a century and a half later, maybe. He got the steam engine to work, and in fact there were some improvements possible. [But] the problem of exactly how the steam engine worked and what made it more efficient or less efficient wasn't really cracked until the middle of the nineteenth century, when thermodynamics became a part of useful knowledge.

Now thermodynamics was directly and demonstrably inspired by people watching steam engines at work. So they have this thing, and they say, "Gee, this works. How could that be?" And from that is born the field of thermodynamics. Once thermodynamics is there, people look at it with the knowledge that they can make these engines better. So from there, there is internal combustion, there is diesel, there is electricity generation, there are all these machines that take advantage of thermodynamics in one form or another.

And that's the kind of internal dynamic within useful knowledge that drives history. That is, I think, the message of my book or the main message of my book, and that's the thing I would point out to economists. In some sense it does, in my modest assessment, help open Nathan Rosenberg's black box – we all talk about technology, but we never know what's in there. I haven't solved everything, and there's lots of stuff that I don't know, but this is one way of opening that black box.

AK & NS: You point out in *The Gifts of Athena* that "useful knowledge more often than not emerges before people know what it will be used for." Now this dovetails a little bit with what you were just saying, but it strikes us as an extraordinarily important point, because it means that progress in various fields will be extremely difficult, if not impossible, to predict and – perhaps more importantly – to plan. Is this true, in your estimation? And what would be some other implications of this?

JM: Absolutely. I don't know of a single economist working on this topic who thinks otherwise. The economist Richard G. Lipsey says exactly this: the only way we can think about technology is in evolutionary terms. And evolutionary biology is a kind of science that makes no predictions, except, perhaps, in saying that certain things are not going to happen because they are excluded. But among all the things that are possible, it really has no way of predicting what will emerge and what it will look like. I tend to be very skeptical about the capability of economists to predict, period. I always quote to my students the famous statement that since our second temple was destroyed, the art of prophecy was given to the fools. That doesn't make me too popular among my forecasting colleagues, but hey, I got tenure.

AK & NS: So tenure is good for something.

JM: Right. [*laughter*] What we can say is this: that certain problems seem to be important and that research will be devoted to them. What is far more serious, of course, is that we actually have no way of predicting what new techniques will emerge that aren't suggested by current relative prices. Nobody can convince me that [people felt] a huge need for the iPod. It caught on because it was a nice design and people liked it and it created its own mark, and that's the way things often go. And I think that is the way technology always works.

The interesting thing, of course, is to look back on what futurists and science fiction writers thought was going to happen fifty or a hundred years ago, and to see how almost all of them completely missed what modern technology would really end up being concerned with and looking like. They all predicted a lot of space travel, which we haven't done all that well, and they predicted all kinds of similar technology – telekinesis and stuff like that – but the information communication revolution really wasn't predicted.

I can't find anybody who predicted that – that people would actually leave offices and factories and start working from home or vacation places or red-carpet rooms or wherever they happen to be. The artificial distinction between work and leisure, both in space and in time, was fairly universal in 1914. If you look at the world in 1914, the vast bulk of the labor force – I don't want to say everybody, but the vast bulk, maybe three quarters of the male labor force – was working in a well-defined place according to well-defined hours. Your bell rang at eight o'clock and you were there, and then it rang again at five o'clock and you left, and that was work. The number of people who were subject to that kind of regime is now declining as the result of ICT. And who predicted that? Nobody. Or if somebody did, I don't know about it.

I'll give you one more analogy I like. Suppose you were trying to make a prediction about the evolution of species. Think about the evolution of Homo sapiens. Sixty-five million years ago, dinosaurs disappeared, as everybody knows, and that gave mammals a chance. So mammals evolved for over sixty million years and created all kinds of rather unbelievable forms, most of which – almost all of which – have subsequently gone extinct. It took sixty million years for Homo sapiens to evolve. Now, would anybody have been able to predict back then that an asteroid would hit and all the dinosaurs would go belly-up? If you were around then, would you have predicted that a species like Homo sapiens, with a nervous system vastly more complex than that of any other species, would eventually change the entire biosphere of the planet? Nobody would have predicted that, because in some sense it was an accident. It could have happened 30 million years ago, it could have happened 40 million years ago, it could have happened 16 million years ago, and in most places it could not have happened at all. That is the kind of accidental factor, I think, that remains true for technology as well.

That doesn't mean we can't make any predictions in evolution at all; we can predict, for instance, with certainty that we will never have insects as big as elephants, because that's ruled out by the laws of physics. And lots of other things can be ruled out. Most of the creatures you see in the bar scene in "Star Wars" cannot exist except in our imagination, because most of them violate some law of physics or chemistry or biology. On the other hand, I can make you an infinitely long list of species that are quite feasible but have never occurred, or as far as anybody knows have never occurred, simply because the correct mutation simply never happened. In that sense, I think we are very much in the same ballpark.

Now, I don't want to press this analogy too far, because in fact it can be misleading. Biology is a very special case of evolution in theory. There are lots of other evolutionary systems that are not quite as indeterminate, and I think technology is one of them. But there is still a deep fundamental indeterminacy there that makes prediction essentially impossible. And that, of course, is why it's so much fun.

AK & NS: It's not fun for people who want to plan for the future, though.

JM: No, but you take your chances, you pay your money, as the saying goes.

AK & NS: You spend a lot of time researching and writing about the Industrial Revolution. You call it the "Industrial Enlightenment." Why is it important that we understand the origins of the Industrial Revolution, and why have you termed it the Industrial Enlightenment?

JM: My forthcoming book is called *The Enlightened Economy*, and it will be a long discussion of the economic history of Britain between 1700 and 1850. In the book I vastly expand my argument that we have deeply underrated and underestimated the ideological roots of economic change. I think that gets to the heart of the issue that you raised earlier about institutions. The point is something like this: a lot of people believed with Karl Marx that what people believe, what their ideology and ideas are, is essentially determined by economic infrastructure – the means of production, technology, population, things like that. And it's not just the Marxists; there are a lot of fans of neoclassical economics who essentially say that people believe in their pocketbooks, right? Workers will believe in socialism, and the upper class will believe in capitalism, and that's the way the world is. Except that that's not the way the world is. Over most of history people have not voted their pocketbooks – Marxists included. The Marxists came from the bourgeois class.

What I want to argue is that ideology has a life of its own, that it evolves through its own dynamic, and that it affects the economic system, and here's how. I'm going to give you only one part of the story because the other part is actually in the book, but here's a part I've left out. If you look at Europe in 1650 or 1700, what you see is a very sophisticated set of economies. They have just basically finished exploring the rest of the world, and there has been great deal of commerce and trade – joint stock companies are emerging, insurance is emerging. This is a fairly sophisticated commercial economy. The problem is, there are lots of special interests trying to get exclusionary arrangements that are good for them but bad for the economy. This is a system in which property rights are well defined and enforced, as Douglass North loves to say, but also rather distortive in the sense that you have lots of exclusionary arrangements. In other words, for the economy to function well, you don't just need good property rights, you also need what we could call, somewhat vaguely, "economic freedoms." You need labor mobility; you need to get rid of guilds; you need to get rid of monopolies, both local and global; you need to get rid of all kind of regulations; and above all, you need free trade. And if you don't have that, you're going to end up in a society that will not be able to grow.

Nowadays we have a different term for this. We call it corruption. We always say, look at countries like Russia or the Central Asian nations – these countries will never have good economies because they are corrupt. But corruption is really just a special form of what we call, in economic jargon, "rent-seeking." I argue in my book that one of the things that happens in eighteenth-century Europe is a reaction against what we today would call rent-seeking, and that this, to a great extent, is what the Enlightenment was all about. The Enlightenment wasn't just about freedom of religion and democracy. It wasn't to be about democracy at all, but never mind that. It was about freedom of religion, tolerance, human rights – it was about all of those things. But it was also a reaction against mercantilism, and you find that attitude in certain people who were very important in the Enlightenment. Above all, of course, the great Adam Smith.

Adam Smith isn't, you know, as original as people sometimes give him credit for. In fact, most of his ideas were [already] around by the middle of the eighteenth century. All these people were saying essentially the same thing: we need to get rid of guilds, monopolies, all kinds of restricted regulatory legislation. And above all, you need free trade, both internal – which Britain had, but the Continent did not – and international. [And yet] the movement was important, not because the ideas themselves were different, but because people were convinced. This movement had a huge influence; you cannot live in America without realizing that the way our political system, our institutions, which were set up in 1789, were deeply influenced by Enlightenment writers. If American colonies had rebelled in 1680, we would not be anything like what we are today. There's not the slightest doubt about it. In fact, some of our founding fathers are celebrated in Europe as great Enlightenment thinkers themselves. Benjamin Franklin, James Madison, Jefferson – these guys were in Europe. They were influenced by European thought, and in fact they probably considered themselves Europeans.

What is interesting is, when you look at the few places in Europe where the Enlightenment either didn't penetrate or was fought back by existing interests, those are exactly the countries that failed economically. You think of Spain and Russia, above all. These were two countries where Enlightenment ideas were brought in, but the reaction against them was so strong that eventually the forces of enlightenment were defeated and these countries sank back into reactionary governments. And these countries – well, Russia is still waiting, and Spain has only been going like mad in the last thirty years, after the death of the last of the Spanish reactionaries.

In that regard, if you look at the countries where the Enlightenment had an impact, they are the countries that formed the convergence club of 1914. They are countries that by that time were industrialized, urbanized, technologically sophisticated. And the countries where the Enlightenment did not catch on, for them the process had to take a very different route. Some made it, like Spain; some didn't, like Montenegro or Serbia or Bulgaria. Eventually they might, but the point is, if you look at Scandinavia or the Low Countries or Switzerland, these were all countries in which the Enlightenment did catch on, once, in one way or another, and by 1914 they are rich countries.

The same, I think, is true in Britain. The interesting thing about Britain is that the big wave of reforms starts in the 1770s and 1780s, but then it stops. It stops during the French and Napoleonic wars, largely as a reaction against France and out of concern that bully radicalism is going to overthrow the state. So there's a sharp setback between 1793 and 1815, but when the dust settles, especially in the middle of the 1820s, you start seeing Britain being influenced more and more by reformers and you get what I call the ten miraculous years between 1824 and 1834. If you look at the history of the governments in Britain between 1824 and 1834, they really overhauled their entire institutional system from top to bottom.

What came out of that is a free-market, liberal Victorian economy. It had some good things and some bad things – which people started recognizing at the time – but the alternative was a rent-seeking, repressive, highly regulatory economy. That economy, I think, would have stalled.

AK & NS: Can you imagine the Industrial Revolution taking place without the printing press and the way it increased the storage capacity and the communication capacity for knowledge? And to follow up on that, do you think that today computers and the Internet can have a similar impact?

JM: Well, that's a hard one. There still are people who believe that the printing press is the atypical invention in history, that without it nothing would have ever happened. But I am far from convinced of that. Almost anything has good substitutes. Without the printing press, what Europe would have had to do is spend a considerable proportion of its labor force to train people to become scribes and copy things by hand. That's something far more expensive, depending on the relative price of labor and on how fast people could write, and it would have been an impediment, but remember that before 1750 or 1800, the vast bulk of books that were printed didn't help technology very much or at all. Sure, there were books about technology and books about engineering and about chemistry and so on, but they were a tiny fraction of all books printed. The vast bulk of books printed dealt with religion or were novels or pornography, or they were political tracts and pamphlets.

Much of the communication about technology is in fact through personal transmission. It's through people traveling and looking around at other people's factories and engineering work. It's through master–apprentice relationships, which are personal transmissions of knowledge through conversation or imitation and not necessarily through books. You can only learn so much from books, even now. I'm aware that it might be a lot in many cases, and as far as more theoretical topics are concerned, that is not negligible. But yes, I can imagine the industrial revolution without the printing press. I can imagine it without steam. I can imagine it – and I have imagined it – without cotton. I don't think there's anything that is really indispensable.

The one exception I would make, with some hesitation,

is the core process of making wrought iron, because that's the one thing for which I can't think of a very good substitute. Iron is something for which we've never found very good substitutes in the modern age

AK & NS: My next question has a couple of parts to it. You have claimed that something that you call Cardwell's Law implies that no one society retains technological leadership indefinitely. What's the basis for this law? And do you see the U.S., which is currently the leader, falling victim to Cardwell's Law in this century? If so, to whom?

JM: Well, once again, I eschew any kind of prediction. I am not saying that in a hundred years the United States will be like the Roman Empire at the time of Attila the Hun or something like that. Anybody who makes that argument is just stupid.

What I can tell you is this. Looking back at the record, it is quite clear that nobody has held technological leadership for a very long time. The reason for that is primarily that technology creates vested interests, and these vested interests have a stake in trying to stop new technologies from kicking them out in the same way that they kicked out the previous generation. And that leads to a political struggle. If everything [went] through the marketplace, there [wouldn't be] a problem, right? Because when the marketplace decides that you guys are less efficient, out you go. You're a dinosaur and that's it. But of course, the old technology doesn't want to rely on the marketplace. They want to rely on known market mechanisms, particularly politics. And they have all kinds of mechanisms. One is regulation, in the name of safety or in the name of the environment or in the name of protection of jobs. They will try to fend off the new to protect the human and physical capital embodied in the old technology.

So there is always a political struggle between the people who want the new stuff and the people who want to preserve the old, and sometimes one side wins and sometimes the other side wins. The ultimate example of that, of course, is Ming China, in which the entire institutional setup was very, very new-phobic and very much against any kind of technological innovation, which, of course, led to these societies falling behind and eventually having their rude awakening in the nineteenth century when they saw how the West had pulled ahead.

I think about that every time I look at what's happening in the United States. I see signs that the system may turn against innovation in one form or another, and I always worry. Now, I'm not claiming that I know the outcome of this struggle. But I see the same arguments being made now. The arguments against stem cell research and cloning were made 150 years ago against anesthesia. They said we shouldn't give a woman a painkiller when she's having a baby. God meant them to suffer, and we can't be playing God.

We didn't create the laws of nature. That God may have done. But we use them, and we change the environment, and we change the way species look. We did that long before we knew genetic engineering, you know. God didn't create poodles; we did. But I see these arguments being made. They're being made from a religious point of view – we shouldn't be playing God – and they are being made from a populist point of view, which is that these new technologies will take people out of jobs and disrupt communities. Technology has always disrupted communities. When people domesticated animals and went to organized agriculture, they disrupted the communities of hunters and gatherers. These communities were hopelessly disrupted. It wasn't good for the guys who wanted to keep those communities, but that's what technological progress is all about. The Industrial Revolution disrupted communities like nothing before.

My argument, in fact, is not that Cardwell's Law predicts that this will happen. It only happens in closed societies. The more open the economy is, the less likely it is to happen. Now some societies are very good in closing themselves off hermetically. Albania did, and North Korea, and places like that. But Albania has regretted it and North Korea will, if they haven't already. And in the rest of the world, it's very hard to stop technology, because if you don't do it, somebody else will. That, I think, has been the most important source of technological dynamism in world history: no country can be conservative on its own unless it is willing to take a terrible risk.

That's exactly what happened in Japan when Admiral Perry showed up in 1853. For two centuries the Japanese had closed themselves off to the rest of the world; they said, we don't want any change. We want to keep things as is. They banned guns, you know. Japan had guns in the sixteenth century, but they got rid of all of their firearms in the seventeenth century. Then there were no guns in Japan. This is a technology they didn't like, and I sort of sympathize with that. But then Admiral Perry showed up and the Japanese said, "You know, there's a big world out there and they've been moving ahead while we have not, and that's not a good situation. Let's go and imitate them." And of course the rest is history. I think that is the difference between a closed and an open economy: in a closed economy, Cardwell's Law is almost inevitable, but in an open economy, in an economy that trades and competes with the rest of the world, this is unlikely to happen.

Here's one more example. It's way outside my field of expertise, but let's look at the American automobile industry in the 1950s. Absolutely zero technological change. The cars they made in 1960 were essentially the same as the ones they made in 1950. The tail fins came off, they came [back] on, but the cars weren't any better. And when I came to America in the late 1960s they were still making things like the Vega and the Pinto, which were the worst cars ever made. But that is exactly what happened. The industry got complacent. It's not that they didn't have new ideas; it's that they suppressed [the new ideas]. If Studebaker wanted to make a better car, they got rid of him.

But then something happened: the Japanese showed up. The Japanese were not part of the American anti-innovation movement, and the Japanese made better cars from better materials. They made them cheaper. The cars lasted longer. And guess what? Today's American cars are far, far better than they were in the late 1950s to early 1970s – not because Americans couldn't have done it earlier, but because openness forced them to do it

That, I think, is what Cardwell's Law really says. It doesn't make predictions; it only says that the more open the world is – the more free trade, the more ideas and people can move from one country to another – the less likely it is that technological progress will come to an end. Who will have leadership is almost indeterminate, and not necessarily important, because it may well be that America will remain the world leader in the development of certain things, like software and how to cook a hamburger, and the Chinese will make laptop computers and automobiles, and that's just fine with me.

AK & NS: You have written that "institutions help determine on which margins the efforts and time of the most resourceful and ambitious men and women will be applied. Entrepreneurs, innovators and inventors will try to make their fortune and fame wherever they perceive the rewards to be most promising. There are many potential avenues where this could be done. Commerce, innovation and finance or plunder, extortion and corruption." Based on that, what are the strengths and the shortcomings of the new institutional economics?

JM: I think the strength has been, above all, to give us a far better story about how politics and power interact with economic variables, which we really paid no attention to [before]. I think the weakness is that we don't really have a very good theory of institutional change; we're making an effort, but we're still not very good at it. And we have no good theory – it is very hard to do – of how institutions and culture are related. In fact, economists are [only] now discovering culture.

I think we are not very good at understanding why some countries come up with one kind of institution and other countries come up with a different kind of institution. We understand that there's a great deal of inertia and persistence in institutions, though they do change over time. But we don't have a very good understanding of why some countries come up with good institutions and other countries come up with bad institutions. And our ability to predict them is absolutely zilch.

That is where I would like research to go, and my own book on this, *The Enlightened Economy*, takes a shot at it. I argue that there is an arrow, a causal arrow, going from belief, ideology, convictions, ideas – call them what you want – to institutional change, and that one way institutions change is by persuading each other. I have one theory about what institutions should look like, and you have another theory, and we try to persuade each other; and if we can't persuade each other, we try to persuade third parties, and eventually the third parties find one argument more attractive than another on the basis of logic or their interests or evidence or some combination of the three, and they make a decision, and then the institutions change and you get reform. That stuff needs to be made much more precise, much more formal, much more rigorous, and needs to be integrated with other things, and we haven't made much progress in that.

AK & NS: How confident are you that the institutions that are conducive to economic growth can be developed where they don't currently exist or, more precisely, transported there?

JM: I am hugely skeptical about it. Precisely because if you change the institutions but don't change the culture, you're not going to change institutions.

I am not optimistic – certainly in a matter of years or decades – about changing any countries' institutions; but having said that, of course, I don't believe that the West has any sort of genetic or biological inclination toward having better institutions. It's all history. Given enough time, Turkmenistan, Moldova, Belarus, all these other countries that are at the moment so poorly governed may well develop in ways we can't imagine. This is not going to happen in our lifetimes. That's the only prediction I'll make, and even that I will carefully push in by saying, I could be wrong.

AK & NS: I would like it if you would discuss what I call, from your book, the "brake analogy": that culture can serve as a brake against innovation, growth, and progress. In describing how this brake works, you say that [a culture] can be compared to a parking brake, in that over time, even if a parking brake is on, it can be worn down. Is there evidence of that actually being the case? Can you illustrate that?

JM: I would put it this way: look at the role that religion plays in technological development. Religion is the most striking part of culture, and it also has an institutional aspect. Religion is a good way of demonstrating the difference between [culture and institutions]. We have religious beliefs and convictions, not necessarily only about God but about all kinds of other things, and then we have religious institutions, churches, congregations, synagogues and whatnot, where you can be a member of one but not another. I've been told, whether this is true or not, that something like 90 percent of all Jews who go to synagogue are really atheists. I find it very amusing, but the reason they go to synagogue is that they want other people to believe in God, because they think that's good for society. Religion, I think, can in some sense act as a brake on technology because in the final analysis, as I said earlier, technology has a metaphysical aspect that we should always think about. We *are* playing God. We are changing the environment, we are causing the extinction of species, sometimes inadvertently and sometimes on purpose. We extinguished the smallpox virus, or we hope we did. But if we didn't, it's not for lack of trying. And if we could extinguish the HIV virus, by God we'd do it.

We are playing God. Now, the underlying presumption is that we have developed a set of beliefs [such] that religion is okay with [us playing God]. It's the basic idea that the creator made the world but put us in charge of it, so by manipulating it and by changing it, we're not sinning against the creator but are, in some sense, illustrating his greatness. That is the early medieval interpretation of Judeo-Christianity that underlies much of our technological creativity. Except, of course, that a lot of religion points the other way and says no, certain things we should not do, and some people believe that about cloning and some people believe that about stem cell research and some people believe that about nuclear power, you name it. In that regard, culture can operate very much as a brake.

Timur Kuran argues that in the Islamic world, this is very much the case – that the impact of religion, on the whole, has been a major brake on economic development. Now, there's Islam and there's Islam, and some places it's better and some places it's worse. It has not prevented Turkey and Indonesia from developing, but in the Middle East, in particular, it's very hard to argue that it hasn't been a brake on technological development.

Religion isn't just a statement about your relation with a higher entity. It also is a social question. As I see it – and this is very much an amateur's view, because I'm hardly an expert on religion – religion is a statement about your relationship with earlier generations; that is to say, religion is deeply historical in the sense that books and principles established many, many generations ago are held in great veneration. That seems rather obvious once you think about it, right? The Christian religion looks back at the New Testament, and the Jewish religion at the Old Testament, and Islam at the Koran. But then, that is what religion is all about. It isn't just about God; it's about the people who came before us – to whom, we believe, God was revealed.

Now, the degree to which we hold fast to the wisdom of earlier generations is an incredibly important element in how innovative a society is, because if you think about it, every act of invention is an act of rebellion. It's an act of disrespect against earlier generations, right? And a highly religious society that believes that all wisdom was revealed to our forefathers isn't going to be very innovative, because by inventing something you implicitly say, "Look, the way my father and my grandfather and other generations have done this particular thing is wrong. I can do it better." That may be correct, but it's disrespectful in some deep way. And that helped me solve a riddle that I had never been able to solve before: looking at the history of Europe over the last 1,500 years, why are there so few inventions associated with Jews until the beginning of the nineteenth century, when Jews became more secularized and became like everybody else in some way? Before that you would have expected Jews to be at the forefront of innovation, because they were literate and because many of them were artisans and craftsmen and merchants. They were deeply involved in the more progressive parts of the economy, but they didn't invent anything. I have looked high and low but until then, there isn't a single Jew of any importance as a scientist or engineer or inventor.

At that level, I think, religion really matters. I think our own secularization started with the Enlightenment, or maybe before; I don't know exactly. I'm not sure how to measure secularization, but I know it's happening. But our secularization has been accompanied by a total loss of respect for the wisdom of earlier generations. That's something we take for granted, but it isn't granted. Most religions actually say, No, these ancient people were smarter than we were and they knew more, and if you want to understand them, you've got to go and reread your Aristotle, or whoever your member of the canon is. We don't have a canon. We don't have a canon for almost anything. People have very little respect for the wisdom of earlier generations, and I think that deep down, that's a metaphysical phenomenon. It's a phenomenon that is essentially religious. That is a good example of how religion and, maybe, human culture served as a brake. And that brake, as I said, can be relieved and it can be weakened; I think it is being weakened today. I have mixed feelings about this. It isn't obvious that it's an entirely good thing, but it's happening.

AK & NS: Let's get back to useful knowledge one last time. Given the fact that often we don't even know what [a new piece of] knowledge will be useful for when it first emerges, is there a role for governments in subsidizing basic research and the creation of new and useful knowledge? How can that be done without there being a corruption in the process?

JM: Well, you know how it is with governments. It's a tough issue. We know that the free market is not going to deliver the right amount of research and development and useful knowledge because of all the market failures that everybody knows about. And obviously, when you have a market failure, then the standard neoclassical economists will say, "Well, then we need public policy," and we probably are a little bit better off with public policy than we would have been without it. But I think that in this particular case, anyone searching for optimality or efficiency is going to have to face the fact that no matter how you look at it, the evolution of technology is inevitably going to be a wasteful process. Evolution is always a hugely wasteful process. Of all the mutations, 99.9 percent end up going nowhere. They are wasteful. Life is wasteful; it is not efficient. The only people who see the world as efficient are economists and strategists, but it isn't efficient and it isn't going to be efficient. We muddle through. The only thing is that some places muddle better than some people, and some places muddle worse. I have some ideas about how I would like research policy to go, but none of them involve efficiency or a good system.

I think corruption both in the government and in the private sector is totally inevitable, and we had better live with it. But what I can say is that there is a certain kind of public policy, along the lines I was talking about before, that I think is unambiguously bad, and that is ruling out avenues of research on ideological or similar grounds. That's where public policy can step in and say there are no taboos, there are no sacred cows, and we should let research go wherever it wants to go – but then the question is, who is going to pay for it? And there things get difficult. There is no obviously optimal policy.

Think about how few of the scientific papers that are published ever get read by anybody. More than half of them never get cited – so yes, they're wasted. You spend a lot of time writing the paper, and nobody reads it. I've written papers like that, more than I care to list. I've written papers. Nobody's read them. It's a terrible waste, but you know, it's part of the process. I accept it because that is the nature of any evolutionary process; it isn't going to be efficient.

I think that open economies are better than closed economies, and I believe that there should be no taboos. If people don't like a particular technology – say, stem cell research – they can always say, "I will buy nothing that has that technology." I'll give you another example. The Americans aren't the only ones. Take the European resistance to genetically modified foods. That is really the kind of thing I'm talking about. Genetically modified foods may be the wave of the future.

AK & NS: The wave of the present, in some places.

JM: Yes, some, but you ain't seen nothing yet. This is going to be huge, and I don't think Europeans are going to able to be able to stop it. I respect people who say look, I don't want to buy lettuce that is genetically modified to resist bugs because I like bugs in my salad. Fine. There ought to be places for you to buy that stuff. And in fact, we do that now. We have a whole market for organic foods; you can buy eggs laid by chickens that haven't been treated with antibiotics and hormones and God knows what else, and they're more expensive, but you can buy them, and that's fine. If you have that technology, you don't have to participate in it. But ruling out things strikes me as a bad idea, so I don't like the Americans' attitude towards cloning and stem cells and I don't like European attitudes towards genetically modified foods. There is plenty of blame to go around here.

Those are the kind of things that I would recommend. I have no specific suggestions about where research money should go, because that involves me pretending to know things I don't know. That's a bad way of making policy.

AK & NS: What research areas would you recommend for a young economist today?

JM: Well, what else but economic history. I think economic history is important to remind the formalizers that this is about real things. This is about real people, real events, real places that you could have touched and that could not be expressed in mathematical symbols, about somebody whose picture you can see. I think that is a way of illustrating what this is all about. There are certain economists who are really good at this, who do formal economics and modeling but always keep in mind historical realities. I think about a guy I really admire, Daron Acemoglu. He is not an economic historian by training or by specialization, but he really reads [history] and thinks about it and is interested in it. The guy is unbelievably smart. That's the kind of stuff that I think people should do. They should study economic history to give meat and sinews to the formal models that they're studying, so that we do not become, God forbid, a branch of applied mathematics. I don't think that'll happen, but the danger is somehow always there if people don't study the kind of things that I do.

134

Chapter 4:

BUGS IN THE
SOFTWARE LAYER

IN HIS BOOK *The Power of Productivity*, William Lewis writes:

> Foreign direct investment in retailing in India is prohib-
> ited. Import duties protect the Indian steel industry from
> global competition. Licensing protects incumbent milk
> processing plants from new entrants. About 830 prod-
> ucts are reserved for manufacture by firms below a cer-
> tain size. Unequal taxes and tax enforcement favor
> low-productivity, small-scale enterprises from steel to
> retailing.
>   ... It is not clear who owns land in India. Over 90
> percent of land titles are unclear.[35]

India's software layer is filled with bugs. Lewis sees these bugs
as being responsible for India's poverty. At the time he wrote,
India's per capita income was only 7 percent of that of the U.S.
and only 59 percent of that of China.[36]

Another dramatic example of the effect of bugs in the software layer is the difference between Communist and non-
Communist countries. In the aftermath of World War II, some
countries, notably Germany and Korea, became divided along

ideological lines. North Korea and East Germany were Communist countries. South Korea and West Germany were capitalist.

The results of this "natural experiment" were striking. By 1997, North Korea's per capita GDP was $700, while South Korea's was $13,590, or nearly twenty times as high.[37] In Germany, according to Jaap Sleifer:

> Before the Second World War the East German economy had the signs of a blossoming landscape. At that time per capita national income amounted to 103 percent of West Germany, compared to a mere 31 percent in 1991. In the industrial sector labor productivity dropped from 91 percent of the West German level in 1936 to merely 31 percent in 1991. East Germany is a case of an economy that was relatively wealthy, but lost out in relatively short time.[38]

Another telling phenomenon is the immigration of workers from Latin America to the United States. Crossing the border appears to make the productivity of a low-skilled worker ten to twenty times higher, based on the wage differential for low-skilled workers in Mexico or Central America and the United States.

What these examples show is the importance of the economy's institutions, or what we call the protocols of its software layer. In the better economies, the latest recipes are used and resources are deployed more efficiently than in the malfunctioning economies.

This does not mean that economists have a simple solution for underdevelopment. We do not know how to quickly and easily implement software protocols that will bring the benefits of high productivity to formerly poor counties. Even the fall of the Berlin Wall and the merger of East and West Germany did not immediately solve the problem of East Germany's backwardness. East Germany's adoption of West German institutions accomplished relatively little. A massive migration of workers from the former East Germany to the former West was the main factor leading toward equalization of incomes. This suggests that it is easier to move people into a new institutional setting than the other way around. Anyone who has tried to rework computer systems to enable merged businesses to use the same information technology would tend to agree that adapting software from one environment to another is difficult.

An economy based on knowledge ought to benefit previously poor countries. A lack of natural resources should not be such a large handicap. The low cost of copying and imitating successful recipes ought to make it easy for lagging societies to catch up to the leaders in the food court economy. Better recipes, however, are not sufficient to enable people to escape the Malthusian constraints of the meadow and enjoy the abundance of the food court. The software layer also must include the protocols that safeguard property, foster impersonal exchange, and encourage innovation.

The fundamental problem for less developed countries is that incentives are not aligned to reward productive effort. As Douglass North put it, "if the institutional framework rewards piracy then piratical organizations will come into existence; and if the institutional framework rewards productive activities then organizations – firms – will come into existence to engage in productive activities."[39]

For economists who share North's view that a nation's institutions or its system of protocols matter, the phenomenon of cross-border differences in productivity is compelling evidence. The fact that one can take a worker from Mexico or Brazil and dramatically increase his productivity by moving him to America is significant. William Lewis and others have shown that productivity differences are not accounted for by a difference in capital per worker. Moreover, differences in capital per worker may themselves be ultimately due to differences in incentives that are created by the economy's protocols.

To understand why protocols matter, let's consider some hypothetical extreme cases. Let's compare a society governed by criminal extortion with one that is governed by an ideal rule of law, and consider how incentives operate in the two societies.

In one society, an organized crime syndicate holds power. Ordinary citizens who appear to have valuables are subject to shakedowns and extortion. No business enterprise can operate in safety and confidence. It is dangerous to invest in any business, because there is no assurance that the business will survive long enough to pay a return. It is pointless to improve real property, because the crime syndicate will confiscate any valuable farmland or attractive buildings.

The criminal society will reward violence and personal loyalty. The crime boss has to ensure that no rival is in a position to gain support and stage a coup. Ambitious people will want to demonstrate loyalty to the crime boss, including a willingness to intimidate and kill rivals.

In contrast, in a society governed by the rule of law, extortion is punished and property is protected. People can improve property, knowing that they will be able to enjoy the benefits of the improvement. Firms can make credible long-term commitments to workers, customers, and investors. Ambitious people will want to build businesses that cater to consumer needs, in order to earn profits and achieve success.

In reality, all countries fall somewhere in between these two extremes. No country is under the thumb of an organized crime boss, although some petty tyrants come fairly close. No country operates under an ideal rule of law, totally free of crime and corruption.

Nonetheless, there is a tendency to move in the direction of one extreme or the other. In a country where the government is relatively corrupt and predatory, citizens will tend to adapt to the situation. People expect bad government to persist. They respond to corruption by trying to participate in it rather than by trying to expose it. Meanwhile, in a country where government officials generally believe that their job is to serve the public, people will view corruption as exceptional. They will make an effort to root out corruption when it appears.

There are a number of bugs that can affect a country's software layer. Let's examine five of them in detail.

1. TRIBALISM.

Humans evolved to hunt and gather in small bands. We naturally form close bonds within groups of up to 100 to 150 people. When people are tightly bound to their tribe or clan, the same leaders monopolize political, religious, and economic power. Communitarian values within the tribal village are strong, but outsiders provoke strong xenophobia.

Tribalism tends to cause resistance to innovation. People in isolated villages view new productive techniques as threats. In part, this is because innovations are associated with outsiders. Moreover, innovations threaten to disrupt local traditions that have sustained community cohesion for many generations.

Tribalism tends to cause warfare. Although the weapons of modern societies are extremely lethal, traditional hunter-gatherer societies show a greater rate of violent death per capita. In dealing with outsiders, tribal societies have fewer occasions to form bonds of friendship and fewer peaceful avenues for resolving conflicts.

Paul Collier, in his book *The Bottom Billion*, sees civil wars as one of the most significant factors in poverty. Civil wars themselves reduce the standard of living. In addition, there is usually great difficulty in achieving reconciliation afterward, so that civil wars are rarely followed by periods of good government.

Amy Chua, in her book *World on Fire*, sees tribalism, democracy, and capitalism as a volatile mix. When an ethnic minority achieves economic success, the majority may choose discrimination, or even genocide, to redress the imbalance.

2. INSECURE PROPERTY RIGHTS.

In many countries, ordinary citizens find it difficult to obtain business licenses or clear title to real estate. The Peruvian economist Hernando de Soto has been a major proponent of the view that secure property rights are a key to economic development.

With no business licenses, entrepreneurs operate in the underground economy, or what economists call the informal sector. This has a number of disadvantages. Long-term contracts lack credibility. Even short-term agreements require extraordinary levels of trust, because there is no third-party enforcement mechanism. Disputes will be resolved by violence, rather than in courts.

In the United States, consider the market in illegal drugs, or alcohol under Prohibition. With no business license, dealers establish territory through violence. Contracts are not reliable, so that business relationships require personal loyalty. When promises are broken or property is stolen, the aggrieved party has no recourse to the police or the judicial system.

In many poorly governed countries, ordinary businesses are as tenuous as drug-dealing in the United States. In some countries, taxes on licensed businesses are so high that entrepreneurs can only afford to operate in the informal sector. In other countries, the cost of obtaining a business license itself is too high. In the worst tyrannies, there is no way for anyone outside of the inner circle of power to operate a large business. The threat is that the tyrant will confiscate the business in order to give it to his cronies.

De Soto has pointed out that many citizens of underdeveloped countries reside on property that has no clear title. Because they lack legal title, the "owners" cannot borrow against the value of their property. They cannot be certain that they will profit from improvements to their property. Overall, de Soto has calculated that there is more than $9 trillion in what he calls "dead capital," meaning the value of real property that cannot be sold or borrowed against.

A few governments actively discourage private property. More often, however, the government lacks the will or the resources to create a system under which residents may obtain legal title to their dwellings.

In India, according to William Lewis in *The Power of Productivity*, "[a]bout 90 percent of land titles are unclear as to who really owns the land. . . . [T]his distortion causes competition among real estate developers to be over finding and acquiring land with clear titles rather than over construction productivity."[40]

Nobel laureate Friedrich Hayek used the term "spontaneous order" to describe the way that markets can solve problems without central direction. For example, in the United States, flexible prices for gasoline have allowed consumers and producers to adjust to changing conditions of supply and demand. In contrast, during the oil market turmoil of 1974–75, price controls on gasoline caused major disorder, with consumer hoarding, long lines at gasoline stations, and so on.

The absence of secure property rights means disorder. It is easy to take what others produce, and consequently it is less profitable to be a producer.

A spontaneous order can emerge in the form of local customs regarding property. Indeed, de Soto sees this phenomenon occurring in squatter communities in large cities in underdeveloped countries. However, governments often work against, or at least fail to reinforce, the customs that develop spontaneously among the squatters.

This is how Lewis describes the disorder in India's electrical power sector:

> Although many industries in our 118 industry studies in 13 different countries are performing below their potential, electric power in India is the worst.
>
> ... The reason India's performance is so bad is that the electric power industry is 95 percent government owned.... Since 1991, private firms have been allowed in electricity generation. Very few have shown up. The reason is that they have grave doubts they will be paid for the electricity they generate....
>
> ... [T]he state government's Electricity Board owns the distribution system.... They are bankrupt because, believe it or not, they lose 35 percent of the electricity they take from power plants.... Sometimes the Electricity Boards simply have not placed meters on customers' lines. Other times, the electricity is stolen through illegal (and dangerous) taps into the electricity wires.[41]

Lewis found that in Brazil, the high tax rates needed to support the large public sector cause many businesses to not register with the government. Of course, these informal businesses also pay a "tax" in that they have less recourse when they are abused or defrauded by others.

3. CORRUPTION.

In many countries, bribery and extortion are a way of life for government officials. This inhibits development in several ways.

First, citizens have little incentive to obey the law. One can be punished without committing a crime, and one can commit a crime without being punished. Paying the bribe is what keeps people out of trouble with the authorities.

Second, corruption tends to make property rights insecure. A successful business or tangible consumer assets are an invitation for a government official to undertake a shakedown.

Third, corruption means that government services will function poorly. Most of the money intended for education, transportation infrastructure, or health care will instead be siphoned off for the private benefit of the officials.

4. THE CURSE OF UNEARNED INCOME.

Economists have coined the phrase "the resource curse" to describe countries whose wealth consists primarily of diamonds or oil. The problem is that resource wealth is more characteristically stolen than earned. Natural resources do not reward hard work, capital accumulation, or innovation. They reward those who can establish and maintain control over the resource.

Some economists believe that foreign aid, because it is unearned, can be a similar curse. When aid is channeled through the recipient government, it gives the leaders an incentive to remain in power, in order to control the wealth represented by the aid. Just as the owner of a diamond mine tries to hang on his franchise, the leader of an aid-dependent nation tries to exclude others from power.

Thus, unearned income serves to undermine the work ethic and the public service ethic. Resources and government aid offer rewards to those skilled at taking things rather than those skilled at creating or improving things. Unearned income makes corruption relatively easy and profitable.

5. LACK OF KNOWLEDGE AND SKILLS.

In a modern economy, knowledge and skills are required in order to be a productive worker and an intelligent consumer. Cognitive skills, self-control, and social skills are important.

Education and training are needed to make the most of one's abilities.

At an individual level within countries, measures of cognitive ability are highly correlated with income, although the correlation is far from perfect. Similarly, although measures of average cognitive ability in different countries are hardly precise, there does appear to be some correlation – far from perfect – between average national income and average national performance on intelligence tests.

Because of environmental influences on cognitive ability, it would be unwise to attribute all of the correlation between average scores and average productivity across countries to causality running from cognitive ability to economic growth. There probably is causality running in both directions.

There are a number of channels by which average cognitive ability could affect average national income. If individuals with higher cognitive ability tend to be more productive within nations, then it stands to reason that nations with more cognitively gifted individuals will tend to have higher average productivity. In addition, consumers with higher cognitive ability may be more receptive to innovation. The role of "venturesome consumers" in innovation and economic performance has been suggested by Columbia University economist Amar Bhide. Finally, individuals with higher cognitive ability may be more intelligent voters, which in turn may push government in the direction of better policies and reduce the likelihood of the ascension to power of a charismatic demagogue.

Cognitive ability is not all that matters. Taking cognitive ability as given, the knowledge and skills that people develop will be affected by their cultural environment. To take advantage of learning, societies must overcome xenophobia, hostility toward the education of women, unscientific ways of thinking, suspicion of new ideas, and fear of failure. The low rate at which productive technologies have spread to parts of Latin America,

Africa, and the Middle East can be explained in part by these cultural factors.

The protocols needed to enable a nation to take advantage of knowledge, innovation, and trade among strangers are easy to take for granted when they are well entrenched. However, they are quite difficult to establish when a country has a long history of bad government or strong tribal enmity.

Even among developed countries, one can observe differences in the software layer. The United States is the most dynamic economy in the world, with the highest rates of business failure and new business formation. Ultimately, this probably reflects cultural attitudes, which in turn are reflected in the structure of financial and regulatory systems.

In Japan and Europe, financial institutions move more slowly to shut down failed businesses. Firms are slower to shed excess workers, in part due to legal constraints. Designed to increase economic security, these features of the software layer in those countries turn out to be bugs from the standpoint of innovation.

The United States tolerates a high failure rate among businesses and a high rate of churning in employment. In recent decades, this has enabled the U.S. to grow more rapidly than Japan and Europe. The leading sectors of innovation, such as computers and biotechnology, are most aggressively pursued in the United States.

The three ideal elements of a prosperous society would be self-reliant families; effective institutions of civil society, including business firms; and good government. These elements are more likely to be present together than individually, because they are mutually reinforcing.

Self-reliant families will be able to contribute to civil society. They have the ability to start businesses, participate in charitable organizations, and join clubs. They also will have high expectations for public servants and little use for corruption.

Strong institutions of civil society enable families to be self-reliant and government more effective. Active business and social entrepreneurship can provide consumer information, public goods, and other services that address market failures. The institutions of civil society will tend to compete with, and put a check on, the growth of government.

Good government allows families to enjoy the fruits of their labors, enabling them to be self-reliant. It provides a legal framework under which business and non-governmental organizations can operate freely. It provides a fair and efficient mechanism for resolving disputes.

Because of these mutually reinforcing mechanisms, we would expect self-reliant families, effective civil society, and good government to go together. We are unlikely to observe simple causal chains or single-factor explanations of national success. We are likely to see countries cluster at either the high end of prosperity or the low end of poverty. Transitions between these extremes should be relatively rare, and many changes may have to occur at once in order for a transition to take place.

For economists, some humility is called for in discussing bugs in the software layer. We claim that government regulation can be stifling, and yet in the United States there is considerable regulation of food, housing, medical services, and other major industries. We claim that increasing private ownership of enterprises is a good thing, but in Russia privatization worked very poorly. We claim that free trade is essential, but India maintains high tariffs and has grown rapidly over the past 15 years.

Institutions that work well in some situations may falter in others. For example, Japan's industrial policy, in which large banks worked closely with government to finance the development of key industries, was very successful from the 1960s through the 1980s. But the Japanese economy performed poorly from about 1990 through 2005.

Similarly, in continental Western Europe, a highly concentrated financial system that promoted large industrial firms achieved a rapid recovery after World War II. However, America's more diversified financial system and better access to capital for upstart firms has produced faster growth in more recent decades.

At this point, all we can say is that there are a variety of protocols that reward productive activity. There are also a variety of protocols that reward unproductive activity. We cannot say that a particular set of institutions is optimal for all nations to adopt. Instead, we suspect that citizens and government leaders have to engage in a trial-and-error process in order to debug the software layer of the economy.

Interview with
DOUGLASS NORTH

DOUGLASS NORTH is the Spencer T. Olin Professor in Arts and Science at Washington University in St. Louis. He was awarded the Nobel Prize in economics in 1993. His major interest is the evolution of economic and political institutions and the effects of institutions on the development of economies over time. He is the author of Structure and Change in Economic History *(1981),* Institutions, Institutional Change and Economic Performance *(1990), and many other books.*

ARNOLD KLING & NICK SCHULZ: People often talk about Douglass North and the "new institutional economics." What about the phrase "new institutional economics" do you like, and is there anything about that phrase that bothers you?

DOUGLASS NORTH: Yes. It should be the "new institutional social science," not the "new institutional economics."

AK & NS: And why is that?

DN: Because we're trying to broaden how we think about problems, and the frame is not economics; it's all of the social sciences. You cannot separate economics from political science and sociology at all. All of the interesting issues are on the borders between them.

AK & NS: Your sense is that certainly in the academy, but maybe more broadly speaking, we separate disciplines to a fault?

DN: Yes. In the academy, we've divided it up into disciplines – economics, political science – and that is fine for trying to separate them out. But in the real world, the problems overlap so much: politics, economy, norms, and sociology, all of them are mixed up. And the good theory you want to develop in the new institution overlaps one to the other.

AK & NS: You came to this conclusion gradually, I imagine, as you started . . .

DN: I'll tell you a story about it. When Ronald Coase and I started the new institutional economics, I proposed that we call it the "the new institutional social science," but Ronald said, "if you do, I will not be a part of it." And so I said, "OK, I withdraw." Obviously I want Ronald to be with me on it, but I think it was a mistake. And as I get on in life, I think it's a bigger and bigger mistake, because it is confining our discussion much too narrowly.

AK & NS: And do you know why – what his position was?

DN: Well, I think Ronald is a traditional economist, and for him, economics is economics. For me, it never was.

AK & NS: Does "institutional economics" refer entirely to institutions of government or to other institutions as well?

DN: Any kind of institution – any way we structure human interaction, which is what institutions are. They're a device that structures human interaction.

AK & NS: The word "change" appears in several of your book titles. Is the focus on change something that sets you apart from ordinary economists in the postwar period? Why are you so focused on change, and why did you wind up interested in institutional change?

DN: Because economics as it exists now is about a theory of choice, and it's static. It's about a once-and-for-all kind of change in a moment of time. All of the interesting issues that we can't solve in the world are a result of the fact that it's a dynamic world in which change over time is at the heart of the issue. Therefore, until we deal with change over time, we are not confronting the important issues of our time.

AK & NS: You argue that learning over time is important for economic growth. Can you talk a little bit more about the importance of time?

DN: Time is the crucial issue because if you're just concerned with a static view of the world, the problems are easy to solve. We're evolving through time, and that's where learning, of course, is all-important: as we evolve, our understanding of the world is changing. And the world [itself] is changing, and we keep on trying to understand that changing world. The only way you understand it is by learning, by adding to your knowledge about how the world is working. And so, time and learning are crucial parts of the whole story.

AK & NS: Your understanding of the importance of this –
how long has it been with you?

DN: Well, it's gradually evolved. I'll tell you another story. When
Ronald Coase and I got honorary degrees at Columbia in
1988, I think it was, we each had to give a talk. And Ronald
gave a talk about the kind of work he was famous for, which
was taking into account transaction costs and so on. We had
a much deeper understanding of economic organizations.
And I gave a talk about how this whole framework of transaction costs really was the framework we should think in for
dealing with societal change overall. And Ronald came up to
me afterwards and said, "I never thought about that." It was a
whole new concept and it's what I've been doing ever since.

AK & NS: You have written: "Individual beliefs were obviously important to the choices people make, and only the
extreme myopia of economists prevented them from
understanding that ideas, ideologies and prejudices mattered." Now this myopia you talk about, does it still exist
among economists?

DN: Absolutely.

AK & NS: What other obstacles prevent economists and
policymakers from seeing what really matters?

DN: Until they understand that our understanding of the world
is very fragmentary, is not complete, is – I believe – partially
incorrect, no matter how intelligent we are, we're not going
to make sense of the world. You cannot explain the September 11 attacks, and all the diverse ideologies from Muslim
fundamentalists to witch doctors that exist around the world
if you assume that people are rational in the sense in which

economists use the term. They've excluded 90 percent of what's interesting about the way the mind works, and because they do, they're becoming increasingly obsolete.

AK & NS: Is it your sense that there's some change prompted by you and others, in the academy and more broadly speaking, to understand these things?

DN: Oh yes. Behavioral economics, which has gotten a couple of Nobel prizes in the last couple of years, is the beginning of a recognition that traditional economics is too narrow, and cognitive science is now becoming a flourishing area of interest to social scientists. I take a lot of the credit.

AK & NS: It is your view that taking the human mind seriously actually changes how we must conceive of economic and political institutions.

DN: Right.

AK & NS: How do we know that that's true?

DN: We don't.

AK & NS: We don't know?

DN: Let me put it this way: in the physical sciences, which is what we borrowed from when we started economics, you could reduce a subject to its fundamental unit, whether it was elements or neurons or genes or whatever. And then if you had a new problem, you build up from this fundamental unit.

Now, economics and social sciences don't have any such fundamental unit. What they have is the brain and the mind, and obviously that's a fundamental unit. But what you have to understand is how it works, and you have to be able to explain when people are "rational" as much as you have to explain 9/11. They're all pieces of the way in which human beings act and interact in particular settings. It's obviously crucial, and it's just myopia on the part of economists that they haven't realized this for a long time.

AK & NS: Maybe you could talk a bit about the holes in our present understanding of the brain and cognitive science that make further progress towards a full understanding of institutions and economic change difficult.

DN: Well, we still don't understand how beliefs get formed, how they change, why they change when they do, and how that underlies the choices people make. I have partial knowledge of that now, mostly as a result of work in the last ten to 15 years. But we don't understand an enormous amount of it, and particularly, what is most crucial, we don't understand how tentative our knowledge is and must be; after all, what we do is through the senses – sound, sight, hearing, feeling. We interpret from the external world. And our brain then constructs explanations of that.

Now that explanation has always got to be at least partially wrong, and maybe always wrong. If you look at things like Muslim fundamentalism and why people should buy into that, it's obvious that there's an enormous amount that has got to go into our understanding before we completely comprehend that. We've made a lot of progress. We now understand quite a bit about particular actions of the brain, and particularly now that we're doing brain imaging and scanning, we even can see how the brain is working, which helps a lot. [But] we're still a long ways from understanding it.

I work with people like Vernon Smith, who does experimental economics. What I do is give them a problem that we should solve. And then we see if we can find some empirical test of ways in which we can explain it. So we're gradually putting together a more intelligent, more thorough understanding of what is an immensely complicated subject that we'll never completely comprehend. And as soon as you do – I talk about it now in static terms: as soon as you think about how the brain evolves over time, and the way in which it can change and so on, you've got an even much more complicated problem.

And I'm going to make a complicated problem still more complicated – if you realize that the world is changing, so that the way you understand the world today is not going to [work for] the world of tomorrow, as technology, institutions, information costs, and so on keep changing – then your understanding of the world may have been right yesterday but it's wrong today. All of that makes for an enormous challenge, which I think most economists only have a very rudimentary understanding and appreciation of at this point.

AK & NS: People are comfortable thinking about change, that the world changes, that individuals can change or groups can change. But there's also the notion of the rate of change, the velocity – for example, now we are in an era where the rate of change is accelerating due to technology and technical change. How does that, if at all, factor into your analysis?

DN: It factors in in that I keep on saying it's a non-ergodic world, which means the world is changing. And therefore, we're always behind. And if we're way behind, of course, our theories are completely wrong. And indeed, all of economic theory is predicated on models that are derived from the past. Now the models, if the world isn't changing very rapidly, may be perfectly fine. But if the world is changing very rapidly, the models are out of date.

AK & NS: One reviewer of your last book said, "North's new book is an inspiring reinvigoration of the research program of Smith, Hume and Hayek, what used to be called 'the moral sciences.'" Is that a fair characterization of your research project? Maybe you could talk about this idea of the moral sciences and how it plays into our understanding of economic change.

DN: I think Smith, Hume, and certainly Hayek – who I think is the most important social scientist of modern times – have been enormously influential in the way I've evolved. I'm not sure I understand the moral character of it. I do think that one of the frontiers is exactly the degree to which moral views are embedded in the way in which the mind has evolved or not, and I don't know the answer to that. It's something I'm reading a lot about.

Evolutionary psychologists have a view, most of them do, that it's built into the way in which the brain and mind evolves in three million years of being hunters and gatherers. Maybe so, maybe not. I just don't know. But I think it's an important issue because the degree to which we solve problems in the world and don't blow each other off the face of the earth at least in part concerns the degree to which fundamental moral attributes may indeed constrain the way we engage each other. I'm not sure that the modern world is a good illustration of that, of course, given the fact that we seem to be having a good time blowing each other off the face of the earth very effectively.

AK & NS: You mentioned Vernon Smith a moment ago, and you said that in collaborating with him, you'll suggest problems that would be good specific areas for research and help develop questions for possible testing. Could you give an example of that, just to give people a sense of what would be a problem that economists or social scientists don't know the answer to?

DN: For example, views about the degree to which trust evolves in a society are terribly important, because if people trust each other then you have low cost of transacting and markets work a lot better. So one of the things we've done a lot of work on with Vernon's group is [the question of] under what conditions you tend to evolve more trust.

There are a lot of questions like that at the frontiers of knowledge, things we need to know much more about. And as I come across those things, we talk about them and I try to get them to do more research on them.

AK & NS: In your Nobel lecture you said: "The organizations that come into existence will reflect the opportunities provided by the institutional matrix. That is, if the institutional framework rewards piracy, then piratical organizations will come into existence; and if the institutional framework rewards productive activities, then organizations – firms – will come into existence to engage in productive activities."

You study economic history. What are some examples, really concrete examples of this in action that would hammer home this point to people about this process?

DN: Well, my illustration about piracy came out of a lot of my recent work – not recent, but I worked for about eight or ten years studying productivity in ocean shipping. And when we looked at the increases in productivity in ocean shipping, they came from eliminating piracy. The question is, how did we eliminate piracy and how did it fit the story? Things like that were not just casual references; they are things that are taken out of my [work in] economic history.

AK & NS: Another quotation from your lecture concerns "the admixture of formal rules in formal norms and enforcement characteristics that shapes economic performance. While the rules may be changed overnight, the informal norms usually change only gradually." You have pointed out that informal norms give formal rules legitimacy. Is there a way to change or influence informal norms more than gradually and in ways that are conducive to growth, or is it all just a crapshoot?

DN: You've touched on an area where we're trying to do a lot of work these days. It's an empirical area that we're very interested in. We're interested in how norms get formed repetitively, how they change and how they shape performance. All those are frontiers which – both in experimental economics and in empirical work of other kinds – we're very much interested in, because they are the very frontier of improving the performance of societies.

AK & NS: In your Nobel speech you talked about "adaptive rather than allocative efficiency, which is the key to long run economic growth," and you say, "we do not know how to create adaptive efficiency in the short run." Please explain what you mean by "adaptive efficiency," because I think this is an important concept, and why it's so important. And then can you speculate on whether we might ever learn how to create adaptive efficiency in the short run or long run?

DN: Adaptive efficiency is crucial if you recognize that it's a non-ergodic world. The world keeps changing. But institutions change very slowly, so you're going to always be in danger that your institutions are no longer going to solve problems for you. The question is, how could you build into the structure a system that would tend to make you keep up with the changing world? And since you don't know which way the world is changing and you don't know what's right or what's wrong with these things, one characteristic of adaptive efficiency is that you must permit lots of trials and errors in the world. That means that you encourage institutions that allow people to make mistakes, that allow them to try new ideas, and you encourage the destruction of institutions that don't work, because one of the problems with organizations that are created by institutions is that they tend to create vested interests and then you can't get rid of them.

So, adaptive efficiency is a world in which you encourage trial-and-error and creating new organizational institutions, and then you eliminate those that don't work.

AK & NS: Why has Latin American growth been so disappointing in places like Argentina, for example? And what can we learn from the experience in Latin America?

DN: In our new book, called *Violence and Social Orders*, we argue that the natural state evolves naturally in any society because it's a mixture of mutually interdependent economic and political interests that reinforce each other. The economic interests are the elites that produce economic activity. But they tend to support political groups that, in turn, will protect them from too much competition. The interplay is the elites in the political world protecting the economic elites from too much competition and giving them monopolies, while on the other hand the economic elites provide the funds that support the political elites. And the interplay is all over Latin America. It's a disease, but it's a disease that is a natural thing and it's very hard to get rid of.

AK & NS: What about Russian economic performance? Since the fall of Communism, it's been disappointing. Has it been disappointing for the same reason?

DN: It's going in the wrong direction. One of the things we've learned is that the crucial part is not so much economic institutions and organizations, it's political institutions and organizations. If you're going to have a dynamic world in which you have competitive economic markets, you must, as a precondition, have competitive political markets, and that's what's been missing in much of the world, certainly in Latin America. In Russia, of course, Putin has wiped out whatever beginnings were made towards creating political competition. And the result is that it's moving in the wrong direction.

AK & NS: What was it, then, that enabled Asian economies to grow so quickly since the 1950s, and why hasn't that experience been duplicated in Africa, say, or in the Arab world?

DN: Would you like ten hours?

AK & NS: Well, is there a Cliff Notes version? [*laughter*]

DN: Yes, but my Cliff Notes version is China, which we have detailed in some length and where I have spent a lot of time. China did everything wrong up to the Cultural Revolution. And then, gradually, they began to learn, and they learned not by aping the West and the United States but by building on what they had, modifying it in directions that pragmatically improved performance. They started out with the household responsibility system. As a result of the fact that they had 30 million peasants dying of starvation, they [tried] out giving them a little bit more freedom and greater control over resources and being able to sell products.

I can go on and on. You had a setting where, pragmatically, people have been open to trying out new experiments. If you ask me the tough question of how do we create it elsewhere, the thing we have learned is that you cannot generalize from the West as to how to do it (which is what we've done when we've tried to do economic reform), because you've got to build on the existing institutional base, which, in turn, is a function of a belief system that is involved. If you try to do something that is alien to that [system], it's not going to work. The reason China is a success story is that they build from the ground up, modifying the institutional framework gradually to do those things.

Now, don't misunderstand me, China's got a long ways to go and whether they continue doing that is a big question.

AK & NS: Could you put odds on that, one way or the other?

DN: Fifty-fifty.

AK & NS: Fifty-fifty? And how about India?

DN: Same thing. India – with a completely different background and evolution – shows that the things that will or will not make China work are going to be different with India.

AK & NS: What are your views on math and economics and the importance of math to the economics profession? Or let me put it differently: what do you make of the emphasis on math in economics?

DN: It was vastly overdone. Math should be a tool, and what's happened is that it's become an end in itself. We build elegant models, using very elegant mathematics, but they are so abstracted, so divorced from the problems we're trying to confront that they don't deal with them at all. We borrowed again from the physical sciences, and in the physical sciences, elegant mathematics is essential. That's not so clear for most of the social sciences. I'm interested in the dynamics of societies over time. Here math has very limited value.

AK & NS: When you were younger, you were a Marxist. Is that correct?

DN: That's right.

AK & NS: Could you just talk about the evolution of your views? What shaped your views and how have they evolved over time?

DN: That's easy. When I went to college, I was curious and I was looking for answers. And in the social sciences, I didn't find many answers. Marx came along and had elegant body of theory explaining everything. And economics certainly didn't say anything that made sense of the Great Depression and what was going on in the world. So Marxism tended to be a very natural sort of thing to buy.

I still am influenced by Marx. He was a very perceptive and visionary theorist. But as I gradually evolved, it became clear to me that Marx had good questions, but he didn't have very good answers. Some of his theory was right – like the importance of technology for social organization, I think he was absolutely right about that. But over time, I evolved out of it, and that's what I've been doing ever since. Then I became a good neoclassical economist, then I became a good institutionalist, and now I'm becoming a cognitive scientist, I guess.

AK & NS: What's next?

DN: Who knows? I think I've reached a dead end.

AK & NS: Well, let's hope not – not anytime soon. What one or two things do policymakers need to know or better appreciate as they look at problems of economic growth and development?

DN: Well, I think the first thing is, we want to understand how economies and societies evolve. Until we understand that, we obviously can't fix them – and we don't understand how they evolve. The beginning of wisdom is having a better understanding of that. The second thing is, you can't understand how economies evolve without understanding political science and sociology. You have to understand how political systems work and political economy works, and you have to understand how social organizations work. You need a whole new framework to think about that, and we're still in the midst of devising a new institutional social science. We're a long ways from it. It takes you back again, every step along the way, to how the mind and brain interpret the external environment.

AK & NS: And it's your view that no matter how much we study, we may always be somewhat limited in our understanding of these things.

DN: There's no question about that.

AK & NS: The fact that we will always probably have some shortcomings in our understanding – especially given that we live in a world of continuous change, where our understanding of institutions and our institutions themselves

162

must change – does that fact put any constraints, or should it put any constraints or obligations, on politicians, policymakers, and even academics?

DN: Oh, very definitely. We should be very tentative about how we understand the world. That doesn't mean you don't do things. You've got to do things, but you've got to recognize you may be wrong. We don't know enough. And so it's terribly important to recognize that you can be wrong, and to be, therefore, very susceptible to modifying the theories you hold in the light of new evidence.

Now as I said, that doesn't mean you don't do anything; you've got to do things. It does mean that you're willing to be adaptively efficient [in the face of] change and to rethink the problems as you evolve.

A K & NS: In your book *Understanding the Process of Economic Change*, you write, "What I have termed adaptive efficiency is an ongoing condition in which the society continues to modify or create new institutions as problems evolve. . . . It has certainly characterized United States societal development over the past several centuries." You point to the United States and its success in adaptive efficiency. Are there things the United States isn't doing or could be doing better with regard to that?

DN: The United States is very lucky because it didn't have the institutional restrictors that evolved in Europe – the carryovers of all kinds of obsolete institutions that still hamper them. We were very fortunate to start from scratch, and while we inherited institutions like property rights and so on, in new environments with new experiences, we evolved pragmatically over a long period of time and we had everything going for us. We still made a hell of a lot of mistakes, but we do keep things going for us. And that's very unlikely ever to be duplicated in history.

AK & NS: That being the case, are you optimistic or pessimistic?

DN: I'm moderately pessimistic about the future of the world. I'm not altogether pessimistic, because I'm impressed by the way in which we respond to change, by the dynamics of the process, and by our efforts to confront it, but I think we may always be behind.

What particularly bothers me is that the world is evolving more rapidly now than it ever did before. The degree to which we can catch up with it and deal with it, I think, is more and more strained now that we've devised ways to blow each other off the face of the earth. The time horizon we have to solve problems is much more abbreviated than it used to be; whereas before we could make mistakes and kill a few hundred thousand people, now we can blow everybody up. And we don't seem to have gotten very far in solving social disorder. I hope I'm wrong.

Interview with
WILLIAM EASTERLY

WILLIAM EASTERLY *is professor of economics at New York University and Co-Director of NYU's Development Research Institute. He is co-editor of the Journal of Development Economics. Easterly is the author of* The White Man's Burden: How the West's Efforts to Aid the Rest Have Done So Much Ill and So Little Good *(Penguin, 2006) and* The Elusive Quest for Growth: Economists' Adventures and Misadventures in the Tropics *(MIT, 2001). His areas of expertise are the determinants of long-run economic growth, the political economy of development, and the effectiveness of foreign aid. He has worked in most areas of the developing world, but most extensively in Africa, Latin America, and Russia.*

ARNOLD KLING & NICK SCHULZ: You've spent much of your professional life in foreign-aid circles. You've been studying aid and learning, in the process, what works and what doesn't. You conclude that while an enormous amount of money has been spent on foreign aid, it has not been to much positive effect. Is that a fair characterization of what you found?

WILLIAM EASTERLY: Yes. It's a fair characterization. There's been $2.3 trillion spent over the last fifty years in foreign aid. And that's in today's dollars. And really, there's surprisingly little to show for it. The main objective of foreign aid, of course, was the permanent reduction of poverty; the main objective was to promote economic growth. And unfortunately, there's no connection at all between aid and economic growth according to the empirical evidence that we have.

Just to boil it down to real cases, the countries that have been the most intensive recipients of aid are in sub-Saharan Africa. And that's the region that has also had the worst economic growth since independence. In fact, of that $2.3 trillion I mentioned earlier, $568 billion of that has gone to Africa, in the 43 years since independence began. Over that period, the income of the average citizen of the average African nation has virtually not increased at all; whereas countries like Singapore and Hong Kong, which got virtually no aid whatsoever, have had economic miracles, have – in the course of my lifetime – moved out of poverty into prosperity, into being just as rich as Western Europe or the United States.

Most recently, we've had rapid economic growth in China and India. And both China and India get a really small percentage of their income from foreign aid. Something less than half a percent of their GDP is their total aid inflow, whereas the average African country is getting close to 20 percent of GDP in foreign aid and yet not getting any economic growth out of that.

AK & NS: It's fair to say that when you started your work in foreign aid, you weren't expecting to find this to be the case. Is that right?

WE: That's certainly fair to say. I joined the World Bank in

1985 with a lot of idealism, really wanting to do something, to make a difference for poor people. Most of my experience has been on Africa and Latin America. I actually lived in Africa for a year when I was 12. My father was teaching at a university in Cape Coast, Ghana. And I think that had something to do with wanting a career that was involved in working on the problems of the world's poorest people. That definitely was the motivation.

But I got very frustrated and disillusioned as I made my way through the course of a career at the World Bank for sixteen years. I was kind of a slow learner, because it took me sixteen years to become dangerous enough to no longer fit well into the World Bank. [laughter]

I can remember a meeting, sometime in the middle of the 1990s, where we were all gathered around a table, all the senior economists working on Africa. And there was this big program of aid to Africa that was conditional on economic reforms. And everyone around the table actually agreed that this was not working. And I said something like, "Well, this is not working, so I guess we should do something very different and abandon this program, right?" And they said, "No, we just have to keep doing this. Because that's what we do." That was an eye-opening experience for me.

I was in the research department at the World Bank the whole time. So I was a little cloistered from the real field-level operations people, but not totally cloistered. I went on field missions and saw how things were not working. The reforms either were not happening or, when they did happen, they were poorly designed by people in Washington who took cookie-cutter approaches to designing other economies. And the economic growth did not happen. So when I saw that the response to failure was just to do more of the same things that were already failing, that's when I really started to question the whole operation of the foreign-aid system.

AK & NS: Let's return to this idea of a response to failure. You write in *The White Man's Burden* that when aid agencies try to tackle developing world problems like malaria – which imposes a huge disease burden on the developing world and is a big killer – they're sometimes thwarted in strange and seemingly unpredictable ways.

For example, bed nets are known to be helpful in combating malaria by ensuring that people, when they're sleeping or at home, aren't exposed to mosquitoes. So one solution is to give out bed nets. One of the things that you found in some programs to give out bed nets is that nets are often diverted to a black market. They wind up being used as fishing nets or wedding veils and the free nets don't always get to the people who need them. What are the implications of a finding like this for people in the wealthy West who are interested in helping poor countries?

WE: What we have to recognize is that rich people, when they're trying to help poor people, are intervening in another country's very complex economy and society. And of course none of us, in the very different environment of the American society and economy, really understand all that well what the local environment is.

Take a basic problem like that: if you give out nets, will people be motivated to use them? That turns out to be a very complex problem that depends on a lot of local knowledge and education. Things that we take for granted in rich countries cannot necessarily be taken for granted. The people have to understand very well that malaria is transmitted by mosquitoes. And you need even more complex layers of knowledge than that. You have to realize that it's not just in the rainy season, when it's hot and there are a lot of mosquitoes, that you need to be protected; actually, a lot of malaria gets transmitted during the dry season, when there aren't as many mosquitoes. There's still malaria. So you need to know that. The people using the nets need to know that they need to use them year-round and not just during rainy season.

You have to be willing to work with local people and educate them about what's in their best interest health-wise, which is not that easy to do, even in rich countries. I mean, we have lots of efforts devoted to trying to educate all of us to take better care of ourselves and to engage in safer and healthier behaviors. My doctor is always trying to get me to eat less butter so that my cholesterol won't be so high. You have people in rich countries not doing the things that are in the best interests of their health – driving too fast on the highways, being overweight, smoking, and so on. Well, these problems are equally severe in poor countries, if not more severe. And you need to know a lot about the culture and the values of people you're dealing with.

There might be some people who won't use bed nets and some people who will. You want to get the nets to people who will use them. One way that we do that in economics is to charge a price for the nets. Then only people who intend to use them will be willing to pay something for the nets. That's a technique that has been tried in Africa quite successfully.

AK & NS: In Malawi, right?

WE: In Malawi, there was a technique that was discovered by some Malawians who worked for an international charity. They were in the local office in Malawi, and they decided that they would sell the nets through the ante-natal clinics where pregnant mothers went for checkups. That kills lots of birds with one stone: the mothers have to pay for the nets, so the nets only go to those mothers who are intending to use them for themselves and their small children – and they are the main risk group. So it's a neat way of targeting the main risk group: pregnant women and small children.

Also, since it's taking place in what is already a medical consultation – the mothers are going in to talk to the nurse about their pregnancy – the nurse can also pass along information about why it's so important to use nets when you're pregnant and why it's so important to protect your young children, so that they don't get malaria and die. These nurses are local people who are much more in tune with the values and the culture and are much more able to communicate than some arrogant aid official who's driving around throwing nets off the back of a truck, expecting that that's going to actually be effective in protecting people from malaria.

AK & NS: In your book you draw a crucial distinction between "planners," on the one hand, and "searchers," on the other. Could you describe the difference between them, and why that difference matters?

WE: Yes. Planners think that the end of poverty requires a comprehensive, administrative solution. They're trying to do something that's a lot like central planning in the old Soviet-style economies, in the context of poverty reduction. They're trying to identify consumer needs and then assign quantitative plan targets to producers, none of whom has any financial incentives to actually do anything, which of course was the whole problem with central planning – that you did not have people who had the incentive to actually meet the needs of consumers. It was just an administrative thing where you were meeting plan targets.

That is so much the mentality of the whole foreign-aid community right now, in exercises like Jeffrey Sachs's big comprehensive plan to solve the problems of all the world's poor, or the United Nations campaign to achieve what are called the Millennium Development Goals, which is basically a certain target for reducing poverty by the year 2015. It's really just central planning all over again.

It's as if central planning has been totally, mercifully extinguished everywhere else except [in the areas with] the world's desperate, poorest people, who can least afford such a dysfunctional solution to their problems – [areas] where it would be much better to imitate the mentality of free markets, which are all about giving financial incentives and motivating people to meet consumer needs. And the way you do that in foreign aid is to have much more accountability for whether the poor are actually satisfied after the aid program is over; after you do an aid project, you ask the poor if they're better off, and then you hold the aid agency accountable for whether they did a good job or not. And there are financial rewards and penalties. People are rewarded for doing good projects and are not rewarded, even penalized, for doing projects that fail completely to meet the needs of the poor.

There's also a huge knowledge problem, which planning is never able to solve but searching, which is much more like a market, can solve. It's the same knowledge problem with central planning that was pointed out by Friedrich Hayek: the central planners at headquarters can never have enough information about what consumers really want and need in every little locale. They just can't process all that; it's too much information to process. The genius of the market is that it's like a decentralized brain for the economy, passing along signals from what each little consumer in each little locale wants and then attracting suppliers to meet those needs.

If there were accountability in foreign aid, you would get much more searching. If agencies knew they were going to be accountable, they would search for the right method to get people to actually use malaria bed nets to protect themselves against malaria. And you wouldn't just be churning bed nets out of the factory to meet the plan target for a number of bed nets; you would be actually trying to find out which consumers, where, want them and are going to use them, and you would be motivated to find a method that actually makes the people who deliver them get them to the people who want them.

AK & NS: The economist Amar Bhide, who's written a lot about both large business firms and then also entrepreneurs, says that in the U.S., for example, large corporations use planning to undertake new projects, while small entrepreneurs, by contrast, opportunistically adapt to their specific circumstances. So in a certain sense, large corporations seem to act a little like the planners you've been talking about, whereas small entrepreneurs act like searchers. Does that ring true to you? And if it does, what does it say about the kinds of organizations that are suited to playing the role of searchers in economic development?

WE: Actually, I think the metaphor of the large corporate hierarchy has led to a lot of misunderstanding about planning. In fact, Henry Ford's success in automating production and building a large corporation on top of the assembly-line production of cars was actually one of the inspirations for some of Lenin's methods and the attempts to design a planned economy in the Soviet Union.

But what was missing – what Lenin did not get, and what all the subsequent planners who have been inspired by what appears to be corporate planning did not get – was that what corporations are really doing is searching for something that works. And when they find something that works, they try to reproduce it on a very large scale. So there's always searching in the private market for things that work. The corporate planning and the large corporate hierarchy – what that is all about is really just scaling up the little thing that you found that does work, that does seem to meet the needs of consumers at a profit for the owner of the corporation.

But you always need the chaos and anarchy of the free market to keep searching for what works and to keep checking on whether the solution that you are scaling up is still working. So large corporations often turn into dinosaurs, because their original idea – which originally was a brilliant idea about how to do things right, how to make a great profit from meeting consumer needs – gradually becomes obsolete, and then they can't adjust.

So corporate planning is just about scaling up a solution after you find something that works. But what the planning mentality, as a whole, always misses is that you can't use planning to find what works. So if you build a whole system like foreign aid around planning, you're never going to find things that work. Because the planning is only a method for scaling up something that you have already found to work.

AK & NS: One reason that scaling up can work in the private marketplace after the solution is found – and that if market conditions change, even large firms have to adapt, or they suffer the consequences – is the discipline of competition. There doesn't seem to be anything like that in foreign aid. Is it possible to build the discipline of competition, or something like it, into foreign aid to make it work better?

WE: Well, first of all, I agree with your diagnosis. I think one reason that mistakes persist so long in foreign aid is that there is no competitive pressure exerted there like there is in the free market. In fact, although there are many different aid agencies, they act more like a cartel than a competitive industry. They all cooperate. In fact, they stress cooperation

and coordination as a virtue, as a goal to be attained in foreign aid, whereas I actually think it would be better if there
were, say, a central pool of aid funding, and those agencies
that were doing a better job getting results got more of that
pool, while the agencies that were not doing such a good job
lost some of their share. That would bring some competitive discipline that might keep aid agencies more honest, so
you wouldn't get them doing the same old failed thing over
and over again.

AK & NS: Are there [certain] institutional conditions that
are necessary in order for searchers to be able to function
effectively? In other words, do you need to have things like
property rights, the rule of law, and minimal corruption for
the searchers that you talk about to function? Or do you not
even need to have those?

WE: The ultimate vehicle for getting out of poverty is a func-
tioning free market, which creates lots of indigenous searchers who solve all kinds of problems for poor people, get poor
people what they want, and give jobs to poor people, who
then can earn incomes and get out of poverty. And for free
markets to operate, of course, you do need property rights,
the rule of law, basic domestic peace, the control of crime
and lawlessness, and so on. Now, that doesn't mean that if
those institutions are missing, there's no hope whatsoever
for poor people. I think that there are still workarounds available even when the government and the institutions are
totally dysfunctional. First of all, poor people are not given
enough credit for how creative they are in forming their
own bottom-up associations and solutions in basically law-
less societies.

You know, people in poor countries do form the equivalent of neighborhood-watch associations to deal with crime. They form rotating savings and credit associations, even when financial markets are completely missing, to provide some of the same functions as financial markets. Poor people do have a lot of ingenuity about getting around the missing institutions and dealing with lawlessness.

And aid workers can also be somewhat ingenious about getting around dysfunctional institutions. One of the most stubborn mistakes of the aid industry is to insist that aid always has to go through the sovereign national government. Most governments in poor countries are not going to spend aid money in such a way that it's going to achieve results for poor people. I think it would be a lot better for aid workers to bypass dysfunctional governments and institutions and think up schemes that would get money directly to poor people. Get goods directly to poor people – medicines, bed nets, vaccines. To put in drilling wells to give poor people access to clean water, you don't necessarily need to have the government involved. That can be done by an aid agency or a non-governmental agency.

Lots of that stuff can be done from the bottom up. I think we place too much emphasis on trying to work through the government and make the government work better. I don't think that's really something that outsiders are very good at doing. I don't think that any of the conditions that are put on aid are very effective in making dysfunctional governments in poor countries behave any better than they would have in the absence of those conditions.

And so I wish that the aid agencies would be a lot more creative, and not always just insist on working through what they religiously intone to be the sovereign national government. Governments in poor countries are often pretty weak and don't actually affect poor people's lives that much, other than by being missing in action and not providing the formal institutions and public services that governments in rich countries do.

AK & NS: In your experience, how important is cultural history in economic development? Is it possible to create a searcher-friendly entrepreneurial society by simply changing the characteristics of the government and the administrative systems? Or are deeper cultural changes required?

WE: Cultural values and behavioral norms, social norms, are extremely important in whether markets work well or not, and thus whether prosperity is even possible for free markets. Most market transactions require some level of trust between the parties doing the transaction. Whether people trust each other or not, whether people behave in a trustworthy manner, whether people keep their promises, whether people do what they said they were going to do, whether they show up on time – those are very important factors in how well free markets work, and thus how much prosperity is possible.

But I don't think that anyone has figured out how to create or change values, or even understands very well the origins of different value systems in different countries. Why do some societies have so much more trust than other societies? Obviously, there are lots of other norms that matter also, such as hard work and how much you sacrifice for the future and for your children. These things obviously matter, but I think that social scientists are really at a pretty primitive state of knowledge as far as the determinants of these values and how to change them.

We do see big differences in social norms between societies, but we really can't explain them. And we really don't know which causes which. It might be that poverty causes values, rather than values causing poverty – that if you're poor and you live in a dysfunctional society, then the payoff for working hard is not very high. So you might not value hard work. That might be an example of how poverty would create the value that you don't value hard work very much.

I think the foundational belief that you have to start with is that people are pretty much the same everywhere, at the core: they're motivated by wanting to better their lives. Some of them are just unlucky enough to be trapped in dysfunctional societies, which could include bad values and cultural inhibitions. Others are lucky enough to be in well-working societies.

AK & NS: What research findings in development economics have advanced our understanding the most in the last thirty years? And what do you think are the biggest issues that still require research?

WE: I think the discovery of institutions by economists has been an enormous leap forward, starting with people like Douglass North. And then there's been a continuing stream of work by a younger generation of economists that have tried to prove statistically and econometrically North's insight that institutions really do explain a lot of the differences in development outcomes – institutions like property rights and the rule of law, freedom from corruption, and so on. I think that's really enormous.

And I think that the whole field of political economy has been a huge leap forward in development; when I started at the Bank, people would engage in mindless moral exhortations for governments to behave better without understanding the determinants of bad leaders being chosen, or why bad leaders stay in power. And without understanding what causes bad governments to become entrenched in power, it doesn't really help to engage in moral exhortation for better economic policies and institutions.

AK & NS: With regard to areas that you think require greater research, are there any that stand out in your mind?

WE: I think the values [question] that we were just talking about is certainly one. Although governments are certainly to blame in many extreme cases of mismanagement, like Robert Mugabe's Zimbabwe, I think government is actually a little over-emphasized in the usual development discussion. We don't understand enough of what's going on way down below, where people's lives are affected much more by rules and norms and the behavior of their neighbors than they are by some distant government official. What causes societies to informally follow certain rules, some of which are conducive to prosperity, and others not – that's something we still don't understand very well at all. And that is an area where I think progress would be possible. There are value surveys and so on that have been done already, [but] much more could be done to get at understanding what is determining the spontaneous order of society – society as a kind of decentralized system, where people follow certain rules just because they value this social pressure to follow the rules. But the rules are different in every society.

That's another reason I'm a fan of Friedrich Hayek; he was amazingly ahead of his time in his understanding of an economy as a kind of spontaneous order. Nowadays, we get lots of people who are excited about the decentralized way in which in the Internet has evolved, who are writing about the emergence of spontaneous order and so on. That is stuff that Hayek anticipated fifty years ago, which I think shows

amazing intellectual prescience. And that [inquiry] is coming back into economics now – trying to understand that
spontaneous order and what makes it happen.

AK & NS: As you look at the developing world and the question of economic growth, are you an optimist or a pessimist,
and why?

WE: I guess I'm a gradualist-optimist. I think that excessively
high expectations for development were created by the
pseudo-scientific version of development economics, which
claimed that it was possible for countries to leap out of
poverty into prosperity in a very short time. Those turned
out to be totally unrealistic expectations. It's really not possible to do shock therapy, like people tried to do in the ex-
Communist countries, or to do what was called the "big
push" in foreign aid, in which you would just launch societies in a very short time out of poverty into prosperity.
I think that's not possible and never will be possible. Some
people would say that this makes me a pessimist, given the
original expectations of development. But I think that those
were just mistaken expectations.

A realistic expectation is that some, not all, poor societies will have the same kind of gradual rise in living standards that the countries that are now rich have attained in
North America and Western Europe. There was never a big
push in the U.S.; there was never shock therapy in the U.S.
There was just gradual muddling along towards greater
individual freedom and freer markets and more democratic
politics and better government. And as that happened, there
was a steady rise in living standards that, over several generations, got people out of poverty into prosperity. I think
that the same process is already happening in many places

in the developing world and will continue to happen. But it will be homegrown rather than designed by aid bureaucrats in New York or Washington.

In that sense, I think I'm an optimist. I think that the same process that led rich countries to escape poverty is possible in a lot of poor countries. But it's not inevitable, either; it's not going to happen everywhere. I don't think that there's some iron law that all societies naturally evolve out of poverty into prosperity. I think there will always be some societies that are dysfunctional, that get stuck with bad governments, that get stuck with bad institutions that never seem to improve, or that get stuck with the bad values and the bad outcomes of the spontaneous order that we were just talking about.

Chapter 5:

THE HEART THAT
PUMPS INNOVATION

THE ROLE OF THE ENTREPRENEUR

Much of the innovation in the world comes from American business. Much of America's innovation in turn comes from entrepreneurs. Entrepreneurs are the heart that pumps innovation into the economy. The dynamism and faster growth of the U.S. economy relative to other industrialized countries in recent decades is due to its strong entrepreneurial heart.

Edmund Phelps, the 2006 Nobel laureate in economics, writes:

> There are two economic systems in the West. Several nations – including the U.S., Canada and the U.K. – have a private-ownership system marked by great openness to the implementation of new commercial ideas coming from entrepreneurs, and by a pluralism of views among the financiers who select the ideas to nurture by providing the capital and incentives necessary for their development. Although much innovation comes from established companies, as in pharmaceuticals, much comes from start-ups, particularly the most novel innovations.[42]

Continental Europe is set up to preserve large public sectors, large banks, and large corporations. For individuals, the promise is stable jobs, a stable business environment, and collective sharing of the costs of unemployment, retirement, and health care. For the economy as a whole, however, the result is stagnation relative to the United States, inefficiency, and a burdening of the working population, who must support an unproductive sector that is becoming increasingly unsustainable.

It is easier for large businesses to fail in America. This benefits entrepreneurs in two ways. First, it means that a new startup can hope to dethrone an existing champion, which provides an incentive for entrepreneurs and financiers to make the attempt. Second, it means that large businesses are nervous about their futures. (As former Intel C E O Andrew Grove put it, "Only the paranoid survive.") The threat of failure forces large enterprises to turn to the products and services of small startups in order to improve productivity and remain competitive.

America's financial system is more diverse and competitive than that in other countries, where only a few banks dominate. A large bank focuses on its largest corporate customers, not on small entrepreneurs. In the United States, entrepreneurs have better access to capital, through venture capital funds, loans from small local banks, and ultimately a broader and more active public equity market.

The role of entrepreneurship in the economy is often underappreciated, even by economists. According to Economics 1.0, one role of the entrepreneur is to organize production. It is as if the entrepreneur runs a bakery, and each morning he or she has to decide whether it will be more profitable to increase the production of muffins or the production of doughnuts. The entrepreneur responds to market signals, thereby helping to ensure that the right goods and services are produced using the most efficient methods. Economics 1.0 also gives a nod to entrepreneurial risk-taking. A chef who starts a restaurant takes more risk than a chef who works for a salary.

Economics 2.0 identifies an additional role for entrepreneurs. The entrepreneur's task is to overcome resistance to change. We have seen that economic growth comes from the adoption of new ideas and the discarding of unsuccessful or obsolete practices. This in turn requires that people accept change. Consumers must adopt new goods and services. Workers must adapt to new ways of organizing production, and often this involves changing jobs, learning new skills, or leaving an industry altogether for a new career. If consumers and workers instead stay rooted in traditional habits, the potential for economic growth will be stalled. In Economics 2.0, entrepreneurs are the drivers of the process of adaptation.

The process of economic development requires change. Farming must become more efficient before people can rise above the level of subsistence. As a nation's workers begin to move from farming to manufacturing, at first they are used unproductively, because labor is cheap. (We see this happening in China today. China's current competitiveness in manufacturing comes from surplus labor migrating from rural areas.) Eventually, the available cheap labor is used up. At this point, efficiency in manufacturing becomes important. As productivity rises in manufacturing, labor shifts toward services.

In developed economies, resistance to change can keep productivity low in key sectors. William Lewis, in *The Power of Productivity*, finds that productivity in the retail sector is low in many countries, such as Japan, because government protects traditional small retailers from modern competitors. In the United States, resistance to change may account for some of the rising cost of education and health care. Doctors have been slow to take advantage of the potential of computer technology to reduce administrative overhead. Only a few colleges and universities have made creative use of computers in presenting course material, and some of the most interesting efforts, such as Carnegie-Mellon's online learning initiative, have not been imitated.

The necessity to overcome resistance to change means that entrepreneurs have peculiar characteristics. While other economic actors study and plan, the entrepreneur experiments and adapts. Entrepreneurship is an approach to ambiguous situations that embodies trial-and-error learning. Entrepreneurial experience tends to include failure as well as success.

Consider Steve Jobs, who along with Steve Wozniak started Apple Computer. In 1976 and 1977, they sold only about two hundred Apple I computers over a ten-month period. The original Apple II, introduced in 1977 with a cassette drive and only 4 kilobytes of RAM, also was unsuccessful. Only when the cassette had been replaced by a floppy disk and RAM had reached 48 kilobytes did the Apple II take off.[43]

Next, Jobs orchestrated the development of the Lisa, which was introduced in 1983. This highly innovative computer cost $50 million to bring to market (with another $100 million to come up with the software) – and flopped. A year later, the Macintosh succeeded where Lisa had failed, but not in time to save Jobs, who was ousted in 1985.[44]

Jobs went on to start another computer company, NeXT computer, which never achieved commercial success, although it was subsequently bought by Apple, paving the way for Jobs' return to Apple as CEO. At the same time that he started NeXT, Jobs also bought Pixar, the highly successful animation studio. Back with Apple, Jobs had mixed results with the computer business. But the iPod, Apple's dedicated MP3 player, was a huge hit, as is its iPhone.

Jobs' career illustrates that entrepreneurs are likely to experience failure. Those who adapt and adjust correctly are successful.

If entrepreneurship requires personality traits that are suited to improvisation, it also requires a culture and institutions that provide flexibility and support to experiments in business. Regulations that entrench existing practices and impede innovation will stifle entrepreneurship.

The process of innovation resembles the biological process of evolution. What appears afterward to be intelligent design is often the cumulative result of random mutations and natural selection. Business consultant Gifford Pinchot III has studied a phenomenon that he calls "intrapreneuring," by which he means experimentation undertaken by individuals within the context of large organizations. Pinchot has written that:

> The reason corporations have such trouble with innovation is that most planning systems fail to take into account the unpredictability of innovation. They are too inflexible to allow quality intrapreneurs to turn on a dime as circumstances change. . . . Despite the apparent rationality of later recountings, innovations never happen as planned because no one can accurately plan something that is really new! Instead, the early stages of innovation consist of groping toward a vision, counting one's progress by what can be learned from mistakes, until at last one grasps a pattern worth repeating.[45]

What Pinchot describes is an inherent conflict between those who grope toward a vision by trial-and-error and the bureaucratic organizations that embody formal planning. This is the same as the conflict between searchers and planners that is described in William Easterly's book *The White Man's Burden.* As Easterly writes,

> Planners announce good intentions but don't motivate anyone to carry them out; Searchers find things that work

and get some reward. Planners raise expectations but take no responsibility for meeting them; Searchers accept responsibility for their actions. Planners determine what to supply; Searchers find out what is in demand. Planners apply global blueprints; Searchers adapt to local conditions. Planners at the top lack knowledge of the bottom; Searchers find out what the reality is at the bottom. Planners never hear whether the plan got what it needed; Searchers find out if the customer is satisfied.[46]

Pinchot believes that there is a certain personality type that is drawn to intrapreneuring – that is, trying to innovate from within a large organization. The characteristics of this personality can be inferred from what he calls "The Intrapreneur's Ten Commandments":

1. Come to work each day willing to be fired.

2. Circumvent any orders aimed at stopping your dream.

3. Do any job needed to make your project work, regardless of your job description.

4. Find people to help you.

5. Follow your intuition about the people you choose, and work only with the best.

6. Work underground as long as you can – publicity triggers the corporate immune mechanism.

7. Never bet on a race unless you are running in it.

8. Remember it is easier to ask for forgiveness than for permission.

9. Be true to your goals, but be realistic about ways to achieve them.

10. Honor your sponsors.[47]

This sort of determination, commitment, and willingness to defy authority is necessary for the intrapreneur, because the intrapreneur is trying to overcome resistance to change within the organization.

However, in most mature, successful corporations, following Pinchot's commandments is *not* a sound approach. For the sake of its shareholders, a firm must limit the ability of individual workers to risk corporate capital. Management has to check the free-wheeling risk-taking of its employees.

What is in the interest of the individual intrapreneur may not be in the interest of the shareholder of the corporation. Suppose that there is a new project that will gain the corporation $10 million if it is successful but will lose $10 million if it fails. If the project has less than a 50 percent chance of success, it is not a wise undertaking from the shareholders' point of view.

The incentives to undertake such a project might appear very different to an individual intrapreneur. If the project fails, the intrapreneur keeps his or her job and salary, and the only downside might be a below-average annual bonus. If the project succeeds, the intrapreneur stands to gain a significant promotion with an upgrade in salary, along with an above-average bonus. Even with a relatively low probability of success, the fact that the personal upside exceeds the personal downside gives the intrapreneur an incentive to undertake the project.

The intrapreneur is someone who tries out a risky new idea while betting the corporation's nickel. Given these incentives, from the point of view of the firm's owners, widespread intrapreneurialism is a disaster waiting to happen. The intrapreneur personally bears too little cost and too little risk, and the shareholders bear too much. This is especially true if all costs are properly taken into account. Often, the cost of integrating a new product into existing corporate systems for marketing, operations, management information, and accounting is something that intrapreneurs overlook.

Often, an intrapreneur has a good idea but the corporation cannot provide the focus and support needed to bring the idea to market. A classic example is Xerox, where many of the features of the modern personal computer were developed. Despite being the first company to develop a graphical user interface, a mouse, and other important inventions, Xerox had little commercial success in the personal computer industry.

To control intrapreneuring, corporations set up bureaucratic filters through which new ideas must pass. The bureaucracy is designed to kill most new ideas, because most new ideas offer a poor return on investment. Corporate decisions are made by committees. In a typical committee, no individual has the power to say "yes" to a new project. On the other hand, almost every member of a committee has the power to veto a new project. Harvard Business professor Michael Roberto describes this phenomenon at IBM:

> Lou Gerstner coined the phrase "culture of no" to describe the situation he inherited at IBM in the early 1990s. In this type of culture of indecision, dissenters essentially have veto power in the decision-making process, particularly if those individuals have power and status. The organization does not employ dissenting voices as a means of encouraging divergent thinking, but rather it enables those who disagree with a proposal to stifle dialogue and close off interesting avenues of inquiry. Such a culture does not force dissenters to defend their views with data and logic, or to explain how their objections are consistent with the organization-wide goals as opposed to the parochial interests of a particular division or subunit. A culture of no enables those with the most power or the loudest voice to impose their will.[48]

Observers of organizational behavior have noted that in committees one is more likely to be regarded as intelligent and a good team player by one's peers by arguing against a new idea than by arguing in favor of it. Middle managers who fight for new ideas are regarded as troublemakers, even if they succeed in convincing corporations to undertake the projects that they propose.

A corporate middle manager who fits Pinchot's description of an intrapreneur is likely to be driven to leave a large organization to start a new enterprise as an entrepreneur. In entrepreneurialism, the incentives are better aligned. If, as often happens, the entrepreneur is overly optimistic about the return from investing in the new idea, the entrepreneur will bear a large share of the loss.

In leaving the corporation to start a new business, the entrepreneur is more exposed to two possible sources of adversity. One is bad luck – even with a sound business concept and a credible effort at execution, an enterprise my fail due to unpredictable sources of competition or customer resistance. The concept of a personal digital assistant failed when Apple tried it with the Newton, but it took off a few years later with the Palm Pilot. Alternatively, failure may be due to lack of skill – the concept itself may be flawed, or any number of mistakes can be made in attempting to execute the business. Netscape Communications had the market-leading Web browser software in 1995, and this gave it the opportunity to attack a number of lucrative markets. However, Netscape descended into mediocrity in all areas, and the company failed to realize its potential.

Because luck is one element of an entrepreneur's success, some people argue that the uneven distribution of income that results from entrepreneurship is unfair. Why shouldn't the lucky winners be taxed, with some of their fortunes redistributed to the unlucky losers? As Brad DeLong put it, "If it is luck or talent, the 60% of me that is a social democrat thinks that this is grossly unfair, and that we should think very seriously about powerful public policies that will level the distribution of income."[49] The difficulty with this sort of redistribution is that it is not possible to completely sort out luck from skill. Successful entrepreneurs often "make their own luck" by adapting to adverse conditions that would set back other entrepreneurs. In any individual instance of remarkable success or failure, one could find elements of both luck and skill that contributed to the result.

Because luck and skill are impossible to measure separately, a redistribution system inevitably would tax the skillful as well as the lucky. By the same token, redistribution would subsidize the unqualified entrepreneurs as well as the unlucky ones. Of these two mistakes, it is subsidizing the unskillful that is the most potentially harmful. Suppose that there are ten entrepreneurs, one of whom will develop a business that is worth $10 million and the other nine of whom will develop a business that is worth zero. If you think that the success is due mostly to luck, then you might want a system in which each entrepreneur receives $1 million, regardless. The problem with such a system is that it will encourage the nine failing entrepreneurs to persist with their unsuccessful enterprises, as well as induce many other entrepreneurs with even less plausible business models to attempt to start firms.

Redistribution would create exactly the sort of problems that corporate bureaucracy is designed to prevent. It would insulate entrepreneurs from downside risks and thereby increase the incentive to attempt new businesses that have poor prospects. At a more subtle level, redistribution would change the game in ways that would lead different sorts of people to become entrepreneurs. If entrepreneurs were insulated against downside risks, then new businesses would be started by people who lack adaptability, persistence, and other qualities that are necessary to make new enterprises successful.

What are the characteristics that differentiate a natural entrepreneur from someone less likely to succeed? The ideas presented here are based on personal experience, the writing of Gifford Pinchot and other business consultants, and the work of Amar Bhide, author of *The Origins and Evolution of New Businesses*. The characteristics that stand out most have to do with colorfulness, eagerness to confront customers, opportunism, and persistence in the face of adversity.

Entrepreneurs tend to stand out as people. They make a memorable impression on others. They express their opinions with passion and flair. Entrepreneurs are the sort of people who acquire colorful nicknames, for example, and they in turn use nicknames to refer to other people. Many entrepreneurs display an intensity that would not be tolerated in a middle manager. CEOs such as Oracle's Larry Ellison or Apple Computer's Steven Jobs would be considered too difficult and disruptive if they were placed in a team setting.

Economics 2.0 says that a key role for entrepreneurs is to overcome resistance to change. To do so, entrepreneurs have to engage the attention and win the loyalty of customers, employees, and potential investors. They cannot afford to be bland or ill-defined. Pinchot expresses this idea in the question, "Do you have more than your share of both fans and critics?"[50] The intrapreneur (or, in our case, the entrepreneur) is someone who elicits a strong reaction from people, one way or the other. You may not like the entrepreneur (many people could not get along with Jobs or Ellison), but you do not forget your encounters with him or her.

Bhide points out that most entrepreneurs engage in face-to-face selling. In that setting, personal persuasiveness can matter as much as or more than the characteristics of the product or service being sold. People are more likely to listen to a salesperson who is amusing, employs stories and metaphors, and uses theatrical vocalization and body language.

For all of these reasons, a successful entrepreneur is more likely than not to be a colorful, charismatic figure. People who are dull and forgettable will fail to motivate customers, business partners, or others who are crucial to the success of the enterprise.

The eagerness to confront customers is another characteristic of the entrepreneur. When first developed, most new products and services do not meet customer needs effectively. Instead, offerings have to be modified, reconfigured, and tuned to suit users' demands. The software industry has formalized the process of confronting consumers with unfinished products by following the rituals known as "alpha-testing" and "beta-testing." During these processes, consumers propose new features, suggest improvements in design, and report bugs. Even outside the software industry, although they may not use the same terminology for their tests, entrepreneurs make extensive use of feedback cycles to hone products and services to meet customer needs.

Facing consumer criticism takes fortitude. One cannot overreact to every customer's quirk. But the worst entrepreneurs are those who avoid interacting with customers. The cliché that says, "if you a build a better mousetrap, they will come," is wrong. Entrepreneurs need customers in order to learn what makes for a better mousetrap.

Often, the process of observing customers will lead the entrepreneur to focus on an unanticipated market opportunity. One famous example is Ray Kroc, who began his business career as the proprietor of a milkshake-making machine. He found that one of his best customers was a small hamburger restaurant. As he observed this little hamburger stand, called McDonald's, he decided that this was a business that could be replicated and marketed to many more people. He switched his focus away from his milkshake-maker, and the rest is history.

Thus, opportunism is another quality of entrepreneurs. An entrepreneur is always on the lookout for an opportunity to launch a successful business. To be sure, an entrepreneur needs to know when it is time to settle down and focus on a promising business idea, rather than continually searching for better ideas without executing any of them. But it is quite common for successful businesses to be based on opportunities that differ from what the entrepreneur initially tried to exploit.

Bhide describes entrepreneurs as "improvisational." They begin an enterprise with relatively little planning, and they adjust on the fly to customer needs until they have found a successful business formula. Entrepreneurs are sufficiently adaptable to be able to extract opportunity from failure. When an entrepreneur sees something that is broken, or has an unsatisfying experience as a consumer, he or she will view this as an opportunity to profit by fixing the problem.

One often hears that it's hard to find a reliable plumber or air conditioning repair person. Not surprisingly, entrepreneurs have tried to step in with web sites where consumers recommend good service technicians to one another, like Angie's List (www.angieslist.com). The rising cost of health care is another problem that represents an opportunity for entrepreneurs. Small clinics, with names like Redi-Clinic and MinuteClinic, operating in retail stores such as Wal-Mart and Target, are trying to address this problem. Relying for the most part on nurse practitioners, these retail clinics attempt to give consumers a cheap, quick solution to everyday health care problems.[51]

The ability to handle setbacks, and to thrive under adversity, is another crucial characteristic of entrepreneurs. Many of the qualities of Pinchot's intrapreneur pertain to a willingness and ability to deal with adversity: being willing to be fired, doing any job needed, finding people to help you, being true to your goals but realistic about ways to achieve them. Most start-ups run short of cash before they achieve success. Stories abound of entrepreneurs who had to juggle credit card debt, accounts payable, or other unconventional forms of finance in order to keep their businesses afloat.

The table below summarizes the characteristics of what one might term the entrepreneurial personality. To clarify these characteristics, the table has a column labeled "un-entrepreneur" to describe the opposite characteristics.

CHARACTERISTIC	ENTREPRENEUR	UN-ENTREPRENEUR
Personal vividness	Colorful, charismatic, polarizing	Inconspicuous, bland, neutral
Orientation toward customers	Eager to confront customers, learn from them, and adapt to them	Shrinks from customers, tries to pay as little attention to them as possible
Ability to change direction	Opportunistic, seizes new chances, shifts strategy and tactics in response to the situation	Sticks to the plan no matter what
Handling adversity	Works around obstacles, tries to extract opportunity from failure	Focuses on avoiding failure and on avoiding blame for failure when it does happen

If you look carefully at the right-hand column, you will notice something more than just the fact that these characteristics describe someone who is not well suited to being an entrepreneur. Someone who fits the description of an un-entrepreneur would be perfectly suited in another role – as a bureaucrat.

The Heart That Pumps Innovation

A stereotypical bureaucrat, whether in a government agency or a large corporation, strives to remain inconspicuous and insulated from customers. Bureaucrats seem to prefer planning to action, and they become unhinged by adversity. They examine failure in order to pin blame and warn against recurrence, rather than to look for new opportunities.

Bhide points out that large enterprises are best suited to making progress along predictable lines, such as adding new capacity. The decision to build a new electric power plant or oil refinery requires careful planning, but it is not fraught with ambiguity. Corporate bureaucracies are effective at making these sorts of decisions.

But in ambiguous situations, in which radical innovation may be appropriate, trial-and-error improvisation tends to be more effective than bureaucratic decision-making. In ambiguous situations, decisions made on the spot, in response to customer feedback, are more accurate than decisions made at a central headquarters. The effectiveness of trial-and-error efforts has important implications for thorny real-world problems. What Easterly argues is that the problems of economic development are too ambiguous and idiosyncratic to be solved by remote planners. Planners have too little knowledge of the local needs and conditions, have too little personal incentive to achieve results, and can too easily evade being held accountable for failure. Instead, economic development is best served by searchers, who take their cues from local customers, can be held clearly accountable for results, and will receive rewards that are tied to success.

Economics 2.0 says that the abundance that arises from innovation and economic growth depends on the work of entrepreneurs and searchers. We see economic activity as an ongoing battle between upstarts and incumbents. Incumbents try to consolidate and defend the existing modes of operation. Upstarts try to apply new knowledge and techniques. When the upstarts succeed, incumbents are reluctantly forced to follow.

As William Lewis points out in *The Power of Productivity*, one of the most frustrating aspects of world poverty is that the know-how to dramatically improve the standard of living in poor countries already exists. In principle, all that people in India or Brazil need to do to boost their incomes is copy the production techniques used in the advanced countries. Yet the upstarts who would do so are often thwarted by politically powerful incumbents or by other institutional impediments. Overall, a country's economic performance depends on how well the upstarts are able to push forward the application of knowledge. The easier it is to enter an industry and compete on a level playing field with incumbents, the faster will be the pace of innovation and improvement. The climate for entrepreneurship in turn depends on many legal, political, and cultural factors.

America has historically been a hospitable environment for people with the entrepreneurial personality. It is almost as if in the early seventeenth century, when required by their employers to attend organizational development workshops in "team-building" and "change management," a group of English dissidents became fed up and said, "Forget it. We refuse. We're going on the *Mayflower*." And they sailed to the New World, even though it meant doing without health insurance.

The famous Turner Hypothesis, propounded by historian Frederick Jackson Turner in 1893, is that the frontier served to hone Americans' entrepreneurial temperament. He wrote that it is

> to the frontier the American intellect owes its striking characteristics. That coarseness and strength combined with acuteness and inquisitiveness; that practical, inventive turn of mind, quick to find expedients; that masterful grasp of material things, lacking in the artistic but powerful to effect great ends; that restless, nervous

energy; that dominant individualism, working for good and for evil, and withal that buoyancy and exuberance which comes with freedom – these are traits of the frontier, or traits called out elsewhere because of the existence of the frontier.[52]

One could argue that the advent of the personal computer, and particularly the Internet, created a virtual frontier that once again has provided an outlet for entrepreneurs. The Internet environment is well suited to unplanned innovation originating from the edge, with relatively little central organization or control.

The Internet has lowered the cost of capital for start-ups. As Daniel Pink, author of *Free Agent Nation*, has observed, the Internet has allowed many workers to achieve the Marxist dream of owning the means of production. An individual with a personal computer and a connection to the Internet has the means for starting a business, such as trading on eBay. Just as "heading out for the territories" provided an outlet for individualists in America's early days, the lower cost of starting a business provides an outlet for today's frustrated corporate workers. More people have the option of becoming entrepreneurs.

According to the Kauffman Foundation's index of entrepreneurial activity, in 2005 an average of 0.29 percent of the non-business-owning population started a new business each month. That would be 3.5 percent of the population per year, which would mean that with a static population, in thirty years everyone would own a business. While this is not going to occur, it does seem likely that close to a majority of Americans will start businesses at some point in their lives.

All societies have people with entrepreneurial inclinations and people with bureaucratic inclinations. Economics 2.0 says that societies where institutions present the fewest obstacles to the entrepreneurs are the ones where the standard of living will be highest. Nobel laureate Phelps, cited earlier, points out that continental Europe's "corporatism" stifles the entrepreneurial spread of knowledge. Collaboration among unions, business, and government strengthens incumbents and helps to institutionalize resistance to change.

In Economics 1.0, innovation descends on the economy like manna from heaven. Anyone who has experienced either intrapreneurship or entrepreneurship knows that the reality is far different. Introducing change requires significant emotional energy and persistence. Entrepreneurialism is essential to the process of pumping fresh supplies of innovation into the economy.

Interview with
EDMUND PHELPS

EDMUND S. PHELPS is McVickar Professor of Political Economy at Columbia University, director of Columbia's Center on Capitalism and Society, and the winner of the 2006 Nobel Prize in economics. He is a fellow of the National Academy of Science and both a distinguished fellow and a former vice president of the American Economic Association. In 2001 Phelps founded, with Roman Frydman, the Center on Capitalism and Society at Columbia (now a unit of the School of Arts and Sciences) to conduct and promote research on capitalism.

ARNOLD KLING & NICK SCHULZ: In an article called the "Dynamism of Nations," you asked and answered an interesting question: "What is needed for high performance?" You answered, "Basically, it is productive change which I call economic dynamism." Give us an example of an economy where there is no economic dynamism.

EDMUND PHELPS: I suppose France is a somewhat good example of a highly productive economy [without] very much indigenous innovation of the commercially successful kind going on. There's very little turnover in the list of the top fifty firms, so the firms are not being bumped off their perch. If there's not much innovation, then the work-place is probably pretty dull, so you'd look for reports of low job satisfaction – and you find them. You see that in the data.

AK & NS: You argue that dynamism actually transforms workplaces and leads to more satisfying jobs, and that there's increasing evidence for this. Is that what you found?

EP: Yes. I think there's evidence. I don't want to say it's over-whelming or indisputable. But the countries that rank high by some standard indicators of dynamism, such as turnover of firms and toting up innovations on the back of an enve-lope, tend also to rank high in job satisfaction and employee engagement.

AK & NS: In an interview with the *Financial Times* you said of capitalist reality: "It's a system of disorder. Entrepreneurs have only the murkiest picture of the future in which they are making their bets and also there is ambiguity. They don't know when they push this lever or that lever that the outcome is going to be what they think it is going to be. There's the law of unanticipated consequences." And then you said something interesting: "This is not in the economic textbooks and my mission late in my career is to get it into the textbooks." How could something that is so seemingly fundamental to economic activity and change, how could this not be in economic textbooks? And what practical dif-ference does it make if it's in there or not?

EP: Well, that's a very good question. If the system were fully in place and safeguarded against being hijacked, then I guess it wouldn't be all that crucial to mankind to understand it right. But I'm afraid that if we don't understand it, that may hold some dangers when it comes to defending the system against people who want to change it. People may not like parts of it and want to change it correspondingly, not realizing that [while] some of those changes may be for the good, some of them may be very much for the worse. I think we really ought to understand capitalist systems much better than we do. It's hard, too, because no actual economic system out there is exactly capitalist.

AK & NS: Is it your sense that those critics don't understand this aspect of entrepreneurship, or do they willfully ignore it? Is it a failure of comprehension or a failure to have had it pointed out accurately?

EP: I'm sure they understand that there are entrepreneurs in the capitalist system. Mussolini must have understood that there were entrepreneurs in the capitalist system. He thought they were no damn good. [*laughter*] He thought he could do better with a more statist, *dirigiste* system, and it was left for a few subtle minds like Friedrich Hayek to try to explain to these guys that, look, there are some subtleties here that you are probably not aware of and that you had better understand more deeply before you chuck out this system.

AK & NS: What sort of reception do you get when you support adding these considerations into the standard economics texts? Do you get resistance?

EP: There's two or three reactions. I think one is to say that will be awfully difficult to do and . . .

AK & NS: Why is that?

EP: Well, I think we understand rather little about uncertainty, about ambiguity. We're not very sure what kinds of things might be deducible from a pretty good model and what kinds of things might be not deducible. So the first reaction is skepticism that progress in that direction will be large and [will come] soon.

The other reaction borders on hostility because many people have a lot invested in the stochastic, steady-state models with rational expectations. They don't like being told that all the results they got are of dubious value at best and that some are of absolutely no value whatsoever. And they don't like to be told that what they did didn't turn out to illuminate the world.

AK & NS: Sort of a classic incumbent's problem.

EP: Right. [*laughter*]

AK & NS: Resisting the innovators.

EP: Very definitely. Although, maybe a more sophisticated position is that you never really know. It could come much sooner than we imagine it. It could come like an avalanche. I think that there are one or two giant steps that, with luck, could be taken pretty soon, and if that happens, then great, we're off to the races. But it might not happen.

AK & NS: In your Nobel talk you said, "Various attributes of a country's economic culture serve to animate entrepreneurs and more broadly to encourage them by offering a willing work force and a receptive market place for their innovations." This notion of economic culture is interesting, since it may mean different things to different people. Could you discuss with a little more specificity what you mean by this culture, its characteristics, how we identify it, and so forth?

EP: A couple of years ago I would have said that it means a yen for novelty, tolerance for uncertainty, and a kind of acceptance – maybe even delight – in ambiguity, in not being quite able to figure it all out but taking action anyway. What did Keynes call it? "Animal spirits."

A few years ago I was thinking along those lines, but then in the spring of 2006 I got the idea that I had to throw some cultural variables into the right hand side of the regression equations that I sometimes fool around with in my efforts to try to predict productivity, unemployment, job satisfaction, and other indicators of economic performance. I was able to line up a couple of very sharp research assistants from Eastern Europe, and I asked them to rummage around for the data. They found some data from the University of Michigan, world values surveys. And I didn't, by any means, find everything I wanted. But there were a couple of intriguing things there that I hadn't imagined could be found. The respondents were asked questions about their willingness to exert leadership, their willingness to accept followership and taking orders, how they feel about competition for their job, how they feel about change, and, when they are looking for a job, how important is it to have a job that's interesting.

So we threw in these variables which calculated average values for each country, the percentage of respondents who expressed themselves strongly on these issues. Sometimes there was a reason to think that something would affect productivity but not, say, unemployment. And sometimes there was a reason to think that one of the cultural attitudes would affect unemployment but not productivity. So we threw in these [variables] – I think of them as workplace attitudes – and lo and behold, almost every one of them made a significant difference in explaining some performance variable. I came away with a general impression that differences across countries with respect to certain well-defined institutions were not as important as the prevailing differences in economic culture.

AK & NS: I want to ask you about three interesting things you mentioned in your Nobel speech and ask you to explain what they are and why they are important. First, what is a Nelson/Phelps Manager?

EP: A Nelson/Phelps Manager is a reference to the 1966 paper that Richard Nelson and I wrote in which we pictured a manager – let's say, a manager of a farm who has just received new information in the mail about a new fertilizer. And so the question is, is he going to adopt it, is he going to try it or not? The Nelson/Phelps thesis is that it would make a big difference if the manager of the farm is somebody with a relatively high level of education, let's say, a liberal arts education.

The idea goes back to Alexander Meiklejohn, who was president of Amherst College for a while in the 1920s. I said, "Why do we go to college? What's the point here?" His view was, "It's not [that] what we are going to learn here, we are going to go out and apply. It's rather that what we learn here is going to set us up to be better able to learn new things than we would otherwise be." New things that would be important to learn depending on whatever new stuff, novel stuff unfolds over our lives. His one-liner was, "College education is all about learning to learn." So Nelson and I argued that an effective manager would be one who has the little bit of chemistry that might be necessary, or maybe the little bit of economics that might be necessary or helpful, for understanding whether or not it would be a good bet to adopt the fertilizer.

Another manager somewhere might benefit from some understanding of foreign languages. This paper was written in a time when one studied foreign languages in college, if you can believe that! More mathematics, too, I suppose. Mathematics could be applied here and there.

Nelson/Phelps Manager is not a term that's in the literature. It was just shorthand for the kind of manager that the Nelson and Phelps paper extolled as important for the diffusion of new innovations.

AK & NS: So these kinds of managers are critical, then, to economic dynamism?

EP: Extremely helpful, I think, to put it mildly – critical is probably right on.

AK & NS: Well, here's another term then. What is an Amar Bhide Consumer?

EP: An Amar Bhide Consumer is a venturesome consumer – to use his words, somebody who gets a kick out of trying new stuff. So that's a little bit different from a Nelson/Phelps Manager. A Nelson/Phelps Manager may get no joy whatsoever out of this decision about the fertilizer, though he's glad he's able to make a better decision than some. The venturesome consumer is a somewhat different idea, [it's about] having fun and going to the mall on Saturday morning to look at the new stuff and then taking some enjoyment in figuring out how to use it well, better and better, at home. That's also very important. If there are no such consumers around then potential innovators are not going to be innovating in the hope of adoption by such consumers.

AK & NS: Are these consumers made or born or somewhere in-between? What accounts for why we have them some places and not in other places?

EP: I'm being somewhat cautious. I wouldn't go around saying that some countries give birth to more of them than others on any systematic basis. I'm inclined to think that either they grew up with a different culture or, if people grow up with the same culture everywhere, then some of it gets banged out of some of them by new-fangled social modes of thought. Not so many centuries ago it would have been said to be frivolous to go to the mall and look at new stuff. You [were supposed to] be thinking about things of higher value in life. In some schools of thought and some philosophies, material goods in general are not really very important. So there have been intervening cultures that may have tempered people's delight in the material and their curiosity about the new.

AK & NS: One last figure that you referred to in your speech was the Marschak/Nelson Financier.

EP: Right. That [refers to] a paper written by Tom Marschak, son of Jacob Marschak, and the same Richard Nelson. It appeared in a journal that absolutely nobody has ever seen except possibly me, and I'm not always sure that I've seen it either. I think it's called *Metro Economic*. In that paper, they addressed what looked like a rather fundamental problem in capitalism theory, namely, why on earth would any financier lend money to a would-be entrepreneur? Given that capitalism theory asserts that there's a lot of ambiguity about how it's going to work, that there's even some ambiguity about whether the development of the thing would be successful, that it's hard to understand exactly what's in the back of the entrepreneur's mind, et cetera, how is it that an entrepreneur is able to get some financing from the financial sector?

No doubt there are several answers, but the answer in the Marschak and Nelson paper was that what the financiers should do is parcel it out, sequentially dribble out the financing, while asking at each step of the way: How's the entrepreneur doing so far? Is he hitting his marks? Now, fifty years later, we are very aware that venture capitalists do set benchmarks and targets. It's a big, fascinating subject.

AK & NS: How does your thinking about these kinds of managers, consumers, and financiers affect your view of the outlook for both Europe and for China?

EP: Well, I think China is a very special case, so let's take up Europe first. I was a bit concerned in 1999 when I started looking at data on the proportion of the [European] labor force with a university degree. I was very concerned that – my God, Italy was in the single-digits in percentage terms. Only 9% of the labor force had a university degree. Maybe Austria was even worse, at 8%, or vice versa. I thought, where are entrepreneurs going to find the workers who relish new problems to solve, novelty and all that, and who can cope with that and who will like it, and where are they going to find consumers who like to try out stuff? I've always found that, statistically, differences in the proportion of the labor force with a university degree do seem to have some explanatory value in understanding differences in economic performance across OECD countries.

You asked about China. Amar Bhide and I wrote a paper

on China in which we said that part of China's distinctive character comes from the fact that Chinese consumers haven't accumulated a lot of human capital, so to speak, in the form of experience with Western consumer goods. You can put them behind the wheel, but they may not know how to get the car going. And so, knowing that they don't know how to get the car going, they may not buy it.

This led us to an old-fashioned idea, absorption capacity, which used to be in the literature in the 1950s and 1960s. The Chinese consumer today can only absorb new stuff so fast. But productivity is going like gangbusters in China. Producers are learning to make a lot of the new stuff. So, with the Chinese consumer always lagging behind, it's kind of inevitable that China will be running a big export surplus. That's our thesis, for better or worse.

AK & NS: Nothing to do with the currency manipulation?

EP: No. [*laughter*] Sorry to disappoint our friends and colleagues.

AK & NS: That's all you hear in Washington.

EP: Maybe that's why the Brookings Institution wasn't interested in this paper a couple of years ago.

AK & NS: What characteristics or institutions of the American economy do you think that Europeans ought to try to adopt, and vice versa? I know that you are a Europhile even though you've been somewhat pessimistic about their prospects, but maybe there are some things.

EP: Larry Summers embarrassed me slightly at a public debate he was moderating. He said, "Can you name one thing that you like about Europe?" Caught me totally by surprise. [*laughter*]

AK & NS: And you couldn't say, "the food."

EP: I couldn't really get out very much at all, which wasn't fair. If I thought about it for a while, I could say a few things.

About the economy – well, of course, some of the small countries pride themselves on their corporatism. They think it's just great to have these good-spirited unions in the company. It just makes everything so much more amicable and cooperative, and it's a great thing to have. Aren't the Americans misguided in not understanding that? Maybe it is something that works well in Austria, where everybody looks pretty much the same to me anyway. [laughter] They've all come from the same place and they all have similar ideas, so I can understand that unions could play some informational role there.

About what I like in the United States – well, nothing is perfect here, so one always sounds so naïve in praising any one thing. Basically, I tend to like the relative openness of the society. People have a chance to do something different and to try to move up the ladder. There is that sense here. Now, whether the data fully support that is another story. I've seen skeptical reports on that, but there's that sense, and we don't deplore people for making it and we don't begrudge them the money that comes with that. I think that's very healthy for everybody concerned, and I also think it's good for the economy.

AK & NS: In your Nobel talk, you say that John Rawls's model of the economy took an austere view of the sources of human satisfaction and that this is a view inherited from classical economics. What do you mean that he took an

austere view? And since you were friendly with Rawls, did
you ever make this point to him? If so, what did he say?

EP: No, no. My last lengthy conversation with him was probably in January of 1997, and then he had some strokes while I
was, unfortunately, snowed under with work. I didn't know
that he had had these strokes. I lost track of him for a few
years, and by 2001, when I was very aware of his condition,
it was really too late. He couldn't talk at that point.

When I made that comment I was going on memory of
chunks of the book – let's say, its first half. It had always
impressed me that when it came to talking about a disadvantaged worker's self-realization, Rawls could not say anything more than, "Well, if he can get a decent paycheck,
then he can be a better parent and take the kid to the ball
game and participate in town meetings at the local church,"
stuff like that. I thought that Rawls didn't have to be so narrow in his view of the opportunities for self-realization
[offered to] the least advantaged. It seemed to me that they
can get something [more] out of participating in the workplace; they can solve problems and experience some personal growth and increased self-esteem and increased
mastery. The natural tendency is for people to say, "Well,
surely, since they are very disadvantaged, they can't do
much." And I understand how that's true, but on the other
hand, they can't do much at home either. It's not as if they
are going to read Proust and the *Complete Works of Aristotle* all day.

A K & NS: Or Rawls, for that matter.

EP: Or Rawls, for that matter. [*laughter*] So I thought that Rawls
could have chosen not to be so austere. But then, I think he
wanted to keep his model simple. He wanted to think in

terms of the wage and [how] the wage then opened up opportunities for self-realization *outside* of work. That was a simple framework which he could make it clear to a hard-working reader, and it worked very well for him. But the thing is, it didn't work very well for me when it came time to thinking about the justice of capitalism. I found myself saying that it couldn't be just. It didn't give any possible self-expression to entrepreneurial types who need to develop a new idea to find their self-realization.

We've got two kinds of deprivation here to worry about: not only the deprivation of the classically least advantaged, but also what could be the deprivation of a whole entrepreneurial class, who don't get a chance to realize the intellectual growth of which they are capable.

In any case, it gets complicated here. Abraham Maslow said somewhere that a person who has reached a higher rung in the ladder of satisfactions would be less satisfied on a lower rung than somebody else who had [newly attained] that lower rung. You can imagine a situation in which the bottom income level has been maximized through tax policy but there are no entrepreneurial opportunities, so that entrepreneurs and hard-hat Joe-lunch-pail types are earning the same low wage. In that situation, the Joe-lunch-pails would be doing a pretty good job of self-realization to the extent that they were able, while the entrepreneurial types would be frustrated, unhappy, and not getting anything out of their jobs.

*AMAR BHIDE is professor of business management at Colum-
bia University. He has published widely in the area of entrepreneurship, strategy, contracting, and firm governance. He is also
the author of two highly regarded books,* The Origin and Evolution of New Businesses *and* The Venturesome Economy. *He
has been a senior engagement manager at McKinsey & Company, vice president of E. F. Hutton, and Associates Fellow at
Harvard Business School.*

ARNOLD KLING & NICK SCHULZ: In *The Origin and Evolution of New Businesses,* you say that "little effort has been
   devoted to systematic research about starting and growing
   new businesses." Why has that been the case?

AMAR BHIDE: Simply because it's too hard to do anything
   systematically. There's ad hoc research from people who do
   management stuff, but there isn't much research from people who do economics, in part because the whole idea of
   entrepreneurship lies outside much of the theory of economics. In economics the emphasis is still on phenomena
   that are stationary, things that don't change, things where

nothing is evolving and where whatever is normal is known, where there is no discovery. I happen to think that it would have been much more fruitful if the Austrian economists – their way of thinking about the world – had been pursued in improving our understanding of entrepreneurship.

AK & NS: And what are some of the touchstones of that [way of thinking]?

AB: Well, [one is] the idea that we shouldn't be studying equilibrium outcomes, that we should be studying change in and of itself.

I'll give you a few telling examples. I was at the University of Chicago when I published my book, and people read it and said, "But how do you measure radical uncertainty or Knightian uncertainty?" The assumption was that if you can't measure it then it's useless. And there was a very nice lecture by Friedrich Hayek in 1974, where he talked about this almost ritualistic preference for only studying things that can be measured. And think of the current best-selling economics book, *Freakonomics*. It's great fun, but Steven Levitt's methods, which are principally statistical methods, can only be applied to phenomena which don't change. And these methods are simply not suited to phenomena which are in a constant state of flux.

The profession of economics simply does not have alternative tools for dealing with these phenomena of entrepreneurship. So you get stuck with relatively uninteresting topics – or at least things that I find uninteresting.

AK & NS: You mentioned that the Austrians have thought a little differently about this. Is it the case that the tools that you are talking about simply don't exist yet and need to be created, or that they are simply not being employed?

AB: I don't think they exist quite yet. So I don't quite know what the answer is, and I think it will require lot of entrepreneurial effort and trial and error to [find those] alternative tools. But I'm pretty confident that our current toolset is not very good. The current toolset is the one with which you have to show proficiency in order to get ahead in the academic world, and that's what you do. Then you find it hard to give up these habits once you get there.

AK & NS: Sounds like it's the equivalent of the drunk who is looking for his car keys under the lamppost.

AB: Oh, absolutely. Absolutely.

AK & NS: So we need more lampposts.

AB: Or we need a different kind of lamppost. We need the courage to say – and in the world of business this is perfectly understood, or in the world of innovation, in the commercial world it's quite well understood – that your first-generation product won't quite work, it will have defects, [although] as long as it produces something useful people [will be] willing to buy it, even with imperfections. And then somebody will come out with a Version 2 and a Version 3. But this kind of open-minded process for discovering the new toolset seems to have been stymied in the academic world.

AK & NS: Really?

AB: Yes.

AK & NS: And is that because . . .

AB: I think part of it is the way scholarly journals operate: unless you have the right and utterly defensible answer you won't get published. So if you say, "Here's something slightly speculative, we don't quite know how it's going to work, but here is a promising line of inquiry and let somebody else after me figure out how to fix it," it doesn't get published. Things have to be proven beyond reasonable doubt. The framework for determining proof beyond reasonable doubt is the existing framework.

I am a member of the Center on Capitalism in Society, and we have several distinguished people, far more distinguished than I, who share this sense of unhappiness that we are locked into a paradigm which isn't getting us very far. One of the things we are about to do is to start a publication, *Capitalism and Society*, in which we will publish stuff that hasn't been proven beyond reasonable doubt.

AK & NS: In your research you found that many successful businesses lacked a strategy for, and sometimes even the goal of, becoming long-lived businesses – that they *evolved* as much as they were planned. Can you discuss that in more detail?

AB: I could tell you story upon story about this, but it [all] goes back to this idea that we were talking about before, that a lot of progress is incremental and all you can see at the time that you start a business is, this little tweak for this little reapplication of this idea in a somewhat different market will make me some money. Beyond that, the future is un-knowable. And since these entrepreneurs aren't risking a lot of capital anyway and they are not beholden to anybody else for raising money, they can proceed in this incremental I-don't-really-know-where-I'm-going way, as long as at each point they are financially self-sufficient.

That's a very different process from what venture-capital backed companies do and, particularly, from what large companies do. So you have to provide a lot of evidence of where this business is going to go, why it's going to go where it's going to go, and so on. At least at the outset, the expectation is that things will follow a plan, though often they don't. But the presumption is that unless you have a credible plan that you can sell to other people, you are not going to get the resources you need to get going.

AK & NS: You also asserted in the book that "the lack of research and planning that we find in many promising startups has a sound economic basis." Can you explain how that is so? That's a striking idea to a lot of people.

AB: Many of the opportunities that these entrepreneurs have are in domains where things are changing so fast that it's impossible to do any research. [And in many cases] the entrepreneurs themselves are severely capital-constrained, so there isn't much money available to do research. The opportunities also often tend to be transient. So quite apart from the costs of doing the research, the out-of-pocket costs, there's the risk that by the time you get around to figuring out what's going on, the opportunity will be gone.

AK & NS: You mentioned Hayek earlier. This discussion makes one think of Hayek's concept of spontaneous order. Would that be a valid connection, in your view? Are you making the case for decentralized innovation rather than central planning?

AB: I think the modern world has a full range of activities. Some of them are actually decentralized, some of them fit the idea of spontaneous order to a tee, and others don't. Just look at the Internet. There are some things within the Internet which have spontaneously emerged, as it were – the growth of HTML and the Web was simply one guy tossing out an idea [that was] picked up by a bunch of other people. On the other hand, there are a whole bunch of infrastructure decisions within the Internet that have been taken [only] after a lot of due deliberation by many parties – where there might not have been an efficient, spontaneous emergence of order. So in some sense, as long as it isn't imposed by some causal force, the world does a pretty good job of figuring out what things need to be planned, what things need to be planned within a hierarchy, what things need to be planned across different hierarchies, and what things are best left to spontaneous order. And even the people who are improvising, they have half an eye out towards the decisions which are taking place in a planned way. I think where people go astray is to imagine that everything can be done through a hierarchical planning process.

But I'm not so fond of the opposite view either. I mean, I like the idea that the grammar is set. That language can and does evolve over time, but that there is some system that has us all speaking more or less the same way – this is probably a good thing.

AK & NS: You pointed out in your book that entrepreneurs "have always accounted for about half of economic activity." Now, that might surprise people on a lot of levels – how is it that something that could have been that significant could have been overlooked for so long?

AB: The great excitement at the time of the Industrial Revolution was the emergence of the large enterprise. It was at the cutting edge of technological change. Small businesses had already been around, but this was a new phenomenon. And the new phenomenon was gaining share. Anything that goes from zero percent of the economy to 50 percent of the economy is going to get a lot of attention.

Even now, the Internet is still not even half of the way information is transmitted. I mean newspapers are still a big deal and old media is still a big deal, but nobody talks about them, right? If the growth of the Internet continues at this rate – let's say it reaches half of media output ten or fifteen years from now – that would be a radical change, and it will be very tempting for people to forget that the other half of it is still old media.

And then you have an additional phenomenon, which is that it is easier to study and document and measure what large companies do because there are relatively few of them, which has amplified and sustained the emphasis on large companies. So in a sense, the evolving norms of academia have sustained this focus on large companies.

AK & NS: There was a time in economics and management circles where people believed that large corporations were, in a sense, omnipotent. As John Kenneth Galbraith once put it, "The big corporations do not lose money." But there has been a sea change in the perception of large firms, which were once thought to be so powerful. What are some of the things that have forced that change in perception?

AB: Companies are not exactly like human beings, but they do have an inherent tendency to decay and die, and I think Galbraith was looking at these firms in their middle-age. We didn't have three hundred years of history when Galbraith was looking at these firms. The game had not fully played itself out.

In a capitalist society, and particularly the American

capitalist society, there is a very strong pressure to either grow or die. You cannot sit still. No matter how large you've become, there's a great deal of pressure from the labor markets, from the capital markets, from your customers, to keep growing. And there's a point in which it is literally impossible to grow, or it's virtually impossible to grow. What I think of as the inevitable mortality induced by this grow-die imperative had not played itself out by the 1950s.

AK & NS: Has the Internet made a difference in opportunities for promising startups? What would that be and how much so?

AB: A great many promising startups take advantage of some external change in the world. And the salient external change of the world in the last four or five years has been the Internet. But it could have been anything else. If, instead of the Internet, nanotechnology had taken off and had become all the rage and there were all kinds of breakthroughs in nanotechnology, I imagine that the promising startups would have been in nanotechnology. It's not the Internet per se. It's whatever feature of our world in which one observes the greatest change.

Promising startups tend to get pulled into the arena of the greatest change. If you were an entrepreneur in Russia, for instance, at the time that communism was collapsing, you probably would have been attracted to privatization more than you would have been to the Internet, simply because at that time and at that place, that was the big deal.

AK & NS: What are India's advantages and disadvantages these days, particularly as far as entrepreneurship is concerned?

AB: That's a tricky one, because until I started studying India all my research on entrepreneurship was based on the United States, which is an economy at the technological frontier. And many of the opportunities that entrepreneurs have exploited in the U.S. came about by helping to advance the technological frontier.

Now, India is very, very far behind the technological frontier, and a lot of the catch-up will simply come about by tracking and adopting techniques and ways of doing things that have already been developed in the United States. So whatever the kinds of opportunities we saw in the U.S., those are probably not the right opportunities for an entrepreneur in India.

As an academic, I can only study what is happening or what has happened. It's hard to tell whether there will be an alternative model where the individual entrepreneur will play a different kind of role. But at the moment, it looks like a lot of the economic and technical change that we see in India is being brought about by large firms, because it's just more efficient to do that.

Here's a striking example of this. When Starbucks got started, it needed an individual entrepreneur, because it was a crazy experiment – who knew whether it would work or not? A lot of trial and error needed to be done before the format and the business model got shaken out. But now that that model has been built, it can be easily replicated on a large scale in other countries like India. And it's much more likely to be a large firm or a wealthy individual who's going to come to the United States, observe Starbucks, and then re-create it in India. And because there is so much low-hanging fruit available through the transplantation of technology, incentives, and methods, it may be that for a while the leading edge of change will be the large firms.

AK & NS: What are the main lessons of your research for those who would like to promote economic growth?

AB: After I did my research in the U.S. and wrote my book, I was asked the question, what can the government do to promote entrepreneurship? And I would scratch my head and come up with virtually nothing. But now that I have spent a couple of years in India doing research there, it strikes me that the reason I could say virtually nothing is that the basic governmental functions in the U.S. actually work. We simply take them for granted. Property rights, the provision of roads, water, electricity. Whether they are directly provided by the government or are provided through a framework or a set of rules that the government enforces, is immaterial; they are provided. But when you go to a country like India and these basic governmental functions don't exist, you see an utter distortion of entrepreneurial drive into things which actually probably do more economic harm than good.

In those countries, I think the promotion of productive entrepreneurship requires two things. One, it requires the government to get out of doing the things that it is unsuited to do. But there's also a second part: it requires improvement in the performance of those functions that the government ought to do. And we are lucky in the United States that we just take it for granted that the basic functions are more or less adequately performed.

AK & NS: One comment in there was interesting to me: that in a place like India – and this would also apply to some other countries – the entrepreneurial spirit is channeled in ways that may do more economic harm than good. What are some examples of that?

AB: If you have a system which offers high returns for corruption, then that's what people will do. So, for instance, historically there have been rules in India that have granted huge tax breaks to small businesses, and so what people do is to set up a large number of small businesses and forgo the economies of scale that one could get by having one large business.

AK & NS: It sounds like a beneficial thing to do – "go and start a small business." But there's this perverse incentive in place.

AB: Right. I think that if you reduced the level of self-employment in India, that would probably be a good thing. There are something like 30,000 rag-pickers in Bombay who go around the streets picking up rags. Their marginal product is pretty low – but they are entrepreneurs. They are self-employed; they take risks and so forth. But if these people were working in a Nike shoe factory, everyone would be better off, I think.

AK & NS: Do you believe there are lessons from your research that are applicable to other areas such as government bureaucracies or international aid and development agencies and the like?

AB: I think the valuable lesson is not the specific results of the research itself, but rather the importance of actually understanding the [local] context and figuring out in detail what is going on before trying to intervene. The aid organizations really ought to be looking much more closely at the specifics of what it takes to start and grow businesses.

Chapter 6:

FINANCIAL INTERMEDIATION

FINANCIAL INTERMEDIATION IS like plumbing: we take it for granted until something goes wrong. In 2007, the top financial news story was about something wrong in the market for subprime mortgage loans. It became apparent that a few million homeowners might soon be facing foreclosure. Moreover, it became apparent that many financial institutions were more exposed to the costs of mortgage defaults than they realized.

Alan Blinder, a professor at Princeton University and former vice chairman of the Federal Reserve, summarized what happened in a column entitled "Six Fingers of Blame in the Mortgage Mess":

> The first finger points at households who borrowed recklessly to buy homes....
>
> Some lenders sold mortgage products that were plainly inappropriate for customers, and that they did not understand....
>
> [B]ank regulators deserve the next finger of blame for not doing a better job of protecting consumers and ensuring that banks followed sound lending practices....
>
> [M]any investors, swept up in the euphoria of the

223

moment, failed to pay close attention to what they were buying . . . .

[C]ollateralized debt obligations, were probably too complex for anyone's good – which points a fifth finger, this one at the investment bankers who dreamed them up and marketed them aggressively . . . .

Investors placed too much faith in the rating agencies – which, to put it mildly, failed to get it right.[53]

Blinder concluded that even after all of the finger-pointing, the subprime mortgage process, "before it blew up . . . placed a few million families of modest means in homes they otherwise could not have financed. That accomplishment is worth something – in fact, quite a lot."

Many other pundits raise the issue that with subprime mortgages, investors did not know what risks they were taking. They complain about a lack of transparency.

Economics 1.0, particularly as it evolved in the half-century following World War II, assumes that everyone is equally aware of all of the risks being incurred in the economy. If you buy stock in a firm, you know the riskiness of all of the projects that the firm is undertaking. If you have shares in a mutual fund that invests in corporate debt instruments, you know the events that could cause default on that debt and the probability that those events will occur. We might refer to this description of widespread knowledge as *complete transparency*.

From an Economics 2.0 perspective, the assumption of complete transparency, in which any individual knows all of the risks being taken by everyone in the economy, is not merely unrealistic, it assumes away the reason for financial intermediation in the first place. If all of us knew the characteristics of every risky investment project, then Wall Street investment bankers would not be among the highest-paid individuals in the world. In our view, *a lack of complete transparency is built into the basic function of financial intermediation.* The managers of a firm are in a position to know more than the investors about the risks that the firm is taking. This is true of any corporation. Indeed, all firms that have outside investors are financial intermediaries.

The modern mortgage market is multilayered. The mortgage broker knows the specific characteristics of the house being purchased, as well as the borrower's financial data and credit history. Investment bankers funnel funds through brokers, using only summary statistics such as the borrower's credit score, the ratio of the loan amount to the appraised value (known as L T V), and the broker's historical performance with the funding agency. Investment bankers then pool loans together. Banks, mutual funds, and pension funds that buy the pools know only the general characteristics of the pool – the range of credit scores, the range of L T V s, and so on. These pools may be further carved up into "tranches," so that if loans start to default, some investors will take an immediate loss while others continue to receive full principal and interest.

At each step in this layering process, some of the detailed information about the underlying risk is ignored. Instead, investors rely on summary information. It is this use of summary information that makes these investments *liquid* – that is, enables them to be bought and sold by many investors. As an intermediary layer is added, while the amount of detailed risk information is going down, liquidity is going up. The result of this process is that the ultimate borrower – in this instance, the homebuyer – pays a much lower risk premium than would be the case in the absence of liquidity.

What happened in the mortgage market is that for many years the risk premium for mortgage borrowers fell. This lowered the interest rates on mortgage rates relative to benchmark interest rates on government debt. Intermediaries discovered that summary statistics, such as credit scores, could be used to make mortgage loans highly liquid.

Yet the loans themselves were becoming increasingly risky, particularly as home prices rose faster than incomes and borrowers had to stretch harder and harder to make monthly payments. The disconnect between the falling risk premium and the rising underlying risk finally became apparent in 2007, when mortgages began to default in increasing numbers. Suddenly, the risk premium for mortgages – and for other forms of lending – began to retrace its steps, with interest rates rising relative to benchmark rates. The loss of liquidity reduced the availability of funds and raised the cost of borrowing.

For starters, it is important to understand that each layer in the subprime mortgage market specialized in processing different components of information. The mortgage originators (often small mortgage brokers) processed information about each loan. They pulled credit scores on borrowers, in order to evaluate their ability to handle their financial obligations. The originators ordered appraisals of properties, in order to determine the value of the mortgage collateral. They then sold the loans to investment bankers.

The investment bankers pooled many loans together. A large pool of loans behaves more predictably than any one loan. Information about the risk of individual loans is no longer a factor at the pool level. All of the loans in the pool are treated as being of roughly the same risk class.

The investment bankers then split the pool into different "tranches" to be sold to institutional investors, including large banks and pension funds. Some tranches were bearing almost none of the risk of mortgage defaults, because only if there were massive defaults would their return of principal be in jeopardy. Purchasers of the low-risk tranches were particularly well insulated from having to obtain information about the underlying loans. Purchasers of high-risk tranches insisted on high returns. Those returns, however, would only be realized if enough of the mortgages paid off on schedule. With large numbers of defaults, the high-risk tranches failed to return investors' principal.

Investors in mortgage-backed securities had little to go by in terms of past experience. Many of the mortgage products were relatively new. Twenty years ago, most mortgage loans required substantial down payments, often as high as 20 percent. Since then, the required down payment has declined steadily, until it became common to lend money for home purchases with no money down. The mortgages themselves often included gimmicks that deferred the payment of principal. Some of these loans even featured "negative amortization," meaning that the outstanding principal owed by the borrower could rise during the early years of the loan.

Often, the default experience for these high-risk loans was predicted on the basis of the recent performance of other types of loans to borrowers with similar credit scores, notwithstanding the fact that the recent performance of mortgage loans has benefited from rising house prices. It had been a long time since the housing market had experienced a period in which home prices were doing anything other than climbing rapidly, so neither the new loan products nor the credit-scoring-based default models had been through a market downturn.

Investors who were not sure about how to evaluate the risk of the various tranches could look to bond rating agencies, which are firms that classify securities on the basis of default risk. But rating investment securities is not an exact science. And the agencies, like the investors, did not have past experience as a guide, given that the innovative securities were too new to have experienced a full housing cycle. In the wake of the subprime mortgage debacle, some pundits have argued that the rating agencies are more beholden to bond issuers, who pay the agencies' fees, than to the buyers of securities. Yet it is ultimately an agency's reputation with investors that makes its work valuable to firms. It seems more likely that the agencies' failure, if any, was one of bad execution rather than bad intentions.

Investors never know exactly what risks they are taking, and financial intermediation is always imperfectly transparent. Intermediaries manage risks on behalf of investors. Each layer knows something different about the nature of the risk management process. No one player can see it all. The mortgage originator sees the entire application of the borrower; the firm that pools the mortgages might only see the credit score and the ratio of the loan balance to the appraised value of the home (the LTV ratio); the financial engineers who create the tranches might see only the range of credit scores and LTV ratios in the mortgage pool; the rating agency might see only these same pool characteristics; and the ultimate buyer of the tranches might see only the agency rating.

This process is designed to create liquidity by insulating the ultimate investor from the need to evaluate all the risks embedded in individual loans. When investors are comfortable about the insulation provided by intermediaries, they require only a relatively low rate of return in order to compensate for risk. When they are not comfortable, they demand higher returns. For a while, prior to 2007, borrowers who lacked much in the way of savings and who had blemishes in their credit histories were nonetheless able to obtain loans to buy. As of the fall of 2007, however, once the problems in the subprime mortgage market became evident, the returns that investors were demanding had become so high that the market had effectively ceased to operate.

From the perspective of Economics 2.0, the subprime mortgage debacle exposed an important characteristic of financial markets. Riccardo Rebonato, the head of quantitative research at the Royal Bank of Scotland, describes it this way:

There is nothing special about mortgages: a similarly intricate and multilayered story could be told about insurance products, the funding of small or large businesses, credit cards, investment funds, etc. What all these activities have in common is the redirection, protection from, concentration, or diversification of some form of risk. . . . [Intermediaries] reshape the one and only true underlying "entity" that is ultimately being exchanged in modern financial markets: risk.

But there is more. All these pieces of financial wizardry must perform their magic while ensuring that the resulting pieces of paper that are exchanged between borrowers and lenders enjoy an elusive but all-important property: the ability to flow smoothly and without interruptions among the various players. . . . Very aptly, this all – important quality is called "liquidity."[54]

As financial historian Michael Bordo has pointed out, there is a long tradition in economics of looking at the changes in confidence in financial intermediation as a factor in the booms and busts in the economy. Indeed, the subprime mortgage crisis can be understood in these terms.[55] Yet Economics 1.0 has turned away from this tradition, coming to treat financial intermediation as nearly inconsequential. Fifty years ago, Franco Modigliani and Merton Miller, in work that earned them a Nobel Prize, showed that if investors know the underlying risks of the projects that a firm is taking, then they are indifferent as to whether those projects are financed with borrowing or with stock. After Modigliani-Miller, Economics 1.0 tended to treat this assumption of complete transparency as if it described reality.

In Economics 2.0, we emphasize the importance of what is unseen and unknown. In the case of financial intermediation, it is the problem of unseen risks that merits attention.

A financial intermediary undertakes specific investments.

When the managers of the firm raise funds from investors, they provide investors with summaries of risk. The willingness of investors to buy and sell securities based on concise summaries of risk is what creates *liquidity*. If no one will lend money against an asset without first undertaking a detailed analysis of its underlying risk, then the asset is illiquid. Without liquidity, asset markets cannot function. If no one will lend you money to buy a house, then fewer people will buy houses and fewer houses will be constructed.

When a typical corporation acts as an intermediary, it raises funds from investors by issuing bonds, shares of stock, or other securities. The investors assess the risk of these securities on the basis of past performance and high-level summaries of the firm's investments. That makes these securities liquid. Any individual investment projects that the firm is funding, on the other hand, are not liquid.

There are many different types of high-risk investments. For example, aggressive start-up companies – such as Apple Computer, Google, and many not-so-successful companies that were started during the dot-com euphoria of the late 1990s – are typically funded by venture capital. Venture capital firms also use risk-pooling, as well as other techniques, to value risk. Venture capital firms raise money from outside investors, most of whom know little about the risks of the investments that the venture capitalist is making; they only know the track record and reputation of the venture capital firm.

An investor who takes risks expects to earn a higher return. That higher return consists of two components. First, there is what one might call a minimum compensation for risk. Suppose that there are bonds with absolutely no risk of default that I could buy today for $100 and that will be worth $105 a year from now. What is the fair price of another bond that will be worth $110 a year from now if all goes well (say, 90 percent of the time) but will be worth only $60 if the borrower goes sour (say, 10 percent of the time)? On average, this junk bond will be worth ($110 × 0.90 + $60 × 0.10), or $105. If I accept the minimum compensation for risk, then I will pay $100 for this junk bond, and on average I will get the same 5 percent return that I could get on the no-risk bond. (Note that if all goes well, my $100 bond will yield $110, or a 10 percent return.)

Of course, hardly anybody is going to accept just the minimum compensation for risk. If I can get a certain 5 percent return on a bond with no default risk, then I would not pay $100 for a risky bond that on average gives me a 5 percent return. I might pay $98 or $99. In fact, if I am highly risk-averse, I might only pay $75 or $80 for the risky bond. The amount of extra padding that investors demand in the return on a risky investment – beyond the minimum compensation – can be called the additional risk premium. We will refer to this extra padding as simply the risk premium.

Risk premiums are not mathematical constants of the sort that one finds in physics or chemistry. They are not determined mechanically in the way that many variables appear to be determined in mathematical economic models. Risk premiums depend on how well financial intermediaries do their jobs – including how well financial intermediaries *convince* investors that they are doing their jobs.

To see how this works, note that there are two ways that a run on a bank can occur. One way is for the bank to suffer losses and stop paying depositors. Word gets around, and pretty soon a horde of depositors rush in to withdraw their money. The second way to have a bank run is for many depositors to *think* that the bank is suffering losses. Word gets around, and pretty soon a horde of depositors rush in to withdraw their money.

Similarly, there are two ways for a risk premium to go down (or up). One way is for a financial intermediary to come up with a new tool for managing risk. For example, when credit scoring was first introduced into mortgage lending in the early 1990s, it improved the ability of lenders to predict the likelihood of borrower default. This allowed mortgage originators to give investors more precise information about the probability of receiving timely payments of principal and interest. With this better information, investors reduced their risk premium.

Another way for the risk premium to go down is for investors to think that financial intermediaries have gotten better at managing risk. What Alan Blinder calls "the euphoria of the moment" for mortgage security investors may have reflected, in part, an overly optimistic view of the ability of credit scoring to predict default rates. Lenders, rating agencies, and investors apparently failed to take into account the fact that these new mortgage products and credit scoring mechanisms lacked any track record over a period of steady or falling home prices.

In Economics 2.0, we see changes in risk premiums – whether due to financial innovation, market psychology, or some combination of the two – as major drivers of investment. The dot-com euphoria increased investment in both the hardware layer and the software layer of the Internet. In the case of fiber-optic cables and other components of Internet hardware, capacity was built in the late 1990s that is only now coming into full utilization. Many web-based companies were launched, many failed, and the survivors learned how to provide valuable services. In the year 2000, investors suddenly took a more pessimistic view of their ability to handle the risk of the Internet economy, sending the risk premium soaring, and stock prices plummeted. Investment declined sharply in both the hardware and the software layer of the Internet.

We suspect that macroeconomic fluctuations can and often do result from changes in risk premiums. The risk premium as we think of it is not a mechanically determined variable of the sort that is typically found in the macroeconomic models of Economics 1.0. Instead, it follows an unpredictable path, and when it moves adversely it drives down investment.

John Maynard Keynes saw investment demand as driven in part by the "animal spirits" of entrepreneurs. We would substitute "the risk premium" for "animal spirits." In terms of macroeconomic impact, the risk premium works like Keynes's original notion of "animal spirits." Textbook macroeconomics today, descended from a reformulation of Keynes's theories by Nobel laureate John Hicks, includes neither animal spirits nor a risk premium. Modern macroeconomic theory is too mathematical and too mechanistic, and it has no room for factors that are difficult to predict using an equation.

The risk premium changes over time because of the evolution of financial intermediation. Intermediaries develop new processes to manage risk. But financial intermediation is not transparent, so intermediaries cannot immediately convince investors that the innovations work. Over time, investors observe the performance of intermediaries, and the innovations that work gradually acquire the confidence of investors.

It appears to be a common phase of the cycle of innovation for investors to become overly confident about how intermediaries are managing risk. Investors became overly confident about venture capital firms and stock mutual funds during the dot-com bubble; they became overly confident about mortgage intermediaries during the subprime mortgage euphoria. If investors do become overconfident, then at some point reality will prove disappointing. This causes investors to lose trust broadly, and they tend to become excessively pessimistic about risky investments of the type that recently burned them.

This emphasis on fluctuations in the risk premium leads Economics 2.0 to take what might be called a Bernankean view on the causes of the Great Depression, rather than a monetarist view. The monetarist view, developed by Milton Friedman, sees a direct link between the quantity of money and national income. Instead, we would view the closing of banks and the crash of the stock market as having disrupted financial intermediation, raising the risk premium and lowering investment. The idea that financial intermediation has real effects was developed most extensively in his younger academic days by Ben Bernanke, the current chairman of the Federal Reserve Board.

In this view, the creation of deposit insurance may have been the best policy innovation of the New Deal. By preventing runs on the bank, deposit insurance allows banks to perform their function as intermediaries. Individuals require little or no risk premium on their deposits, and banks use this advantage to lower the risk premiums that they charge borrowers.

Deposit insurance is not a costless form of government intervention, however. Deposit insurance creates what economists term "moral hazard." Bank managers can take risks knowing that the government will bail them out if they fail. Depositors, whose money is guaranteed by the government, have no incentive to provide any checks against excessive risk-taking. In the late 1970s, deposit insurance in the United States suffered a crisis stemming from moral hazard. Banks and savings and loans that were insolvent were allowed to remain open, and these institutions had every incentive to gamble, knowing that their depositors' losses were covered by Uncle Sam. In the 1980s, after suffering tens of billions of dollars in losses, the insurance agencies reformed their regulations, and until recently the system appeared to be well run.

By providing insurance to bank depositors, the government injects itself into the process of financial intermediation. The depositor is relieved of having to guess about the quality of the bank's portfolio. Instead, government regulators must take on the responsibility of monitoring the safety and soundness of banks. Until the 1980s, regulators used sloppy practices in performing this function. The regulatory apparatus that included risk-based capital requirements, market-value accounting, and encouragement of securitization was considered an improvement. However, although these were considered necessary for correcting the flaws in the regulatory apparatus of 1980, these features have been counterproductive in the current environment. Yet the natural process of innovation always creates pressure, in the form of new risks undertaken by existing intermediaries or new forms of intermediation that fall outside the regulatory framework.

Economics 1.0 does not tell as rich a story of financial intermediation as Economics 2.0. Instead, intermediaries tend to get written out of the show, like a soap-opera character whose actor has just quit or died. One of the most telling examples of the way that Economics 1.0 writes off financial intermediation is the above-mentioned Modigliani-Miller theorem, which states that regardless of whether a firm finances its capital acquisition mostly using debt or mostly using equity, the overall value of the firm and its risk profile is unchanged. A key assertion of Modigliani-Miller is that investors "see through the corporate veil," meaning that shareholders fully understand the risk of the firm's capital investments. Once one grants that assumption, the theorem is straightforward. To use one of Miller's self-deprecating metaphors, the theorem says that if you can see inside a pizza box, then you realize that regardless of whether it was cut into six slices or eight slices, it's still the same pizza.

If investors can see inside the box, then financial intermediation is meaningless. In the Modigliani-Miller world of perfect transparency between investors and the projects that firms wish to undertake, investment is unaffected by whether firms issue stock or issue bonds. Beyond that, investment is unaffected by whether banks are thriving or closing, or by the existence or absence of venture capital firms, junk bond funds, mortgage securities, and other components of financial markets.

The Modigliani-Miller outlook became enshrined in textbooks in corporate finance. As Rebonato points out:

It is because of the ability of investors to know what individual firms are up to and to achieve diversification by themselves that managers should simply concentrate on finding investments ("trades") whose return exceeds their appropriate hurdle rate – or so, at least, standard investment and corporate finance theory teach: "Remember, a good project is a good project is a good project" correctly intone Brealey and Myers in one of the best-known university textbooks in corporate finance . . . this is the end of the story (and I am out of a job).[56]

According to our Economics 1.0 textbooks, financial intermediaries have no business undertaking risk management. In the Economics 1.0 world of approximately perfect markets and essentially perfect information, investors see all of the risks themselves and manage accordingly. The risk premiums we observe reflect only investor preferences and the characteristics of the underlying investment projects.

Economics 2.0 sees financial markets as operating in a fluid and dynamic environment of imperfect information. Financial intermediaries affect the risk premium by how well they convince investors that they are managing risk. This in turn depends on their ability to find ways to manage risk and on their ability to establish and maintain a track record that persuades investors of this ability.

In our view, there has been a long-term secular decline in many important risk premiums. These include the risk premiums faced by homebuyers, entrepreneurs, consumers, and large firms raising capital. The investments made possible by this long-term secular decline in risk premiums account for some of the increase that has taken place in our standard of living. We think that adopting an Economics 2.0 outlook would lead people to pay more attention to fluctuations in risk premiums. Indeed, we think it is impossible to give an account of major financial events, from the Great Depression to the Internet euphoria and crash to the recent credit cycle in the housing and mortgage markets, without focusing on risk premiums.

Nothing in traditional economics textbooks explains the existence of intermediaries or suggests that they add real value. Yet Wall Street financiers are among the most highly compensated individuals in the entire economy. Something does not add up.

Economics 2.0 does not say that every investment banker deserves his or her high salary. But it does explain how financial intermediaries add value by making it easier to undertake risky investment projects. If investors had to fund these projects directly, risk premiums would be high; that is, investors would require high rates of return, because the risks are difficult to evaluate. When investors purchase securities from intermediaries, they charge a lower risk premium, reflecting their confidence in the intermediaries' ability to evaluate and summarize risks.

To some extent, investors have to take on faith what the intermediaries are doing. Investors' faith in different forms of intermediation can fluctuate on the basis of government policy (such as deposit insurance and financial regulation) or the past performance of the intermediaries themselves. A history of good performance can lull investors into overconfidence, and an episode of bad performance can drive investors into risk aversion. In order for risk premiums to continue to decline, the economy needs intermediaries to innovate while maintaining consistent, effective performance.

In the United States, regulation of financial intermediaries has evolved in ways that help to promote stability. Deposit insurance can protect depositors from bank failures. As we learned in the late 1970s, however, deposit insurance does not *prevent* bank failures. Regulators have to set and enforce reasonable capital standards.

The high default rates on subprime mortgage loans in 2007 may have exposed weaknesses in the current financial regulatory structure. Financial regulation will never be perfect. Regulation that is too stifling would reduce innovation and limit the access to credit of established firms and low-risk borrowers. On the other hand, regulation that is too lenient can allow booms and busts in the credit cycle to get out of hand. The challenge for government policymakers is to find the best middle ground.

Chapter 7:

ADAPTIVE EFFICIENCY AND
THE ROLE OF GOVERNMENT

ECONOMICS 1.0 LOOKS AT the many sources of imperfect markets and inefficiency as providing opportunities for government intervention. Economics 2.0 looks at the economy primarily in terms of its adaptive efficiency – how effective it is at incorporating new recipes and discarding outmoded ones. From that perspective, government regulation tends to be more of a threat than an opportunity.

A cliché has it that generals always fight the last war. Economic actors are prone to the same failure of vision. This can be seen in the high rate of turnover among leading firms.

The table below (on pages 242 and 243) gives the companies that were listed in the Dow Jones Industrial Average in various years since 1907.[57]

The Dow represents the most important stocks in the most important industries at a given time. The only stock to survive in the Dow for the last one hundred years is General Electric. (GE has survived by changing focus. Much of its profits now come from financial services, not from manufacturing equipment that generates or relies on electrical power.) Fifty years ago, steel production was the primary indicator of a modern economy. Today, there is not a single steel manufacturer represented in the Dow.

In their book *Creative Destruction*, Richard Foster and Sarah Kaplan write that "[i]n 1987, Forbes republished its original 'Forbes 100' list [from 1917] and compared it to its 1987 list of top companies. Of the original group, 61 had ceased to exist. . . . Of the five hundred companies originally making up the S&P 500 in 1957, only seventy-four remained on the list through 1997."[58]

In January 1969, the United States Department of Justice filed an anti-trust suit against International Business Machines (IBM). The suit dragged on until 1982, when it was finally dismissed. During that time, the mainframe computer, which was the locus of IBM's alleged monopoly position, began to give way to personal computers, a market in which IBM lacked the agility to compete.

The historical pattern strongly suggests that corporations that are large and important today are unlikely to remain so in the coming decades. Eventually, Wal-Mart, Microsoft, and even Google will meet the fate of Bethlehem Steel, Union Carbide, American Motors, and other once-dominant firms.

Economics 1.0 takes the state of technology as fixed and asks about the efficiency of the existing market structure. Does one firm have too much market power? Are consumers unable to obtain important information? These questions relate to what is called static efficiency.

Economics 2.0 instead looks at dynamic efficiency. Are firms with new and better technology able to enter the market? Are firms with obsolete methods forced to adapt or go out of business?

There is considerable research pointing to the importance of dynamic efficiency. Lucia Foster, John Haltiwanger, and C.J. Krizan, summarizing some previous empirical findings, have noted that the rates of job destruction and job creation are high, with annual rates of more than 10 percent in both categories. Moreover, most of these changes take place within narrow industry groups; a worker is more likely to move from one factory job to another than to shift from factory work to doing computer programming. A major determinant of job shifts is entry and exit within an industry – more efficient firms enter, and less efficient firms disappear. The authors cite research showing that for five-year periods, entry and exit account for 40 percent of job creation and destruction. They argue that this process helps drive improvements in aggregate productivity.[59]

Martin Baily summarized a study conducted by economists at the Organization for Economic Cooperation and Development as follows:

> The study stresses, correctly, the high degree of churning in all countries. The importance of the creative destruction process and market experimentation is clear. Compared to Europe, entering firms in the United States are smaller and of lower relative productivity. If successful, however, they grow employment much more rapidly than entrants in the other countries.
>
> In the policy arena this part of the research supports the idea that excessively stringent regulation in both product and labour markets will hinder growth. It illustrates vividly the constant churning that goes on in markets and shows that even though many European countries have barriers to economic change, the change happens anyway. There is an irresistible force of economic change and industry evolution. These barriers, however, may slow down the pace of innovation and the creation of new employment opportunities.[60]

Once we recognize the importance of entry, exit, and industry change in economic performance, our perspective on the role of government changes. In the world of Economics 1.0, where the state of technology is taken as given and firms are presumed to

Companies Listed in the Dow Jones Industrial Average in Various Years

1907	1927	1959	1987	1999
Amalgamated Copper	Allied Chemical	Allied Chemical	Allied-Signal Inc.	AT&T
American Car & Foundry	American Can	Aluminum Company of America	Aluminum Company of America	Alcoa
American Smelting & Refining	American Car & Foundry	American Can	American Can	American Express
American Sugar	American Locomotive	American Telephone & Telegraph	American Express	Boeing
Colorado Fuel & Iron	American Smelting	American Tobacco	American Telephone & Telegraph	Caterpillar
General Electric	American Sugar	Anaconda	Bethlehem Steel	Citigroup
National Lead	American Telephone & Telegraph	Bethlehem Steel	Boeing Co.	Coca-Cola
People's Gas	American Tobacco	Chrysler	Chevron Corporation	Disney
U.S. Rubber	General Electric	DuPont	Coca-Cola Co.	DuPont
U.S. Rubber (first preferred)	General Motors	Eastman Kodak	DuPont	Eastman Kodak
U.S. Steel	International Harvester	General Electric	Eastman Kodak	Exxon
U.S. Steel (preferred)	Mack Trucks	General Foods	Exxon	General Electric
	Paramount Famous Lasky	General Motors	General Electric	General Motors
	Sears Roebuck & Co.	Goodyear	General Motors	Hewlett Packard
	Texas Company	International Harvester	Goodyear	Home Depot

(Continued)

1907	1927	1959	1987	1999
	United Drug	International Nickel	International Business Machines	Honeywell International Inc.
	U.S. Rubber	International Paper	International Paper	Intel Corporation
	U.S. Steel	Johns-Manville	McDonald's Corporation	International Business Machines
	Western Union	Owens-Illinois Glass	Merck & Company	International Paper
	Woolworth	Procter & Gamble	Minnesota Mining & Manufacturing	Johnson & Johnson
		Sears Roebuck & Co	Navistar International Corp.	McDonald's Corporation
		Standard Oil of California	Philip Morris Companies	Merck & Company
		Standard Oil (New Jersey)	Procter & Gamble	Microsoft Corporation
		Swift & Co.	Sears Roebuck & Co	Minnesota Mining & Manufacturing
		Texas Corporation	Texaco	J.P. Morgan
		Union Carbide	Union Carbide	Philip Morris Companies
		United Aircraft	United Technologies	Procter & Gamble
		U.S. Steel	USX Corporation	SBC Communications
		Westinghouse Electric	Westinghouse Electric	United Technologies
		Woolworth	Woolworth	Wal-Mart Stores

be optimally productive, government regulation represents an opportunity to correct market failures. In Economics 2.0, the tendency of government regulation to benefit incumbents and thwart new entrants means that regulation represents a threat to dynamic efficiency.

Markets can fail in many ways. Nobel laureate George Akerlof came up with a famous example, called "the market for lemons." Suppose that most people who put their used cars on the market do so because they are of low quality. If you have a good used car that you happen to want to sell, buyers are likely to price the car as if it were like all of the lemons on the market. Because you cannot get a fair price for your car, you will be inclined not to sell it. This reinforces the equilibrium in which only bad cars are available in the used car market.

Economics 1.0 sees these sorts of market failures as occasions for government intervention. Economics 2.0 sees them as occasions for market innovation. In fact, a number of services have emerged to address the lemons problem. One may obtain a vehicle history report for a prospective used car purchase. Some used cars are sold with warranties. Some companies deal exclusively in used cars, and these companies rely on good reputations and favorable word-of-mouth in order to achieve sales volume. All of these sorts of services help keep used car prices close to their fair values, even for good used cars.

Government programs also can be flawed. The U.S. Internal Revenue Service and state Departments of Motor Vehicles provide notoriously poor customer service. If it were as difficult to get past voice mail and speak to a person at your bank as it is at the IRS, you would switch banks. If a retailer kept you waiting in line for a routine transaction as long as the typical DMV, you would go to a different retailer. Government does not face competitive pressure, and so it does not fix its problems. Obsolete firms go out of business. Obsolete government programs do not.

One well-known example of a persistent government program is the mohair subsidy. This was first enacted in 1955, supposedly because we needed to ensure an ample supply of wool in case another war broke out requiring large numbers of wool uniforms. This rationale was doubtful then, and it is absurd now. Yet the subsidy could not be killed. The original subsidy was abolished in 1993, but it has been reinstated since.

Larger programs are just as difficult to change. Social Security was enacted when the life expectancy for 65-year-old males was about 50 percent less than what it is today. Still, the 65-year age of eligibility for Social Security and Medicare benefits is sacrosanct, even though actuarial estimates show huge deficits looming for these programs.

There are a number of reasons that governments tend to resist change. First, as with any bureaucracy, the internal dynamics tend to favor those who question innovation and put roadblocks in the way of those with new ideas. We have seen that an intrapreneur adopts the philosophy that "it is easier to ask for forgiveness than to ask for permission." That mindset is strongly discouraged within a corporate or government bureaucracy. There, it is easier to fail conventionally than to succeed unconventionally.

Second, the constituents who are threatened by change tend to be more visible and better organized than the constituents who might benefit from change. Thus, the mohair subsidy's beneficiaries are in a position to lobby effectively, while the taxpayers who would benefit from ending the subsidy are diffuse and unorganized.

Finally, the ability of innovators to engage in "competitive entry" is much lower in the government realm than in the market realm. IBM probably did not want to compete in the personal computer market. Their first choice presumably would have been for such a market never to develop in the first place, and for large mainframes instead to continue to dominate the computer market. But given that other firms had demonstrated the potential for personal computing, IBM had no choice but to enter the new market. When private firms pass on innovation, other firms enter the market and drive them out of business. For government, the option exists to choose whether or not to adapt to innovative possibilities. Sometimes, governments are leaders or early adopters. But they have an equally safe option to ignore innovation.

The traditional approach to regulatory policy is to identify an alleged market failure and then charter a government agency to address the failure. The implicit assumption is that government intervention always works to correct the market failure. However, as Clifford Winston points out in his book *Government Failure versus Market Failure*, the assumption that government policy is successful is usually false. According to Winston, some forms of market failure are not as important as they might appear to be in theory, while poorly conceived or badly implemented government regulations have been quite costly:

> In practice, potential market failures such as market power and imperfect information do not appear to create large losses to the U.S. economy .... [G]overnment policy to correct market failures is characterized by two major flaws – that is, government failures – that cost the U.S. economy hundreds of billions of dollars a year. First, government policy has created economic inefficiencies where significant market failures do not appear to exist, such as with antitrust laws and economic regulations that have raised firms' costs and generated economic rents for various interest groups at the expense of consumer welfare .... Second, in situations where market failures do exist, government policy has either achieved expensive successes by correcting these failures in a way that sacri-

fices substantial net benefits or in some cases has actually reduced social welfare.[61]

The conclusion that one draws from Winston's broad-ranging
survey is that while there are many things that can go wrong
with markets, there are also many things that can go wrong
with government efforts to correct market failure. Market par-
ticipants have imperfect information, but so do government
policymakers. Markets sometimes give individuals and businesses incentives that are distorted from the standpoint of
optimal social efficiency, but legislators and bureaucrats also
face distorted incentives.

Economics 2.0 suggests focusing not on current distortions
but on dynamic efficiency. What sorts of correcting mechanisms exist for the sorts of market failures and government
failures that are bound to occur?

When it comes to dynamic efficiency, we believe that the
advantage lies with markets. Government intervention tends
to interfere with dynamic efficiency. The reason is that incumbents have more political power than upstarts. Incumbent firms
and industries are large, politically sophisticated, and cash-rich.
Innovative firms are small, politically inexperienced, and cash-
poor. Greater government intervention is more likely to benefit incumbents than upstarts. In industries where regulation is
entrenched, new entry is likely to be limited. For example, in
the United States, the automobile industry is very difficult to
enter, given the myriad regulations for safety, fuel economy,
and so forth. William Lewis, in *The Power of Productivity*, documents the regulatory impediments to innovative retailing
that exist in Europe and Japan. The ultimate source of these
impediments is the political power that the traditional stores
enjoy, which they use to enact protectionist legislation and
regulations.

In short, markets empower those with innovative solutions to problems, while government tends to empower incumbents who resist change. Thus markets are often more conducive to dynamic efficiency.

EDUCATION AND HEALTH CARE

In October 2004, Maria Casby Allen, a parent in Fairfax County, Virginia, showed her school board a graph comparing the performance of minority students in Fairfax with that of similar students in Richmond. Three years later, Allen described what she reported:

> [B]lack children in Richmond outperformed not only Fairfax children but their counterparts across the state as well, while children who attend our highly regarded schools in Fairfax are seriously lagging behind not only Richmond but the whole state. The data came as a surprise to school administrators, who were convinced that Fairfax County, because of its high reputation, simply was untouchable.
>
> ... The data that I presented did not create a sense of urgency; in fact, the data seemed too quickly forgotten. So, not much later, I returned to share more bad news with the Fairfax County School Board: other school districts in Virginia that were doing good things were also starting to get good results.
>
> I compared scores of the ten school divisions in Virginia, which were urban as well as suburban, with the largest black student populations ... Fairfax County came out rock-bottom, ten out of ten – or at least, tied for the bottom position – on every single state test taken in elementary school, right across the board. Richmond schools were consistently some of the top performers.

Where are things now, a few years later? Frankly, not much has changed.[61]

What Maria Casby Allen was testifying to is the challenge of what economists call the diffusion process. A new, effective process is developed – in this case, the better practices adopted by Richmond and later copied by other school districts for improving the education of poor and minority students. However, incumbent organizations – in this case, the Fairfax County schools – resist adopting the best practices that challenge the status quo. The gradual diffusion of innovation is a process that has long fascinated economists. In 1957, Zvi Griliches showed that over 25 years the share of hybrid seed in corn production rose exponentially, but the process took off at different rates in different states. He emphasized that economic incentives helped explain the different diffusion rates.[63]

In 1990, economic historian Paul David used the history of the electric motor as an analogy for computers. David noted that the electric motor's contribution to productivity had been slow at first, because it took time to enhance the quality of both the device and the processes that used it. He argued that computers, which at that time were not having a noticeable impact on productivity, would follow a similar path and that the productivity gains would follow as the diffusion process worked itself out. His prediction proved to be correct.[64]

In Economics 1.0, the primary benefit of competition is lower prices. A monopoly holds down the level of output in order to increase prices and profits. In Economics 2.0, the primary benefit of competition is faster diffusion of innovation. Organizations prefer stability to change. It is the pressure of competition that forces them to adopt best practices. Wal-Mart's success with computerized inventory management and logistics forced competing stores to adopt these techniques. Statistical quality control techniques, first developed in America by pioneers such as W. Edward Deming, were not adopted by American automobile manufacturers until they were pressured by Japanese competitors, which had been the first to employ Deming's ideas.

What Maria Casby Allen was finding in Fairfax County is that when an organization, such as a school system, is insulated from competition, it will resist innovations, even when they have been proven effective in similar settings elsewhere. We believe that this provides an important lesson for how government should address education and health care in the future.

Education and health care are services that have many shortcomings. We are a long way from solving the problem of how best to educate young people or deliver health care services. There is much to be learned, and most of that learning will take place by trial and error.

Replacing government-run schools with universal education vouchers would help to introduce the pressure of competition into education. Under a voucher system, all it would take in Fairfax County would be one school willing to experiment with the methods that have been found to work in Richmond. If the experiment were to succeed, then parents would use their vouchers to send their children to the progressive school. That in turn would put pressure on other schools in the county to adopt the better methods. That is how competition spurs the diffusion process.

In health care delivery, government holds back the process of diffusion by regulating medical practice. In theory, a large health maintenance organization could organize health care delivery so that more services are supplied by trained technicians, with doctors and other highly educated staff conducting only the most sophisticated procedures. For example, a trained technician can read a throat culture and prescribe an antibiotic, but most state regulations will not allow this. A trained technician could administer routine physical therapy, but state regulations require advanced degrees.

From an Economics 2.0 perspective, the key to better education and health care is the development and adoption of innovations. Competition spurs both innovation and adoption. Government involvement tends to stifle competition. Over the long run, we will see better results with less government involvement.

Interview with
WILLIAM LEWIS

WILLIAM LEWIS is director emeritus of the McKinsey Global Institute. His book, The Power of Productivity: Wealth, Poverty, and the Threat to Global Stability, *is based on an extensive economic, political, and sociological study of thirteen countries over a dozen years conducted by the Global Institute. In this research, Lewis and his colleagues examined some of the conditions that have led to the disparity between rich and poor countries. His findings about why some countries experience robust growth while others remain stagnant are surprising and insightful.*

ARNOLD KLING & NICK SCHULZ: Describe how you and the McKinsey Global Institute came to do the work that went into this book.

WILLIAM LEWIS: Well, it is unusual that a private-sector firm like McKinsey would do this kind of work, and so that story itself is interesting. The other aspect that is relevant here is that none of us anticipated, when we started the McKinsey Global Institute, that 15 years later we would be looking at a book like this or that I would be talking to you about a subject like this.

The basic idea back in 1990 was that there were several big trends going on in the world that were not very well understood. People were beginning to use the word "global-ization," but it was not very well understood and nobody knew where it might lead. There were other changes as well, maybe more in Europe than elsewhere, with the formation earlier of the Common Market and then the European Union. And then of course the fall of the Soviet Union, cou-pled with a lot of other economic experiences had led to a wave of market reforms around the world. So the question was, what does all of this mean and where is it leading? And for a firm like McKinsey, what are the implications for our clients? Our clients are people who can talk to anybody in the world. You name them, they can talk to them. But they weren't getting answers that were very satisfying, and so they were interested in talking to us. We in turn were being drawn into discussions that we were not prepared to help with very much. We read a little bit more than our clients and we were feeding that back to them, but that only can go on for so long. So we faced the question of either deciding to invest in this knowledge-building that was differentiated from what others could do or getting out of the game. And McKinsey made the strategic decision to get into the game.

AK & NS: What sort of specific work did you set out to do?

WL: It was a step-by-step process. I spent six months traveling around the world talking to my partners and to well-informed people of one kind or another, academics and businesspeople and journalists, about what we should do, but I didn't get a very clear picture from that. Then, serendip-itously, I happened to see one Saturday morning before I dashed off to play tennis those statistics buried at the back of the Economist that show the latest figures on GDP per capita using purchasing power parity exchange rates. What they showed (and this is back in 1990) was that the U.S. still was well ahead of Germany and Japan by that measure. Of course, that was in conflict with all the conventional wisdom at the time, which was saying, basically, that Germany and Japan had come out of the war with superior economic models and that the U.S. was going to have to change or fall behind.

What I realized when I saw those numbers was that if they were right, then the conventional wisdom was wrong. That would be a very, very important thing to get straight for all sorts of reasons. The idea quickly emerged in our discussions that if this is true, given that employment is about the same in many countries, it's got to be a productivity difference; and if the U.S. has a productivity lead, it's got to be in services, because everybody knew that U.S. manufacturing had gone to the dogs. That was the conventional wisdom at that time.

AK & NS: The title of the book came to be *The Power of Productivity*. How did productivity come to loom so large in what you studied?

WL: Productivity is the best single measure of what leads to differences in economic performance. Even though GDP per capita is the all-encompassing measure, GDP per capita is determined primarily, almost entirely, by productivity. People basically work in order to have a place to sleep and something to eat and so on and so forth. The huge differences around the world are the efficiencies with which they work – their productivity. So it is the *power of productivity* that determines what the global economic landscape looks like, and because there are such great differences, we have quite a number of severe issues facing us today.

AK & NS: You say in your book that in order to really understand a country's economic performance, you need to conduct analysis at the level of individual industries and
sectors. Why is that?

WL: Japan is the best example of that. I have devoted a whole
chapter to Japan. I put Japan first because it is in many
respects the most interesting country right now to study
economically.

The paradox was that in the 1990s, the stories on the
front pages of the *New York Times*, the *Wall Street Journal*,
and the *Economist* were all about how the Japanese manufacturing industries, through trade, were driving U.S. manufacturing industries into the ground and virtually wiping
them out. And of course, that did happen in consumer electronics – the U.S. basically got out of the consumer electronics business entirely. And the steel industry and the
automobile industry came very close to going bankrupt.
Although not all companies in those industries were in such
bad shape, the industries as a whole were in very bad shape,
in large part because of competition from Japan, which was
able to deliver high-quality products at lower costs. Yet the
GDP per capita numbers at purchasing power parity
exchange rates showed that GDP per capita in Japan was
roughly 30 percent lower than in the United States. How
could this be? The only way to understand it was to look at
the productivity of individual industries in Japan.

What we found is that Japan has a dual economy. It does
have a select few manufacturing industries that have high
productivity – much higher productivity than the corresponding U.S. industries. In fact, they have the highest productivity in these industries of any country in the world. And
yet, the traded part of an economy is always a tiny fraction
of the total GDP. A rule of thumb is that it is at most roughly

15 percent of the GDP. What that says is that the standard of living is determined – because the productivity of the country is largely determined – by what happens outside these traded goods. The productivity of a country in total, the average productivity, is the average productivity of every single worker. In that sense, every worker is equally important. If you have low productivity in the non-traded parts of manufacturing and in the huge domestic service industry – such as retailing and housing construction – you are going to have low average productivity, even if you have a handful of industries like automotive and machine tools and steel in which you have the highest productivity in the world.

AK & NS: What did you find in the case of Japan?

WL: What we found was that, among its industries, Japan had the highest productivity in the traded-goods manufacturing sectors. In the rest, productivity was very low. In retailing, 50 percent of U.S. productivity; in food processing, about a third of U.S. productivity. And food processing, although it's a manufacturing industry and is not heavily traded, has more employment than steel, automotive, computers, and machine tools put together. So it's much more important.

The way this plays into the debate today is that all these sectors are in the same economy. All the so-called Washington Consensus factors are the same for these sectors – the same exchange rate policy, same monetary policy, same rule of law, same set of governing institutions, same high-quality education system, same infrastructure, same availability of capital. All the factors that the World Bank has said are so important over all these years – up until Bill Easterly and a few others did some serious regressions on this – are the same for these sectors, and yet there are huge differences in their relative performance that end up determining the standard of living in Japan, the GDP per capita. Therefore it is necessarily true that there is something huge going on at the micro-level that has to be taken into account when you try to understand a country's economic performance. Because the macro-level conditions – the macroeconomic stability factors, the budget deficits – are the same for these sectors in Japan. You have to analyze the macro-level factors and make sure they're OK. But that's easy; people understand that already. What they don't understand is that there is another equally important factor or set of factors at the micro-level which are very difficult for anybody to get at.

AK & NS: How can there be such a disparity between the U.S. and Japan in these sectors, such as retailing, in terms of productivity?

WL: When you come to understand retailing, [you realize] that the industry of retailing has gone through its own evolution. Fifty years ago or so, retailing was much more similar all around the rich countries than it is today, in that it was primarily dominated by general stores of relatively small scale and mom-and-pop, small-shop operations. What has happened over the last sixty years is that innovations have occurred in retailing and new formats of much higher productivity than these former formats have developed, the most obvious being the so-called big-box stores, epitomized by Wal-Mart, which has productivity around five times that of a normal general store of the 1950s. So the story in retailing is, how many of these high-productivity formats are in the mix of stores, and how much of retailing is still like it was in 1950. In other words, the evolution in retailing has progressed at far different rates in these countries around the world.

In the U.S., the fraction of mom-and-pop, general-store-like operations that are left accounts for under 20 percent of all employment. In Japan it's still over 50 percent. Even in France this fraction is down to about 30 percent. When you put the mix together, of course, you get a much lower productivity. That's at the operational level. Why is productivity different? It's different because the nature of the retailing operations in the different activities of retailing is fundamentally different on a mix basis.

Then you get to the next level. Why haven't entrepreneurs and managers of capital and others who have invested in retailing, who have created businesses of operations and firms and actual formats in retailing, [managed to do it] at the same rate? Why has it been different? There you get into a huge area of micro-level rules and regulations and incentives for managers, so that basically they end up doing different things.

In the U.S., there is much more level and free competition for meeting the leading consumers' demands. So if Wal-Mart moves into an area, it sets up new operations. Because of its higher productivity, it is able to under-price these much less productive operations. And consumers – as nostalgic as they may be about Main Street and the small shopkeeper and the relationships they have with those people – have shown that they will go for the lower prices. The consumer chooses the more productive format because the prices there are lower, and eventually the less productive format goes out of business and those people or their children end up working elsewhere. A lot of them probably end up working at Wal-Mart. Whereas in Japan, there are all sorts of obstacles.

AK & NS: What kind of obstacles?

WL: The big operations have great difficulty in Japan getting hold of land. The local zoning authorities for a long time banned big-box stores outright, stores of roughly more than ten thousand square feet. That ban was put in place through the political influence of the small shopkeepers and others. The U.S. objected to that and finally got it overturned, but it was overturned in favor of something almost equally ineffective, which set up a lot of environmental and traffic and other potential obstacles, with the [local] boards that determine whether to go forward being dominated by local interests, local producers, local retailers.

I read in the paper just the other day that Carrefour, which is probably the most successful international retailer – it has high productivity, has been in the international game much longer than Wal-Mart, and is successful in most places around the world – has actually just given up on Japan after trying for two decades to build stores and to create what they've been able to create in most other places in the world.

At the same time, there are huge incentives for the mom-and-pops not to close down, to continue to limp along. They come from many directions. First of all, the mom-and-pops simply get subsidized loans. And they have no trouble paying off those loans, because they have been sitting on some of the most valuable real estate in the world, especially during the bubble period. When they die, their estate will have no trouble paying off the loans, so they don't have the cash flow problem they would have if they weren't subsidized through these loans. And there is a strong incentive for them not to sell in the Japanese tax code: capital gains taxes are very high and estate taxes are very low, so there is a huge incentive for these mom-and-pops to hang on to their land and pass it on to the next generation. Those are the main factors that have led retailing to stagnate in Japan relative to the U.S. and even Europe.

AK & NS: One finding that might surprise some people is that the education level of the labor force isn't nearly as important for the overall economic performance of a nation as commonly thought. You say in the book that the importance [of education level] has been "taken way too far" – in other words, that education is not the way out of the poverty trap. How did you reach that conclusion?

WL: By sifting through evidence, primarily from two directions. Interestingly enough, we got the first hint of this when we were studying the U.S. relative to Japan back in the early 1990s, when the Japanese were wiping out the U.S. consumer electronics industry and threatening the steel and automobile industries. The conventional wisdom in the U.S. was that this was true, and that it was in large part true because the U.S. labor force was so bad. There were many disparaging comments made in the U.S., and maybe even stronger ones made abroad (especially in Japan), about how the U.S. labor force was getting what it deserved because it was lazy, uneducated, and maybe even dumb. But of course, the Japanese – the capable, competent Japanese manufacturing companies – showed that this notion was wrong by coming here, building their own factories, managing American labor, and taking a lot of other local inputs and coming within five percent of reproducing their home country productivity.

When we first came out with this conclusion, it really staggered Bob Reich and others. Bob Reich was then U.S. Secretary of Labor and a great advocate of the German apprenticeship system, and he felt that we just needed to train American labor better. We showed that something like 40 percent of the unemployed in Germany had been through the apprenticeship system. But more importantly, you can take the U.S. workforce and train it on the job with sufficiently skilled managers to get within a hair's breadth of the highest productivity in world in these industries. That pattern – and our conclusion, back then, coupled with the fact that the U.S. wasn't behind – got a huge amount of attention and really undermined the initial economic platform on which Bill Clinton was elected.

I am a Democrat, by the way, and I voted for Clinton, but he clearly was wrong about the health of the U.S. economy in his first campaign and in the early days of his being president.

The great bulk of the evidence about education came from competent multinational corporations of any nationality, who showed they could go virtually anywhere in the world and take the local workforce and train it to come close to home country productivity. The clinching evidence [came when] we looked at some other industries. We compared the construction industry in the U.S. with construction in Brazil and found that in Houston, the U.S. industry was using Mexican agriculture workers who were illiterate and didn't speak English. They were not any different than the agricultural workers who were building similar high rises in São Paolo, say. And yet they were working at *four times* the productivity.

Just because people are not educated does not mean that they are incapable, which is a mistake educated people in the West often make – and not just in the West but probably in Japan as well. Uneducated people can be trained on the job to accomplish quite high skill levels and quite high levels of productivity. And that's good news, because if the World Bank and everybody else had to wait until we revamp the educational institutions of all of the poor countries and then put a cohort or two of workers through it, we are talking about another fifty years before anything happens. That's not acceptable and it's not necessary, thank God.

AK & NS: Many people don't realize the destructive power that large government bureaucracies can have on economic development. But there is no anti-government ideology evident in your work. And your comments about whom you voted for speak to that. What experiences led you to this conclusion about the role that the large government and government bureaucracies can have in productivity and economic efficiency?

WL: That's an interesting story. I will try to make it short. We got the first hint of this in Brazil, and then we got conclusive evidence in Russia and, of course, found it to be absolutely true in India. And since then, some other work in other countries have shown it, particularly in Argentina.

The problem we found was that the most productive multinationals in some industries were not going into these countries in the way that we expected them to, or were not expanding in these countries nearly as fast as we thought they had the opportunity to do. We tried to get at why this was, given that their productivity was clearly multiple-times higher than that of the domestic producers they would be competing against. We did interviews with these people, because through McKinsey we know these firms in a different way and we could talk to them.

Our interview with Carrefour in Russia was really a watershed, because Carrefour said, "Well, we know all about Russia. We can handle most of the problems in Russia. We don't have trouble with red tape and bureaucracy. We can handle bribes. We know all about bribes. We can even handle any threat to our physical security. We've been in tough situations and we can make our people feel secure. What we can't handle is not making money. And you can't make money in Russia." And of course, that really left us puzzled. So we went away and built up a model of Carrefour's cost structure in Russia – what it would be – and the cost structure of their competitors. And we found that by and large they were right. Their competitors were able to under-price what Carrefour would have to price at in Russia just in order to break even, let alone make money.

We found that Carrefour's competitors were doing a number of things that Carrefour could not, or would not, do in their business practices. Imports were flooding into Russia and many of the local domestic producers were selling smuggled goods, on which they had not paid import tariffs, and counterfeit goods. McKinsey did a study of the vodka industry in Russia and found that 40 percent of the vodka sold in Russia was not made by the company whose label appeared on the bottle – so much for the value of the brand. And then we looked at taxes. Taxes have to be collected on the final sales price, what the customer pays at the cash register. Carrefour, as with virtually all multinationals, pays its taxes because they cannot afford to do otherwise. And it was not just the profit taxes; it was, in fact, other taxes that made the difference. The sales tax, the value-added tax, the employment tax – all of these would be rolled into what the consumer would pay Carrefour for any given goods or services. When you added all that up and compared it with what their competitors were doing – competitors who by and large were not paying these taxes – Carrefour could not make money. So they were right.

That led to the next question. This problem of competing with so-called informal firms, as these kinds of firms were known, has to have been true for the rich countries at some stage of their development also. When they were poor, how did they ever get over this problem? And you think about it and say, well, I wonder if they got over this problem because it didn't matter. Taxes were so low, because the governments were so small, that it didn't matter if there was this uneven playing field. If [a producer] had productivity four times as high [than its competitors], it could make money even though it paid taxes and its competitors didn't, because the taxes themselves were so low.

We did examine the size of all governments in the U.S. and France when these countries were at roughly the same stage of development as Brazil and Russia are at today. We found that whereas the poor countries are up in the 30-percent range for total government as a fraction of GDP, the U.S. and France were below 10 percent. Basically, it didn't matter.

But then you might say: the rich countries today have high taxes and big government. Why doesn't that matter? The reason it doesn't matter today is that everybody is formal. Informal firms fade out because as you grow, the only way to get high-productivity operations throughout the whole economy is to have it dominated by big firms of scale that have a substantial division of labor, high productivity, and so on. And that means that all firms pay their taxes, and then the playing field is again level, because everybody pays the same fraction of taxes.

The no-man's-land that the poor countries have gotten into now is having gone to big governments before they can afford it, before informality has been phased out or driven out by high-productivity operations so that they can have both big government and informality. That's a recipe for disaster for the reasons I have explained, in terms of the competitive dynamics at the micro-level. You might predict, as a result, that informality is increasing. And sure enough, in my chapter on Brazil, there's a chart [that shows that] informality has been increasing for the last 15 years there. Brazil is going in the wrong direction.

AK & NS: What can a developing country like Brazil do to get out of that trap?

WL: It is a problem because once you are there, as everybody knows from simple kindergarten politics, it's very difficult to cut government services for people. And we look for examples. Our instincts are to look to see who has done this before, rather than to try to think theoretically about how this might be done, how this has been done before. There are four relevant countries – Ireland, Canada, New Zealand, and Chile – that have significantly cut their government. And actually, all of them have been successful afterwards – to different degrees, but they have been successful afterwards. Not only because of cutting government, but because of other things that they have done as well.

However, Ireland, New Zealand, and Canada were already rich countries when they did it, and actually they were forced to do it in large part by the bond market. Canadian debt was approaching junk bond levels, so they were facing a financial crisis, and they had to do it. Chile is the only poor country that has done it. Unfortunately, Chile did it under a military dictatorship. But it did what needed to be done. Chile did what Brazil needs to do. Basically, it went from where Brazil is today to where Japan was in 1950. Japan then had a total government of about 20 percent [of GDP]. And nobody has made a good argument to me that any poor country needs to have a government fraction of GDP of more than 20 percent. Twenty percent ought to be enough, and yet no poor country comes close to it except Chile.

AK & NS: Another problem is that we now have instances where the government itself is actively encouraging the informal sectors in some areas. Isn't that true?

WL: That's certainly true, and it gets wrapped up with other kinds of efforts that are well-motivated but really are not going to lead these countries out of their poverty trap –

efforts such as microfinance, property rights for squatters, and so on. All those things are worth doing, but they are not going to solve the problem. Not as long as the bigger conditions exist and are preventing the rapid formation of a formal sector, where you can benefit from economies of scale and the division of labor and training along particular functional skill lines and so on. That's the way countries get rich.

AK & NS: We hear a lot about competition and trade distortions, subsidies and tariffs and that sort of thing. And certainly they exist in the U.S. and Europe and other developed countries. But another finding from your research that might surprise some people is that the distortions to competition are most severe in poor countries. Is that right?

WL: The distortions to competition in the great width of the economy are more severe in poor countries. As you go to progressively poorer countries, that picture shows up without any question. India probably has the most distorted economy of any major economy in the world now. Even more than the old Soviet Union. Brazil has actually removed a lot of the market distortion. Retailing in Brazil is probably close to being as productive as retailing in Japan. But Brazil has this huge problem of informality, and as a result the more productive enterprises either can't enter the market or cannot enter and grow nearly as fast as they have the potential to do.

AK & NS: When you talk about these more productive sectors and firms, a lot of the time you are talking about large Western multinational companies. You mentioned Carrefour. But a lot of these companies are perceived sometimes in the media, sometimes by NGOs and the like, as threats to

developing countries. But you don't see them as quite as big
a threat to these developing countries.

WL: Well, foreign direct investment is a win-win game. It's a win
for the poor countries, because they get the capital to
expand capacity and produce more goods and services. It's
investment in the country, so it employs local labor. And
local labor is always two-thirds of the cost structure of any
operation, so two-thirds of the value created by the new
firms automatically and immediately goes to local labor
through the salaries that are paid to local labor. And their
productivity is so high that these jobs pay well relative to
what you can make as an informal worker in those countries. That's how wages go up as a result of productivity
improvement, and that's how countries get richer. That's
the growth dynamic; that's how growth actually occurs. It's
people taking more productive jobs, which leads to higher
wages, which then leads to more demand for the things that
people with higher wages want. So it's a winner.

The reason it works is that the consumers in these countries end up getting a better combination of price and service and quality and convenience than they are able to get
otherwise, and so they go to shop at these places. The consumer is better off because the consumer gets a better deal.
Now that is not true in every case, and obviously there have
been some multinationals that have not succeeded. But for
the last couple of decades the story of foreign direct investment has been a win-win story for everybody.

Populism is against this in many of these poorer countries. One of the reasons that [populism] has been successful is because the secret enemies of globalization – and in
particular of foreign direct investment – are the local domestic producers. The multinationals have shown that they can

invest substantial amounts of money to the benefit of the economies, the local economies that I have described, across the globe, without question. And they can operate there at a productivity level significantly higher than that of the local producers, and under-price them, and either drive them out of business or force them to improve in the way that the multinationals operate. The domestic producers are against this because they don't want this competition. No producer – *no producer* – has ever asked for more competition. So these domestic producers are really the secret enemies of globalization and they are exerting a lot of influence against it.

AK & NS: Why are consumer interests so weak, not just in developing countries but also in developed nations? You touch on this in your book when you talk about domestic producers and their political clout. What, if anything, can be done to strengthen the relative status of the consumer to the governing elites and the producers in any country?

WL: I tried to figure this out because the literature on this is actually very weak and there is not much of it. I did have a Yale law school graduate do some research here, and I looked into the literature [to see] what had led to the consumer-rights laws and regulations in the U.S. that are so different from those of almost any other country, and certainly any poor country. And the startling thing that emerged from this, first, was how long ago these laws were actually put in place in the U.S.

As I say in the book, the Sherman Act of 1890 probably had more good, pro-consumer competition policy than most countries in the world have today. And of course, it took a long time for the Sherman Act to work its way through the United States. It had to be followed by the Clayton Act and some other acts and then be interpreted by the courts and the Federal Trade Commission. It was another two or three more decades before we really got pieces of the Sherman Act showing up in the actions of the court. But certainly by the late 1920s and early 1930s, when all the reforms occurred in U.S., we were seeing the benefits of this. The example I often give is that it was in the early 1930s that insider trading became illegal in the U.S. Insider trading didn't become illegal in Germany until five years ago. So most of the rest of the world has lagged.

So then the question becomes, why was the U.S. so far ahead, and why has it taken so long for other countries? Now, this is all relative. Obviously, Europe is much further ahead in many respects than Japan on this. And Japan and Europe are both much further ahead than most poor countries. But now I went back to the really serious students of American history. Gordon Wood at Brown is one of the premier scholars of colonial and Revolutionary America. He wrote this remarkable book, which I read at the time, called *The Radicalism of the American Revolution.* It came out in the early 1990s, I think. It's in my recommended readings list, if you want a reference. Wood showed that at the time of the Revolution, consumerism exploded in the United States. And consumerism was associated with fundamental notions of individual rights. Prior to that, at least in the feudal societies of Europe, consumption was viewed as a luxury to which only the land-owning class was entitled. Everybody else was entitled only to subsistence – enough food and enough shelter to survive, and that was it. But at the time of the Revolution, because the Revolution was so rooted in ideas of individual rights and equality of opportunity and equality of desire and equality of demand, everybody said, "why not me?"

So you suddenly had a few million farmers beginning to

view themselves as consumers. And that thinking didn't have much manifestation then, because we were still primarily an agrarian society for the next one hundred years. But certainly by the time the Industrial Revolution got started, the thinking in this country was so oriented towards consumption and consumers – certainly nothing like it is today, but relative to everybody else – that these laws naturally came into being when there began to be a need for them as a result of the Industrial Revolution and the issues it raised about monopolies, special interests, influence on government, special privileges, and so on. Basically, the U.S. was ready, and it was this political philosophy of individual rights that was so important. It is also important in England, of course, and competition law is probably more advanced there than anyplace else, maybe as advanced as in the United States. So it has spilled over to other places.

But the other side of the coin, the modern thrust that conflicted with this so strongly in the first half of the twentieth century and even to mid-century, was the thrust of planning, as I will call it. The Soviet Union illustrated this to the greatest degree, with its fully centrally planned economy. It is interesting how many economists, how many intellectuals, how many people really thought that planning was the way to create a superior economy, because smart people could just figure out what should be done.

I think I have in the book this great quotation from Gunnar Myrdal, from right after he won the Nobel Prize. It must have been back in the 1950s. He said, "What the poor countries or the developing countries need is super planning." That kind of thinking just permeated the poor world and, also, the development institutions. There were vestiges of that thinking left in the middle 1970s when I was at the World Bank, and it still echoed around in Delhi when we were there working on India. Nehru was a great admirer of the Soviet central planning system. He and the leaders in India thought, and in some respects they probably still think, that at least some of them are smart enough to figure out how all this should happen.

And of course, the way you make a plan happen is by having a plan for production, not for consumption. There is no way you can plan or affect the individual choices that people make as individuals when they buy things, but you certainly can affect strongly what they have to buy through production planning. So this whole producer orientation was aided and abetted in modern times by the planning idea. It's easy to see where the idea came from in feudal times – basically, the landowners and the people who owned the capital could control what happens. They were the only ones who had the ability to do anything. This whole battle for individual rights, for political philosophies based on individual rights, and for what immediately comes from those political philosophies – namely, the idea of consumer rights – has expanded around the world to a relatively small degree.

And yet, as you can tell from my argument, that's the only way I can see for the grip of special interests and privileges that is holding back so many of these poor countries – and some of the rich countries – to be broken. The only way it can be overcome is through this notion of consumer rights, because democracy is necessary but not sufficient. It is necessary because it's the only way you can effect change of this kind, but it is not sufficient because democracies have a weakness that lot of people have always recognized: a majority, or an effective majority, can gang up on the minority and, for short- or medium-term gain, can actually extract privileges or special benefits compared with what the other group gets. In Japan, the LDP [Liberal Democratic Party] is a great example of that, even in a democracy. For fifty years, it governed from a coalition of small retailers – the mom-

and-pop shops, the small farmers, the backward construction industry, the doctors and the lawyers. [This coalition] really ganged up on – as I say when I talk about this – the Tokyo housewife, who really gets screwed as a result of this system. And it just gets worse if you go to poor countries.

The way to break that, if you put any stock in the U.S. example, is for politicians (given conditions like that of the U.S.) to learn that they can be successful politically by campaigning on behalf of consumers. Those consumers are a majority. They are the other cross-cutting majority. There is enough evidence in U.S. political history, not just early on but through Franklin Roosevelt and even John Kennedy, that they had a clear consumer orientation. In fact, I have this quotation from Kennedy in the book, from when he was campaigning for president; he said on national television something to the effect that "the consumer is the only person in Washington without a high-powered lobbyist. I intend to be that lobbyist." And Roosevelt had a more eloquent, detailed quotation that I have in there as well. That's the reason I end up saying this business of becoming rich is not easy; it's amazing that anybody does. And we are in for a very difficult fifty-year period as a result of the complexity and the difficulty of doing better economically.

Chapter 8:

CHALLENGES FOR THE FUTURE

THE PERSPECTIVE OF Economics 2.0 points to three fundamental challenges for the future:

1. Determining the status of intellectual property.

2. Achieving a peaceful transition from underdevelopment to modernity.

3. Adapting to technological advances in surveillance capability, bio-engineering, artificial intelligence, and virtual reality.

INTELLECTUAL PROPERTY

Two of the most prominent corporate legal battles of the early Internet era involved defendants accused of giving away something for free. Microsoft was charged with anti-trust violations for giving away a free copy of its web browser, undercutting rival Netscape. Napster, a music file-sharing service, was accused of contributing to copyright infringement by making it easy for consumers to upload and download copyrighted music for free.

These cases epitomize the challenge of dealing with an economy in which value increasingly comes from the software layer rather than the hardware layer. The material portion of our GDP is declining, and the intellectual portion is increasing. This trend serves to increase the importance of intellectual property. Yet the question of whether intellectual property ought to have the same status as tangible property is quite unsettled.[65]

One can make a compelling case for strong laws protecting intellectual property. John Locke, the philosopher who influenced America's founders, argued that man's natural right to physical property comes from "mixing his labor" with the land. One can argue that if property rights derive from mixing one's labor, then property rights apply as much to the intangible fruits of labor as to its tangible output. According to this view, those who mix their labor to compose or record songs are entitled to a copyright. Similarly, tinkerers who mix their labor in order to invent a new product or process are entitled to a patent. Copyrights and patents on intellectual discoveries are the equivalent of titles to land or physical goods.

However, one can also make a compelling case that laws to protect intellectual property are not natural, and that they promote disorder rather than order. They can create conflict where none existed previously. With tangible property, potential conflict exists whenever two people want to use the same thing at the same time. For example, two people cannot farm the same land at the same time. In economic jargon, we say that land is rivalrous, meaning that you and I are potential rivals over land. Similarly, we are potential rivals over a particular hamburger, a particular car, or a particular doctor's time. Tangible goods and services are rivalrous.

Ideas are not rivalrous. I can use a formula, listen to a song, or follow a recipe without interfering with your ability to do so at the same time. I do not have to engage in physical trespass or violence in order to use one of your ideas. If someone takes the book you are holding away from you, they are depriving you of something. But that is not the case if someone unobtrusively stands over your shoulder and reads the book.

Indeed, it can be argued that while tangible property rights serve to *limit* disputes in situations where they might otherwise occur, intangible property rights *create* disputes unnecessarily. It is the person who presses a claim to intellectual property who must engage in physical trespass. I have to stop *your* printing press from printing a book. I have to stop *your* computer from downloading a song. Thus, intellectual property rights seem to confer a sort of reverse property right that diminishes the tangible property rights of others.

Confusing the issue further is the existence of systems that control the use of copies of software, music, or other creative works that are distributed digitally. These systems, sometimes referred to as Digital Rights Management, are privately created mechanisms for crippling a user's ability to copy ideas from one computer to another. The problem with these systems is that rights can be transferred, in effect, by the act of figuring out how to get around the protection mechanism.

There are also contractual mechanisms for managing intellectual property. We can say that your purchase of this book gives you a license to read and share the book but not a license to make extensive photocopies of it. The problem is that I have no contractual relationship with somebody who reads the book over your shoulder, memorizes it, and then proceeds to print and copy it.

Another way to look at intellectual property is from a utilitarian perspective. If we were trying to create incentives for creation and distribution of ideas, how would we structure incentives for the greatest social good?

Unfortunately, this approach does not give a clear answer, either. If the cost of distributing or copying an idea is zero, then a price of zero gives the right incentive to users. Yet if creative works command a price of zero, there is no incentive to invest resources in creating those works in the first place. Information wants to be free, but people need to get paid.

When the distribution cost of a good is zero, all of the social cost is associated with the production of the initial unit. It costs a music group time and resources to compose and record one copy of a song. But all subsequent copies have zero marginal cost. If the price to download the song is set to be equal to the marginal cost (which is the traditional efficiency condition from Economics 1.0), then the creator cannot recover the upfront cost in writing the song.

Pharmaceuticals represent a similar problem. It may take hundreds of millions of dollars to develop and test a variety of molecules, take some of them through clinical trials, and find one that is safe and effective. Subsequently, however, the marginal cost of each pill manufactured to deliver the molecule may be pennies. Is the price per pill socially optimal if it is set at pennies (the price that is equal to the marginal cost) or at hundreds of dollars (the price that may be needed to enable the manufacturer to recover the costs of research, development, and testing)?

The issue is further complicated by the fact that there are alternative mechanisms by which the creators of information "goods" can recover costs. (See Carl Shapiro and Hal Varian's book *Information Rules*.) One method is bundling. Microsoft bundles its software in new personal computers, which simplifies the task of getting paid for software. But the bundling issue is exactly what vexes competitors. Netscape did not want a free web browser to be included in the operating system bundle sold by Microsoft.

Another method for recovering the cost of information goods is through advertising. Many publications and services on the World Wide Web are supported by ads. This allows the creators to distribute the information for free (satisfying the condition of setting the price to equal the marginal cost) while recovering their costs of collecting and organizing the information.

One broad alternative to restrictive patents and copyrights would be for a patronage model to support the development of new recipes. For example, the fans of a particular musical group could form a club that offers rewards to the band for producing new recordings. People with friends or family members afflicted with a particular ailment could form an association that offers subsidies for research and prizes for discoveries that lead to treatments for that ailment.

Overall, what is called for seems to be a pragmatic rather than an ideological approach to intellectual property. It seems both utilitarian and just to reward in some way those who undertake considerable investment and effort to discover a new recipe, such as a new pharmaceutical. On the other hand, it seems foolish to reward somebody for merely coming up with a good suggestion, such as allowing people to handle email over a cell phone network or having a web site store a consumer's credit card data and shipping information so that the next time they order something at the site the consumer can order more easily. The latter two are examples of actual patent fights that involved Blackberry (accused of infringing) and Amazon (who accused others of infringing), respectively.

Aggressive enforcement and frequent resort to the legal process to resolve issues of intellectual property would not appear to be a desirable direction in which to head. Instead, it would seem that the more use we can make of alternative approaches to rewarding creativity, the better.

* * *

THE TRANSITION TO MODERNITY

The most successful economies have been those in which people have been most willing to accept and promote change. Poverty tends to be concentrated in countries where people and cultures tend to resist change. This means that those countries will either remain backward economically or confront difficult social tension.

Amy Chua, in her book *World on Fire*, documents how the rapid introduction of democracy and capitalism can produce violent ethnic strife. If a minority ethnic group achieves economic dominance, the majority may use its political power to install a demagogic ruler who seeks to redress the economic imbalances by force. Examples include the Indonesian nationalization of Dutch firms under Sukarno, the oppression of Tamils in Sri Lanka, the confiscation of farms owned by whites in Zimbabwe, Hugo Chávez's attacks on the political and economic status of those with European rather than native-American features in Venezuela, and anti-Semitic nationalizations in various countries.

EXTREME TECHNOLOGICAL ADVANCE

Looking ahead, Ray Kurzweil and other technologists foresee what we might call extreme technological advance. From a purely economic perspective, this should produce unprecedented increases in productivity and improvements in living standards. However, the potential for social dislocation could be correspondingly large.

One example of a disruptive technology is surveillance. The demand for surveillance is being driven both by a desire for convenience and by concerns about terrorism. For the sake of convenience, many drivers have installed transponders in their cars in order to get through toll booths more quickly. For the sake of convenience, many cell phones have GPS systems, so that their locations can be determined by emergency responders. For the sake of convenience, shipped packages are given radio-frequency identification (RFID) tags, which enables them to be tracked. Because of concerns about terrorism, people routinely expect to be scanned before boarding planes or entering certain buildings, and surveillance cameras are becoming more widely used.

On the supply side, surveillance technology is getting cheaper. RFIDs, cameras, and data mining are all much less expensive than they were a decade ago. As David Brin argued in *The Transparent Society*, there is no way to undo the technological progress in surveillance capability through attempts to ban its use. We need to adapt culturally to the ready availability of surveillance technology.

For those of us concerned about civil liberties, the best defense, Brin and others argue, is to "watch the watchers." Whenever organizations, particularly government agencies, use surveillance technology, other organizations should be conducting audits of the surveillance systems. Misuse of these systems needs to be brought to light.

Bio-engineering is another field that offers both opportunities and threats. Over the next few decades, it may prove possible to design organisms that improve energy efficiency and production, clean up pollution, or perform other productive functions. By the same token, though, it would then be possible to manufacture harmful organisms, and this represents a threat that must be addressed – which is another reason to expect governments to rely more heavily on surveillance technology.

Bio-engineering also may allow humans to modify our brains and our bodies in radical ways. We may be able to slow or eliminate cell decay, extending healthy life. We may be able to improve our stamina, our memories, and our moods. Of course, the desirability of these changes is something that can be debated.

Artificial intelligence could accelerate productivity growth. Computers that can process natural human language, including body language, would be able to interact with humans more quickly and effectively. Computers that can anticipate and predict our needs and our actions could help us be more efficient. However, such technology might also be used by some individuals or groups to exercise stronger control over others.

Virtual reality, finally, may serve to enhance both entertainment and long-distance communication. One wonders, however, whether people will lose themselves in virtual worlds and forget about the natural one.

Interview with

WILLIAM BAUMOL

WILLIAM J. BAUMOL is the academic director of the Berkley Center for Entrepreneurial Studies and the Harold Price Professor of Entrepreneurship and Economics at New York University Stern School of Business. Professor Baumol's primary areas of research include economic growth, entrepreneurship and innovation, industrial organization, antitrust economics and regulation, and the economics of the arts. He is author of more than forty books, including Good Capitalism, Bad Capitalism, and the Economics of Growth and Prosperity *(with Robert E. Litan and Carl J. Schramm) and* The Free-Market Innovation Machine: Analyzing the Growth Miracle of Capitalism.

ARNOLD KLING & NICK SCHULZ: You argue in *The Free-Market Innovation Machine* that entrepreneurs don't just appear or disappear, but are allocated by economic conditions and circumstances into or out of activities that are of greater or lesser productivity. How did you come to this conclusion?

WILLIAM BAUMOL: The answer is that to the best of my ability, I looked through economic history. I might also say that

I have gathered some of the world's leading economic historians to produce a series of essays describing the circumstances of the entrepreneur in different societies.

AK & NS: This is something you're doing right now?

WB: That's right. The two co-editors along with me are David Landes and Joel Mokyr, who are clearly among the leading lights in the field. And we're getting all sorts of fascinating and surprising results.

For example, one preliminary result is that entrepreneurship was encouraged much more by the institutions in Mesopotamia than it was in Rome. And this [next part] may particularly delight you. Abraham Lincoln gave one set of lectures before he became president. He repeated the same lecture over and over again, and it was on innovation and technology. He knew, as most of our contemporaries do not, that the Romans had discovered how to make, and indeed had actually constructed, a working steam engine. Heron of Alexandria, whose precise dates are not known, produced it. Lincoln said, what is extraordinary is that all the Romans did with it is treat it as a toy, whereas anyone today – that's in Lincoln's day – knows what wonderful things a steam engine can do. And that's exactly the role of entrepreneurship.

The thing is, it's hard to get statistics about entrepreneurship, because different entrepreneurs do different things. You can't use the usual metric analysis. So you're driven to examine the history, and that's exactly the sort of evidence that I tried to accumulate.

AK & NS: You mentioned that Mesopotamia did a better job of encouraging entrepreneurs than Rome did. What was it about Rome? They had this invention of the steam engine, but they treated it like a toy. Why?

WB: The answer is simple. In Rome, it was considered very good to be wealthy and very honorable to acquire wealth. And that's what Julius Cæsar went out and did. And the best and most honorable way to acquire it was aggressive warfare, ransom, blackmail, usury . . . I can go on naming these things that were considered highly respectable. What was considered totally disgraceful was to take such a thing and use it in commerce or production. That was something that was not nearly as profitable as conquering a province, and it led you to be sneered at, to say the least. That sort of activity was left to the children of freed slaves.

So those children, as soon they got any money, they got out of that business as quickly as they could, it was so disgraceful. There was more money to be made in military activities, and there was more honor to be gotten. It's the old Willie Sutton joke: they rob banks because that's where the money is.

AK & NS: You've argued in the past that the most promising way to stimulate productive entrepreneurial activity is to reduce the rewards for unproductive or rent-seeking activity – the kind that you were just talking about in ancient Rome. Do you still believe that? And if so, would you say that we're doing a good job of that in the United States?

WB: In a historical context we're doing a relatively good job, but we still have a long way to go. We don't have corruption problems of the scale you find in the Muslim countries, in China, and so on. We don't have the powerful bureaucracy that you have in India, where bribery becomes the only way to get things done. In those senses, we're doing a good job. But there's still plenty of room here to make money through pointless litigation. There's plenty of room to make money by surrounding patents with slightly modified patents, so that technical knowledge cannot be used by others when it legitimately should be. I can think of many examples where there is much room for improvement.

AK & NS: You believe that large firms can't leave innovation to chance. This is one of the main themes of some of your research: [large firms] must pursue innovation to survive. You write about this in the context of oligopolistic competition, but what about firms in a monopoly position?

WB: They're not under nearly such pressure to innovate. The data, such as they are – they are highly imperfect – suggest that neither at the highly monopolistic end of the spectrum nor at the highly competitive end do you get as much research and development effort relative to revenues, or to whatever standard you want to use, as you do at the level of the large but competing firms.

AK & NS: With largely knowledge-based industries, and in a world of increasing returns, do you think that over time there will be a tendency towards monopoly? And do you see this as a problem? Or are there other forces at work that make that not as much of a risk or a problem?

WB: Over the whole of the twentieth century, there is no evidence of any significant change in concentration, less or more. It ended up almost exactly where it had begun. There are many reasons [for this], but in terms of what I'm focusing on, the primary reason is that although the firm that gets an innovation first may indeed gain power over the market, other firms keep trying, and [eventually] innovators come in and take away the market. If you take a list of the giant firms of fifty years ago, you'd be surprised how many of them have fallen behind.

AK & NS: Is it fair to say that you're less bothered by the existence of oligopolistic firms and oligopolistic competition than some others who fear that economic power is too concentrated?

WB: The answer is yes, I am. I do think that the antitrust laws are very important, that you have to watch out, because I've seen plenty of cases of abuse. Under certain circumstances, collusion in decision-making is obviously drastically dangerous for the public interest. But in other cases, it is essential. It is essential for the public interest that every major computer producer exchanges technology with every other major computer manufacturer. Because that means that when you buy your laptop and it's using a new chip and a better screen and a better keyboard – and each of those was invented by a different firm – this means that the one that you buy will have all three of them.

It's not that oligopolistic firms are all good or all bad. They do certain things better than other enterprises, and other things worse. Our job, if we're working for the public interest, is to be selective, to work against the one and not impede the other.

AK & NS: How widespread or large, would you say, is the problem of proprietors of technology and useful knowledge withholding that technological information? There's a perception that if somebody is given a patent or a copyright and has monopoly protection, they may not have the incentive to disseminate it widely. And yet, in some of your

research, you found that the picture is a little more complicated. Can you talk about that?

WB: Yes, certainly. The basic difference is between what economists refer to as complementary and substitute innovations. If you are a drug company and you're putting out a
headache remedy, and I'm working on a headache remedy
that is cheaper and a little better than yours, I'm going to
keep it secret, because it's a case of winner-takes-almost-all.
Whereas if you are working on computer memory and I'm
working on screens, then we're both better off if I let you
have my technology and you let me have yours, because
your invention enhances the value of mine and my invention enhances the value of yours. That's what we call complementary innovation. And that's why you get a huge
amount of technology exchange in the computer field and
much more reservation in the pharmaceutical field.

AK & NS: So there are some instances where firms don't
have an incentive to disseminate their technologies.

WB: Yes, that's right.

AK & NS: What's the best way to encourage them to do so,
or have we done that? Have we done a good job of encouraging them to do so without a corresponding degradation
of their incentive to produce new knowledge and new technologies?

WB: My impression is that we don't have to do much in the
case of complementary technologies, and there's a special
reason why not: in the complementary technologies, there
is the very important problem of compatibility. You want
your electric plug to fit into my socket. So these firms do it

not out of love or goodwill, necessarily, but because they're afraid that if there is no coordination and exchange, you will build a plug that captures the market and it won't fit my socket.

I've published an article in the *Antitrust Law Journal* in which I say that in an ideal world, I would consider requiring the licensing of technology at a price that fully compensates the licensor. And I give a formula for that price, which is a little more complex than we can discuss here. I don't think there's any immediate prospect of this happening. But I would strongly support a change in the law which would say that all patented technology should be licensed to any user on terms that fully compensate the inventor. In other words, give the inventor as much of a return as he would have earned if the other firm were not using the technology.

AK & NS: So the license is made available immediately, and you figure out how much the inventor would make over the life of the patent?

WB: Essentially, the formula gives you what the patent would make per unit. Suppose a patent is used to manufacture widgets. The formula asks how much more you would make per widget if you were the only user of that particular widget-producing machine. And that's what your competitors have to pay you each time they use it. That means that any competitor who is more efficient at using it than inventing it will find it profitable to license it from you. And you will be likely to make even more money than you would have made yourself.

AK & NS: Are there any other changes to intellectual property laws that you would advocate, changes that would yield greater and wider dissemination of technology and knowledge but would not reduce the incentives for investing, creating, and finding those technologies and knowledge?

WB: Well, there is some reason to believe that the Japanese patent rules have pushed things in the right direction by making it less safe than it is in the U.S. if you don't license and safer if you do. For example, when last I looked, they required immediate publication of all of the technical details of an item put up for patent, whereas we require disclosure only once the patent is granted. That means that if you are applying for a patent and you're worried that somebody will invent something close to it on the basis of what you've revealed, your best bet is to make an arrangement [first] to let them use your invention. So there are a variety of things that would move things, in my view, in the right direction – that would, as you put it, retain the incentive for inventive activity while encouraging the elimination of the obsolete through easy dissemination.

AK & NS: You claim that there's evidence that innovative industries, overall, do not earn extraordinary profits relative to other industries. What's the data or evidence supporting that conclusion, and is it a robust finding?

WB: There have been a number of studies that suggest this, data analyses of the returns to investment in the computer industry, taking account of the Bill Gates returns on one end and the ones that went bankrupt on the other. If you average them out, they come out very near to the lowest competitive level of return – a positive return, but nothing to brag about. There have been other studies that confirm the relatively low earnings both of the innovative oligopoly firms and the individual innovators and entrepreneurs. These are statistical returns-calculations of various sorts.

AK & NS: You compare the free market capitalist structure to a machine – you call it the free market innovation machine. And you say that it produces innovation and growth. You claim that the inherent structure of free market capitalism means that it will grow more powerful and productive over time. Is that right? And if so, why?

WB: You may quote me as saying that my one confident prediction of the future is that it will surprise me. I do not predict what's going to happen. What I hope I said is, I see no reason for any slowdown in the process. The mechanism is such that it may very well not only continue but grow more powerful.

AK & NS: What is it about the mechanism that might permit it to grow more powerful?

WB: Because it's a ratchet mechanism. If there are five firms competing in new models of their products every year, they tend to spend about the same amount year after year, until one of them makes a breakthrough. When it makes the breakthrough it pours money into [the product], but then its competitors have to match it. That gives you a new level of research and development spending. And that, in turn, continues until somebody else makes a breakthrough. So it moves upward; it's very difficult to move downward.

AK & NS: What, in your view, are the primary threats to a robust free market machine?

WB: Clearly, continued opportunities for rent-seeking. The standardization of the education process, which teaches everyone to think the same way. I mean if you compare the American system of higher education with that of Europe and the Far East, you'll see that we do much less of that than the others do.

AK & NS: At a higher education level?

WB: Yes. The one piece of evidence there is the fact that in the international map of physics competition, the U.S. always comes out number 27 or 19 or something unworthy like that. And yet, year after year the Americans win more than half of the Nobel prizes. Think of the fact that the Wright Brothers didn't go to high school. That Edison dropped out of school, I believe, at twelve. That Faraday had no formal education.

AK & NS: And you mentioned Lincoln as well.

WB: That's right.

AK & NS: So maybe the lesson is, don't go to school. [*laughter*]

WB: Well . . .

AK & NS: Just kidding.

WB: I know. But it's interesting: at the beginning of the nineteenth century, these [innovators] were dropouts from elementary school. Now they're dropouts from college, like Bill Gates, because the technology is getting more complicated. So you do need some underpinning.

AK & NS: You argue that 20 percent of the total economic benefits contributed by new products and new technology go to the individuals who have invested directly or indirectly in that innovation. That's a "spillover" rate of about 80 percent, is that right?

WB: That's right, but I'm wrong.

AK & NS: Tell me about your being wrong, and then I'll ask you if we know what an optimal spillover rate would be.

WB: We don't. But William Nordhaus has done a very ingenious calculation. His calculation is that less than 3 percent remains with those who have contributed to the innovation.

AK & NS: So your very conservative estimate was 20 percent, but it's really more like single digits.

WB: Yes. And I will admit that it was cowardice on my part, because my crude reckoning led me to say that it was about 8 to 10 percent. And I thought, gee, that's a small number. So I [interpreted] the curve in a conservative direction, evidently wrongly.

AK & NS: Let's say it's 3 percent. Take off your economist's hat for a second, and put on your man-in-the-street hat. Is this a good thing? Or should we want it to go more in one direction or other?

WB: I'll put it this way: I have no strong reason to argue that it's either too low or too high. It doesn't seem too low – look at the rate at which new products are entering the market. It's not too high, because what underlies it is that the bulk of the benefits have gone to raise the standard of living of the general public. And I think we can bear even more improvement in the overall standard of living.

AK & NS: Do you think that the Internet is a big deal in terms of opening up innovation opportunities? For example, does it make small entrepreneurs unusually powerful? Or is their situation relatively unchanged from what it was?

WB: I think it adds a great deal of opportunity, but I'm no expert in the field.

AK & NS: Some of your important work focuses on the process of entry and exit in a market. What conditions for entry and exit are necessary or efficient for healthy economic growth?

WB: Mostly the absence of impediments to entry – legal [barriers], unnecessary and costly licensing, opportunities for incumbents to harass you through litigation. It's really the elimination of any artificial burdens that are imposed on the entrant. If you want to go one step further, government guarantees of bank loans to promising entrants.

AK & NS: And on the exit side, in the education sphere, you have almost no exit.

WB: Yes.

AK & NS: You pointed out that innovative entrepreneurs do not work in the stable heterogeneous markets that the standard economic models describe. Where does the study of entrepreneurship, innovation, and growth belong in the economics curriculum?

WB: I think it belongs at the very beginning. And I'm working on providing the materials right now. I think the innovation and growth are much more important for the state of the economy than things like monopoly and tariffs.

Notes

1 J. Bradford DeLong, *Macroeconomics*. McGraw-Hill Irwin, 2002. Chapter 5, "The Reality of Economic Growth: History and Prospect."

2 Ibid.

3 Robert William Fogel, *The Escape from Hunger and Premature Death, 1700–2100*. Cambridge University Press, 2004.

4 Ibid.

5 William Nordhaus, "The Health of Nations: The Contribution of Improved Health to Living Standards," in *Measuring the Gains from Medical Research: An Economic Approach*, eds. Kevin Murphy and Robert Topel. Chicago: University of Chicago Press, 2003.

6 Fogel, *Escape from Hunger and Premature Death*.

7 Deary, Ian J., *Intelligence: A Very Short Introduction*, Oxford University Press, 2001.

8 Fogel, *Escape from Hunger and Premature Death*.

9 Ibid.

10 William Nordhaus, "Do Real-Output and Real-Wage Measures Capture Reality? The History of Lighting Suggests Not," in Timothy F. Bresnahan and Robert J. Gordon, eds., *The Economics of New Goods*, Vol. 58, 1997, pp. 29–66. http://cowles.econ.yale.edu/P/cp/p09b/p0957.pdf.

11 Gregory Clark, *A Farewell to Alms: A Brief Economic History of the World*. Princeton University Press, 2007.

12 Stephen L. Parente and Edward C. Prescott, *Barriers to Riches*. MIT Press, 2000.

13 Peter C.B. Phillips and Donggyu Sul, "Economic Transition and Growth," Cowles Foundation Discussion paper 1514, June 2005.

14 Lant Pritchett, "Forget Convergence: Divergence Past, Present, and Future," *Finance and Development*. World Bank. http://www.worldbank.org/fandd/english/0696/articles/090696.htm.

15 David R. Henderson and Charley Cooper, "The Top One Percent Includes You," TCSDaily.com, May 20, 2004. http://www.tcsdaily.com/article.aspx?id=052004D.

16 Kirk Hamilton et al., *Where is the Wealth of Nations? Measuring Capital for the 21st Century.* The World Bank, 2006.

17 DeLong, *Macroeconomics.*

18 William Easterly, *The White Man's Burden: Why the West's efforts to aid the rest have done so much ill and so little good.* Penguin Press, 2006.

19 Ibid.

20 Ibid.

21 The original source for this data is Thorsten Beck and Ross Levine, "Legal Institutions and Financial Development," NBER working paper 10417, April 2004. http://cori.missouri.edu/pages/seminars/beck-levine.pdf.

22 Easterly, *The White Man's Burden.*

23 William W. Lewis, *The Power of Productivity.* University of Chicago Press, 2004, p. 235, 239.

24 Simeon Djankov, Florencio Lopez de Silanes, Rafael La Porta, and Andrei Shleifer, "The Regulation of Entry," World Bank Policy Research Paper No. WPS2661. http://econ.worldbank.org/external/default/main?pagePK=64165259&piPK=64165421&menuPK=64166093&theSitePK=469372&entityID=000094946_01091104014189.

25 Ibid., pp. 26–27.

26 Friedrich Schneider, "Size and Measurement of the Informal Economy in 110 Countries Around the World," World Bank Policy Research Paper, July 2002. http://rru.worldbank.org/Documents/PapersLinks/informal_economy.pdf.

27 Jeremy Greenwood, Ananth Seshadri and Mehmet Yorukoglu, "Engines of Liberation," *Review of Economic Studies* 72 (2005), pp. 109–133.

28 The Federal Reserve Bank of Dallas, Annual Report, 2003, "A Better Way: Productivity and Reorganization in the American Economy," http://www.dallasfed.org/fed/annual/2003/index.html.

29 Ian D. Wyatt and Daniel E. Hecker, "Occupational Changes During the 20th Century," Bureau of Labor Statistics, *Monthly Labor Review*, March 2006.

30 Mark Aguiar and Erik Hurst, "The Allocation of Time Over Five Decades," Federal Reserve Bank of Boston Working Paper 06-2, January 2006.

31 Ronald Schettkat, "Differences in U.S.-German Time-Allocation: Why

Do Americans Work Longer Hours Than Germans?" Institute for the Study of Labor Discussion Paper 697, January 2003. http://www.iza.org/en/webcontent/publications/papers/viewAbstract?dp_id=697.

32 Ray Kurzweil, "The Age of Knowledge," *Library Journal*, 1991. http://www.kurzweilai.net/meme/frame.html?main=/articles/art0246.html?m%3D10

33 "Attack of the Two-Headed Scientists," *Wired*, June 11, 2003. http://www.wired.com/science/discoveries/news/2003/06/59137.

34 Alan Greenspan, "Technology and Trade," April 16, 1999. http://www.federalreserve.gov/boardDocs/speeches/1999/19990416.htm.

35 Lewis, *The Power of Productivity*, p. 199.

36 Ibid., p. 197.

37 Brad DeLong, *Macroeconomics*, cited in our chapter on "Economics 2.0 in Practice."

38 Jaap Sleifer, "Planning Ahead and Falling Behind: The East German Economy in Comparison With West Germany, 1936-2002," Kuczynski Prize Lecture, September 2007. http://www.ith.or.at/ith_e/kuczynski_prize_lectures_2007_e.htm.

39 Douglass North, "Economic Performance Through Time," 1993 Nobel Memorial Prize Lecture. http://nobelprize.org/nobel_prizes/economics/laureates/1993/north-lecture.html.

40 Lewis, *The Power of Productivity*, p. 222.

41 Ibid., pp. 218–219.

42 Edmund Phelps, "Dynamic Capitalism," *The Wall Street Journal*, October 10, 2006.

43 Mary Bellis, "Inventors of the Modern Computer: The First Hobby and Home Computers: Apple I, Apple II, Commodore PET, and TRS-80," http://inventors.about.com/library/weekly/aa121598.htm.

44 Mary Bellis, "Inventors of the Modern Computer: The History of the Graphical User Interface or GUI – The Apple Lisa," http://inventors.about.com/library/weekly/aa043099.htm.

45 Gifford Pinchot III, *Intrapreneuring*, Harper and Row, 1985, p. 16.

46 Ibid., pp. 5–6.

47 Ibid., p. 20.

48 "Don't Listen to 'Yes,'" Harvard Business School Working Knowledge, June 6, 2005, http://hbswk.hbs.edu/item/4833.html.

49 J. Bradford DeLong, "Incomplete and Partial thoughts on Greg Mankiw's Updated 'Lazear vs. Krugman,'" http://delong.typepad.com/sdj/2006/07/incomplete_and_.html.

50 Pinchot, *Intrapreneuring*, p. 31.

51 Daniel Yi, "Latest Retail Niche: Clinics," *Los Angeles Times*, July 18, 2006, http://www.latimes.com/features/health/la-fi-clinics18jul18,0, 7656405.story?coll=la-home-headlines.

52 Frederick Jackson Turner, "The Significance of the Frontier in American History," http://xroads.virginia.edu/%7EHYPER/TURNER/chapter1.html.

53 Alan Blinder, "Six Fingers of Blame in the Mortgage Mess," *New York Times*, September 30, 2007, http://www.nytimes.com/2007/09/30/business/30view.html?ex=1348804800&en=7eede1d75958b918&ei=5090&partner=rssuserland&emc=rss.

54 Riccardo Rebonato, *Plight of the Fortune Tellers: Why We Need to Manage Financial Risk Differently.* Princeton University Press, 2007, pp. 8–9.

55 Michael Bordo, "The Same Old Story," remarks at the Chicago Federal Reserve Conference, September 28, 2007. http://michael.bordo.googlepages.com/The_same_old_story.pdf.

56 Rebonato, *Plight of the Fortune Tellers*, pp. 108-109.

57 Global Financial Data, http://www.globalfinancialdata.com/articles/dow_jones.html.

58 Richard Foster and Sarah Kaplan, *Creative Destruction: Why Companies That Are Built to Last Underperform the Market – and How to Successfully Transform Them.* Random House, 2001. http://www.randomhouse.com/doubleday/currency/catalog/display.pperl?isbn=9780385501330&view=excerpt.

59 Lucia Foster, John Haltiwanger, and C.J. Krizan, "Aggregate Productivity Growth: Lessons from Microeconomic Evidence," working paper, June 2000. http://www.bsos.umd.edu/econ/haltiwanger/fhkcriw_062300.PDF.

60 Martin Baily, "The Sources of Economic Growth in OECD Countries: A Review Article," http://www.csls.ca/ipm/7/bailyreview-e.pdf.

61 Clifford Winston, *Government Failure vs. Market Failure*, AEI–Brookings Joint Center for Regulatory Studies, Washington DC, 2006, pp. 73–75.

62 Maria Casby Allen, presentation at a forum on reading instruction, May 22, 2007. http://www.manhattan-institute.org/html/cb_49.htm.

63 Zvi Griliches, "Hybrid Corn: An Exploration of the Economics of Technological Change." In *Technology, Education, and Productivity: Early Papers With Notes to Subsequent Literature.* p. 27–52. New York, Basil Blackwell, 1988 [1957].

64 Paul A. David, "The Dynamo and the Computer: An Historical Perspective on the Modern Productivity Paradox," *American Economic Review* Vol. 80, No. 2, May 1990, pp. 35-361.

Notes

65 See, for example, Stephen Kinsella, "Against Intellectual Property,"
    Journal of Libertarian Studies, Vol. 15, No. 2, Spring 2001,
    http://www.mises.org/journals/jls/15_2/15_2_1.pdf.

Index

Index

Index

Index

Index

DESIGN & COMPOSITION BY CARL W. SCARBROUGH